WAR IN THE FAR EAST

VOLUME 2

Japan Runs Wild, 1942–1943

PETER HARMSEN

CASEMATE

Philadelphia & Oxford

Published in the United States of America and Great Britain in 2020 by
CASEMATE PUBLISHERS
1950 Lawrence Road, Havertown, PA 19083, USA
and
The Old Music Hall, 106–108 Cowley Road, Oxford OX4 1JE, UK

Copyright 2020 © Peter Harmsen

Hardcover Edition: ISBN 978-1-61200-625-3
Digital Edition: ISBN 978-1-61200-626-0

A CIP record for this book is available from the British Library

Printed and bound in the United States by Integrated Books International

Typeset at Versatile PreMedia Service (P) Ltd.

For a complete list of Casemate titles, please contact:

CASEMATE PUBLISHERS (US)
Telephone (610) 853-9131
Fax (610) 853-9146
Email: casemate@casematepublishers.com
www.casematepublishers.com

CASEMATE PUBLISHERS (UK)
Telephone (01865) 241249
Email: casemate-uk@casematepublishers.co.uk
www.casematepublishers.co.uk

Contents

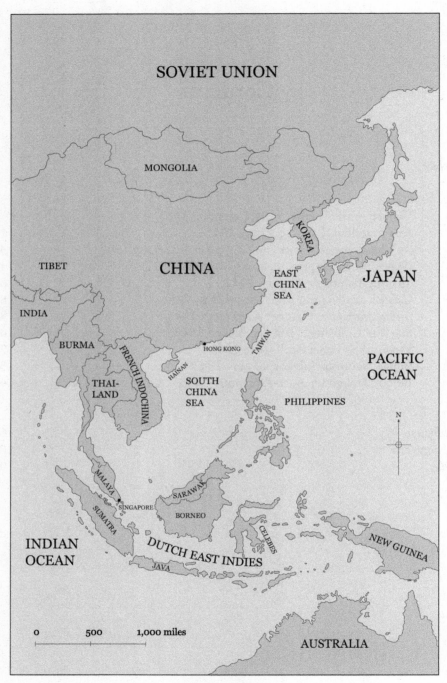

East Asia, 1941

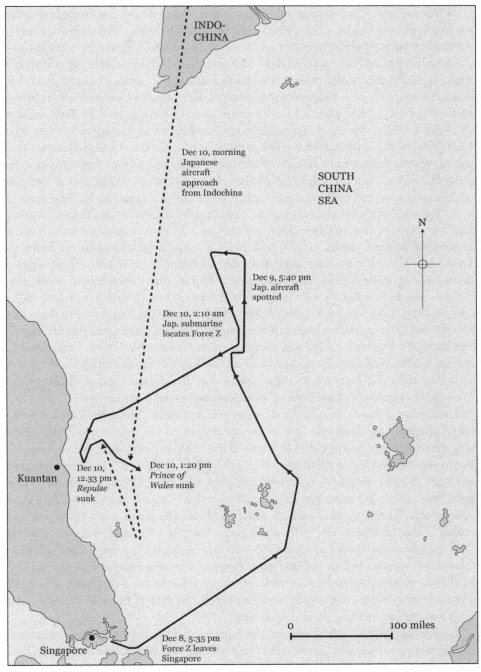

The sinking of the HMS *Prince of Wales* and HMS *Repulse*, December 8–10, 1941

What made Phillips change his mind was a telegram arriving from Singapore shortly before midnight: "Enemy reported landing Kuantan." The city of Kuantan, on the east coast of the Malay peninsula, was located much further south than any previously reported landings, and if the Japanese succeeded in establishing a foothold there, it would drastically change the strategic situation, putting Singapore within much easier reach of rapidly moving infantry. Kuantan was not too far from the route that Force Z had planned for its return journey anyway, and Phillips decided to make a detour for the reported Japanese landing zone. Given everything that Phillips knew at the time, which was not much, it was not an unsound decision. Less sound was his decision not to call for air support from Singapore. He did not want to break radio silence and might have believed that aircraft would be sent as a matter of course, due to the obvious urgent need to contain the Japanese landing force.[9]

As it turned out, there was no Japanese landing force at Kuantan. The intelligence had been flawed, and therefore there was also no intention whatsoever in Singapore of sending fighters to the area. When Force Z approached Kuantan at dawn on December 10 and found no large assembly of Japanese vessels in the process of disembarking troops, it was clear to Admiral Phillips that he had made a mistake, but by now it was already too late. Force Z had ended up in a trap partly of its own making. Unbeknownst to the British officers on board, the *Prince of Wales* and *Repulse* had been spotted, along with their support vessels, once again the day before, this time by a Japanese submarine, and since then Genzan Air Group,[10] stationed in Saigon in southern Indochina, had been on the lookout for the ships. A few hours after daybreak, the Japanese aviators located the British fleet, and at about 11 am the attacks began with a mixture of bombers and torpedo planes.[11]

Lieutenant Takai Sadao, leader of a torpedo squadron, later remembered being taken aback by the complete lack of enemy aircover: "Much to our surprise, not a single enemy plane was in sight. This was all the more amazing since the scene of the battle was well within the fighting range of the British fighters." Even though they were left to their own devices, the British ships were able to put up a tremendous fight, and as the Japanese planes closed in on their targets, the anti-aircraft guns opened up. "The sky was filled with bursting shells which made my plane reel and shake," Takai later recalled.[12] The smell and smoke of the enemy barrages entered the Japanese aircraft, adding to the intensity of the situation.[13] Flight Seaman First Class Uno Susumo was in the first wave of attacks on the *Repulse*, and saw his and his fellow aviators' torpedoes all miss the target. "We and our airplanes attack the enemy as if we were a fireball, and still we failed," he said to himself, in a daze and with tears of rage rolling down his cheeks.[14]

Undeterred by the initial failure, the Japanese planes kept coming, and in the course of two subsequent waves, the *Prince of Wales* was hit repeatedly and reduced to a sitting duck, unable to dodge further attacks. The Japanese pilots proceeded with devastating efficiency, flying into the wall of bullets and shrapnel hurled against them from below. "Such cool-headed and imperturbable firings, the same as those in peacetime training, were seen everywhere, so that it was not by accident that many torpedo hits were scored," the commanding officer of the Genzan Air Group reported later.[15] Similar cold-blooded behavior was displayed on the British side. On board the *Repulse*, American *CBS* correspondent Cecil Brown was struck by the crew's almost otherworldly sangfroid. Each shell delivered to the service gun was handed over with a joke. The men were having the time of their lives, Brown thought to himself, and later wrote in his diary: "I never saw such happiness on men's faces."[16]

The valor displayed by the British sailors could not change the sad fate of both ships, and even the skillful maneuvering of William Tennant, captain on board the *Repulse*, was insufficient: "I found dodging the torpedoes quite interesting and entertaining until in the end they started to come in from all directions and they were too much for me," he wrote later. [17] About 90 minutes into the battle, his ship was at journey's end. "Stand by for barrage," a metallic voice warned over the ship's communication system. The crew could see a plane at 300 or 400 yards, approaching from the port side. As it came closer, it dropped its torpedo, which headed straight for the *Repulse*. "This one's got us," one of the sailors said, watching helplessly as the white stripe darted towards them just below the surface of the water. The torpedo struck about 20 yards astern from where Cecil Brown was standing. "It felt like the ship had crashed into a well-rooted dock," he wrote. "It threw me four feet across the deck."[18]

It was the death blow for the *Repulse*. Captain Tennant ordered all hands to abandon ship, and just minutes later it rolled over. As the men flocked on the upturned starboard side, Tennant left the bridge and joined them. "It was strange walking along what was normally a vertical surface," he wrote later. "Without any feeling of the ship going down the sea came up and took me. Almost at once I was sucked down into water that was very black and no light at all." Seconds later, he bobbed up to the surface and heard a shout from a life raft just feet away: "Here you are, Sir, come on."[19] He was among 796 officers and men rescued from the *Repulse*, out of an original complement of 1,309.[20]

Phillips on board the *Prince of Wales* was not that lucky. Assaulted repeatedly by both torpedo planes and bombers, his ship managed to stay afloat for nearly an hour longer than the *Repulse* but listed dangerously. Some of the wounded were evacuated by gangplank to the destroyer HMS *Express*, where Able Seaman Shiner Wright helped them over the side. He was horrified by the sight of sailors whose skin had been burned off by bursting steam pipes. "They were so badly burnt they wouldn't allow us to touch them," he said later of the gruesome experience.[21] Even the Japanese pilots, circling around the doomed ship like merciless birds of prey, were able to appreciate the tragedy unfolding. "As we dived for the attack, I didn't want to launch my torpedo. It was such a beautiful ship, such a beautiful ship," one of them said later.[22] With only minutes to go before the mighty hull would be devoured by the waves, the crew were scrambling to save themselves, but Phillips was seen on the bridge, slumped on a stool in complete despair. "I cannot survive this," he said, apparently resigned to stay with his ship.[23] At 1:20 pm, it turned upside down and sank. Altogether 327 of the crew of 1,612 went to the bottom. Phillips was one of them.[24]

Only now, when all was lost, did friendly aircraft arrive. Flight-lieutenant T. A. Vigors from the Royal Australian Air Force base at Sembawang near Singapore piloted the first airplane to reach the area after the two vessels had been sunk. He saw hundreds of men clinging to bits of wreckage and swimming in filthy oily water. It would be hours before they could all be picked up, and in the meantime they might be subjected to further air attack. "Yet, as I flew round, every man waved and put his thumb up as I flew over him," Vigors wrote in a report immediately afterwards. "After an hour lack of petrol forced me to leave, but during that hour I had seen many men in dire danger waving, cheering and joking as if they were holiday makers at Brighton waving at a low-flying aircraft."[25]

Half a world away in Britain, it was still morning, and Prime Minister Winston Churchill received the news of the disaster by telephone while he was lying in bed. He had been warned about the risk of sending the *Prince of Wales* to the Far East, where the Japanese Navy enjoyed clear superiority.[26] The British leader had not listened, and now he was forced to face the consequences. It was the most direct shock of the entire war, he later recalled: "As I turned over and twisted in bed, the full horror of the news sank in upon me. There were no British or American capital ships in the Indian Ocean or the Pacific except the American survivors of Pearl Harbor, who were hastening back to California. Over all this vast expanse of waters Japan was supreme, and we everywhere were weak and naked."[27]

It was yet another blow to British pride, of which there had been many over the preceding two years, but in some ways it was worse than the others. Harold Macmillan, the future prime minister, described the "humiliation, almost incredulity" with which the news was received by the British, a maritime nation at heart. "Our people are accustomed to setbacks, even disasters, on land," he wrote in his memoirs. "But a defeat at sea is another thing."[28] One week later, in a bitter reminder of how fast fortunes could change in a time of war, John Kennedy, one of Churchill's chief military aides, received a much-delayed letter that Admiral Phillips had penned during his voyage from the Atlantic to the Far East. Displaying happy ignorance of the misfortunes lying ahead, it said, "It is grand to be at sea again."[29]

★ ★ ★

The Japanese Empire seemed unbeatable in December 1941. Yet, the Japanese people initially displayed an almost apathetic attitude towards the war and only gradually worked up a level of enthusiasm to match the astonishing victories abroad. In the morning of December 8, just hours after the attack on Pearl Harbor, the young

German diplomat Erwin Wickert took the tram through Tokyo, watching his co-passengers read newspapers that had been printed during the night, while there was still peace. None of them talked, and everyone seemed unaffected, although there was little doubt most knew their country was now at war with the strongest power on earth. "They probably had not yet completely fathomed the news and were looking for an explanation in yesterday's reports," Wickert wrote.[30] Robert Guillain, a French journalist, noticed the same subdued mood in Japan's capital and guessed that some might even harbor quiet anger at the predicament their leaders had placed the nation in. "In the streets," he wrote, "people showed surprise as they were reading the first special editions of the newspapers, and muted dismay. Fear was taking hold of them, as they understood the folly that Japan had committed."[31]

Later the same day, shop owners set up loudspeakers outside their stores, and each time news was broadcast, people would gather around to listen, quiet and without moving. Youth groups and paramilitary bands walked to the emperor's palace and the Yasukuni Shrine, where Japan's war dead were commemorated. Some also strode by the German embassy, shouting "Banzai!" in shrill voices. "You couldn't hear much excitement," Wickert commented drily, as many seemed to be showing support for the war out of a sense of duty rather than any inner conviction.[32] The Tokyo Stock Exchange, which perhaps expressed the public mood in the most honest fashion because money was at stake, triggered particular concern, and even before the markets opened the Finance Ministry arranged for supportive buying of shares to take place. It did not help much, and stock prices experienced an initial downward trend in reaction to the war news, only to gain ground again after news started trickling in about sweeping, early successes in the Pacific.[33]

Little by little as reports of the rapid advances became better known at home, the Japanese public began displaying a greater degree of fervor. Crowds were now cheering when newsreels boasted about fresh triumphs, and on the airwaves radio announcements of new advances mixed with an endless stream of patriotic marches.[34] "The town was full of waves of rising sun flags," Sakamoto Tane, the wife of a judge in the city of Kōchi, wrote in her diary, "and we celebrated together the string of imperial army victories."[35] The young and impressionable were especially affected. "I felt as if my blood boiled and my flesh quivered," said Kōshū Itabashi, a middle-school student, recalling his emotions when hearing reports about new Japanese victories abroad. "The whole nation bubbled over, excited and inspired. 'We really did it! Incredible! Wonderful!' That's the way it felt then."[36] Emperor Hirohito himself also displayed growing enthusiasm. The divine ruler, who followed the progress of war with great attention to detail in a special map room established in his palace, had reacted with calm to the reports about the success at Pearl Harbor, but as the victories started accumulating, his mood improved, almost as if he could not believe his own luck. "The results of the war are coming too quickly," he exclaimed after yet another triumph on the battlefield.[37]

The diplomats at US Embassy in Tokyo, turned into enemy aliens overnight, were confined to their compound, and initially had to accept Japanese police officers swarming all over the area, peering through the windows of the buildings, and sometimes even stepping into their private rooms. "The theory that we were prisoners to be treated as criminal prisoners was clearly the attitude of the police from the very beginning," US Ambassador Joseph Grew commented.[38] Otto Tolischus, the Tokyo correspondent for the *New York Times*, was arrested on trumped-up charges of espionage the moment the war began. After the initial scare, he noticed that almost all his prison guards were exceedingly friendly, which he took as a bad sign, since it suggested to him that they were feeling good about the progress of the war.[39] His gut feeling was confirmed when after a period of complete isolation from outside news, police officers showed him photos of American targets destroyed across the Central and Western Pacific. "Well," Tolischus said with slightly veiled sarcasm, "under the circumstances, I can only congratulate you on your success." He later recalled the officers' reaction: "They smiled. I knew they would see nothing wrong in their treachery, and the irony escaped them."[40]

Among Japan's political elite, who were very well aware of their nation's strengths and weaknesses and did not receive their news filtered through a screen of propaganda, the mood was also rising, but with an unmistakable accompanying note of caution. "The military achievements, attained by the Japanese armed forces at the initial stage of the war, including the surprise attack on Pearl Harbor, were brilliant," wrote Kido Kōichi, the emperor's closest advisor, after the war. "The nation was intoxicated, as it were, with an unbroken string of victories, gained by the Japanese armed forces at various fronts in quick succession one after another. I, as one of the Japanese nationals, shared their rejoicings but none the less I could not believe in spite of myself that Japan would be able to emerge victorious from this war."[41]

Japan's military and political leaders had run a huge but, they believed, calculated risk when embarking on war with the Western powers, and initially the gamble had paid off beyond all expectations. However, they all knew that Japan was weaker than the West in all respects, and that this weakness would show up even more clearly beyond the short-term. This put an early end to some of the wilder Japanese ambitions. For instance, in the heady days after the success at Pearl Harbor, the Japanese Navy toyed in a serious way with the idea of occupying Hawaii, but the plan never got anywhere near materializing due to logistical concerns. Feeding an occupying army along with the civilian population would have required a steady stream of supply vessels sailing to the Hawaiian Islands, exposed to the threat of the potent US submarine force.[42] Kido determined even at this early stage to seek ways for peace with America and Britain. "It was my belief," he said, "that Japan would commit an irretrievable blunder if she went too deep in it, elated over her initial successes. This fear haunted me from the very beginning."[43]

Japan's Axis partners in Europe were generally excited, but not universally so. When the Pacific war was just a few hours old, Italy's Foreign Minister Count Galeazzo Ciano received a nightly phone call from his German counterpart Joachim von Ribbentrop. "He is joyful over the Japanese attack on the United States. He is so happy, in fact, that I can't but congratulate him," Ciano wrote in his diary, while keeping a level head himself.[44] German Propaganda Minister Joseph Goebbels noted with some annoyance that his government had not been informed beforehand about the Japanese attack but put it down to the need to maintain secrecy. "Triggering this war, the Japanese have opted for bold tactics," Goebbels recorded in his diary.[45] The Nazi Party mouthpiece *Völkischer Beobachter* blamed "the general agent of Jewdom, Mister Franklin Roosevelt" for the outbreak of war in the Pacific, describing Japan as the natural political center of the nations in the region. "The peoples of these countries are acting in their own interest by cooperating closely with Tokyo," the newspaper said in an editorial.[46]

German dictator Adolf Hitler himself had nothing but sympathy for the Japanese actions. "There are certain situations in the life of a great power when it must resort to arms if it doesn't want to give up completely. This kind of situation has arisen for Japan," he told his closest aides. "They have had an amazing start and can now dominate the Pacific in an almost uninhibited manner."[47] More importantly, Japan's aggression fit completely into Hitler's own plans for the war. Tensions with the United States had intensified over the preceding months, and a state of undeclared war already existed in the Atlantic, where American warships had become semi-belligerents, persuading him that the official peace between the Washington and Berlin could not last. Previously, his plan for German great power status had been to defeat the Soviet Union first and then turn to the United States. With the US administration under Franklin D. Roosevelt becoming ever more deeply involved in its support of Britain, it was clear that the Americans were a threat that needed to be settled much earlier, even before having definitively dealt with the Soviet enemy.[48]

In this light, according to Hitler, the events of December were no inconvenience. Rather, it was unbelievably lucky that Japan had dragged the United States into the war and would keep it occupied for the foreseeable future in the Pacific. "Now the East Asia conflict falls into our lap like a present," he said, beaming with joy.[49] According to the German *Führer*'s logic, the best he could do was to add to America's woes by forcing it into a two-ocean conflict which involved not just the Pacific but also the Atlantic, and on December 11 he declared war on the United States. Thus, in a matter of days, Japan's attack on Pearl Harbor had connected the separate wars in Europe and Asia and turned them into a genuinely global conflict, affecting most of mankind one way or another. "Now," Goebbels wrote in his diary, "this war has become a world war in the truest sense of the word."[50]

★ ★ ★

Half a world away, Admiral Ugaki Matome, chief of staff of the Japanese Navy's main ocean-going units assembled in the Combined Fleet, expressed the exact same thought as the German propaganda minister. "Now it has really turned out to be the Second World War," Ugaki wrote in his diary. "The whole world will revolve around our empire."[51] Japan had opted for a meeting with destiny, but its senior leaders knew that they had to play their cards exactly right or they would lose everything. The Japanese expansion across the Western Pacific and Southeast Asia in the weeks after Pearl Harbor betrayed a feverish, all-consuming ambition, and from an outsider's point of view, it was not always easy to discern any overall logic. Ordinary Japanese soldiers often had little or no understanding of why they were going to war. This conversation taking place among soldiers heading south in December was typical:

"We can't be going east. Our Fleet is moving south. Are we going to Borneo?"

"What on earth for? To join the gorillas and the cannibals?"

"Idiot! There's oil there."[52]

Japan's foes, too, were confused. "Look what they are doing out here, jumping all over the map instead of meeting at one or two places," a British officer said.[53] The Japanese were indeed scattered across the map in the winter of 1941–42, but not in a random manner. It all was according to a carefully laid plan, and despite the disparaging view of many of its enemies, Japan was remarkably successful. Ultimately, the objective was to gain access to the natural riches of Asia. The main prize was the oil in the Dutch-controlled East Indies, without which the Japanese Empire and its war machine would grind to a halt, but it was more than that. Japan's economy, ravaged by a decade of conflict in China, including four years of all-out war, also coveted other resources, such as the tin and rubber of the Malay Peninsula.[54]

The Japanese commanders were under two major constraints. The first constraint was one of manpower. From day one, they lacked soldiers and had to spread their troops thinly in order to implement their plans for conquest. Some units had to be used twice, participating in one campaign only to immediately move on to the next. It was war on a shoestring, and it was only going to get worse. The Japanese could not count on ever being able to match the British, the Dutch, the Australians, and especially the Americans in basic material terms. The United States was temporarily weakened, but soon it would have more of everything. Therefore, it was necessary to essentially win the war psychologically. The US democracy, considered inherently weak by the Japanese, was to be persuaded that continued fighting would entail sacrifice of such magnitude that a compromise solution and a negotiated peace was the only palatable alternative. A *fait accompli* had to be established, and a defensive perimeter was to be set up as far out in the Pacific as possible, before the Americans gathered strength to hit back.[55]

This led to the second constraint the Japanese commanders were facing. They did not have much time. Admiral Yamamoto Isoroku, the commander-in-chief of the Combined Fleet, had hinted at this problem even before the war broke out. "If I am told to fight regardless of the consequences, I shall run wild for the first six months or a year," he had told Prime Minister Konoe Fumimaro. "But I have utterly no confidence for the second or third year."[56] In other words, the war would be decided for Japan during the first 12 months. Its military was on a tight schedule, and the top brass further exacerbated this by imposing on themselves a seemingly impossible deadline. Having disappointed the emperor with the endless quagmire in China, they now wanted to show that they could not just achieve their stated objectives, but even exceed them. Hirohito had voiced doubts that the operation to seize Southeast Asia could be completed within five months. In response, the officers resolved to "pledge on the honor of the southern armies to firmly live up to His Majesty's considerations by completing the southern operation within the term scheduled by Imperial General Headquarters."[57]

In a more profound sense, the urgency the Japanese leaders were experiencing was a problem of their own making. They struggled to complete their conquests as early as possible in order to prevent Allied reinforcements of the areas under attack.[58] By this, of course, they did not mean reinforcements from Great Britain or the Netherlands, which were in no shape to hit back any time soon, the former involved in a life-and-death struggle against Germany, and the latter occupied by the same power. It was America which could and would retaliate. It was a matter of almost diabolic irony that it did not have to be this way. The main rationale for attacking Pearl Harbor had been fear that the United State would interfere with the Japanese conquest of Southeast Asia. In the event, the Japanese blitzkrieg in late 1941 and early 1942 was carried out with such speed that the American Navy would not have made any difference. It suggested that in the Japanese debate for and against attacking Pearl Harbor, the opponents of this rash act might have been right. It had not been necessary to destroy the US Pacific Fleet in order to bring the war in Southeast Asia to a victorious conclusion. Now it had nevertheless been done, and Japan had awakened a sleeping giant.[59]

"A date which will live in infamy," US President Franklin D. Roosevelt had called that fateful Sunday when Pearl Harbor was struck. He gave voice to a feeling of immense anger affecting Americans of all ages and occupations, at home and abroad alike. John Donovan, an American pilot who had volunteered to fly for the Chinese side, was alerted to the news about the war within hours, and on December 8 he expressed the sentiments of many of his compatriots when he argued that what had happened reflected not just Japanese boldness, but also misplaced American softness: "Well, today they have gone and done it. You have to give the guys credit for nerve," he wrote in a letter home. "It should never have happened. A big country like the

U.S. standing by complacently trying to conciliate with the murderers. Yes, that's the trouble with a democracy showing too much kindness to the wrong people."[60]

During the first confused days, the Americans had only limited chances of striking back. The US-held island of Guam, a fueling station for US Navy vessels en route to or from Asia, had been under bombardment since the beginning of hostilities in the Pacific. At 4 am on December 10, a landing force of 400 Japanese waded onto Dungcas Beach, a few miles north of the capital of Agana. The Japanese marched into the central square of the city, where the Insular Force Guard, a unit made up of 80 local recruits, awaited them with nothing more than rifles and a few .30 machine guns.[61] "The Insular Force Guard stood their ground and opened up a fire with machine guns and rifles hot enough to halt the invading force for a short time," Guam Governor George J. McMillin wrote in a post-war account. The shooting lasted for less than an hour: "The situation was simply hopeless, resistance had been carried to the limit." Three blasts were sounded on the horn of an automobile which was standing on the square in front of the governor's residence. "This was not a prearranged signal to cease fire, but it seemed to have been understood by both sides, and the firing stopped immediately," McMillin said.[62]

The atoll Wake, another US possession, was better prepared and equipped and held out for longer, even though the odds were terrifying. Consisting of three small islands located 1,500 miles east of Guam and more than 2,000 miles west of Hawaii, Wake looked lonely on the map, and the troops stationed on the island, 500 US Marines under the command of Major James Devereux, would be excused if they felt like the loneliest garrison in the world. Reinforced by civilian workers employed on construction projects, they had been subjected to Japanese air attack since shortly after Pearl Harbor, and early on December 11, a Japanese fleet consisting of three cruisers, six destroyers and several other vessels arrived from the Marshalls attempting to land 450 men on the island.[63] While the Japanese ships began their bombardment, the Marines lay in wait, with three batteries of coastal artillery under strict orders to hold fire until the very last minute.[64]

When the Americans finally opened up, it worked to devastating effect. First Lieutenant Clarence A. Barninger later described what happened after his battery opened fire on the cruiser *Yubari* at a distance of less than 6,000 yards: "The ship immediately belched smoke and steam through the side and her speed diminished... After some time, she got slowly under way, going a short distance, stopping, and continuing again; she was engulfed in smoke when she crept over the horizon."[65] Another cruiser, the *Hayate*, received three salvos, broke in two, and sank rapidly, with 168 killed and no survivors.[66] The Japanese opted for breaking off the operation and as they retired they were pursued by four American Grumman F4F Wildcat aircraft, which had survived the air raids of the previous days and now also entered the battle, spreading havoc among the enemy ships. Amid unexpected defeat, the Japanese grudgingly admitted they had met stronger opposition than expected.

"Our Navy admires the ability and courage of the pilots and fighters that defended Wake in the operation," naval aviator Captain Yamaoka Mineo said in a post-war interview. "The airplane pilots were very brave and skillful."[67]

While the Wake garrison was fighting for its life, the US Navy at Pearl Harbor worked frantically to organize reinforcement. By mid-December Task Force 14, commanded by Rear Admiral Frank Jack Fletcher and consisting of carrier USS *Saratoga* as well as three cruisers, nine destroyers, and support vessels, was heading west towards the beleaguered island, but it was hampered by the speed of its slowest member, the oiler *Neches*, commissioned in 1921. At the same time, the Japanese were done licking their wounds and prepared a second attack on Wake. It was to take place in the night between December 22 and 23, and this time 2,000 Japanese soldiers were to disembark. In addition to significantly boosting the force that had failed in the first attempt to invade the island, the Japanese commanders chose new tactics. Wake was to be taken by surprise, under cover of darkness.[68]

As the second Japanese invasion force reached waters off Wake, shortly after 2 am Japanese soldiers, wearing white headbands so they could more easily identify each other in the dark, clambered into assault boats and moved quietly towards the shore. By the time they stepped onto Wake, they had been detected, in one case because of their injudicious use of pyrotechnic signals as a means of communicating,[69] but it was too late to halt the invasion. Fierce battles broke out in the hour before dawn. A Japanese intelligence officer described the hand-to-hand fighting with the American enemy for one of the artillery positions: "'Charge!' the commander's voice rang out. We jumped to our feet and charged. Huge shadows which shouted something unintelligible were pierced one after another. One large figure appeared before us to blaze away with a machine gun from his hip as they do in American gangster films. Somebody went for him with his bayonet and went down together with his victim."[70]

Little by little the outmanned and outgunned Marines had to yield key positions. "We secretly circled behind the enemy's line," the unnamed intelligence officer wrote. "Then, hurling our hand grenades, we charged into the enemy. In this manner, the artillery position which had troubled us so much up to the present was captured."[71] Even so, the Americans were determined to put up a fight, and in a bold counterattack, they routed an entire unit of 100 soldiers, witnessing a rare scene of panic among the Japanese: "Some 30 of them eventually attempted to hide or take shelter under and about a single Marine searchlight truck, and were killed where they crouched," wrote the official Marine Corps historian. "None volunteered to surrender."[72]

Successes such as this were only local. There were simply too few soldiers on the US side, and they were spread out too thinly to defend a coastline that added up to 21 miles on the main island alone.[73] A further blow, this time mostly psychological, came with the light of day, when the American defenders saw themselves surrounded by Japanese warships on all sides. Some counted 16 vessels, others 27.[74] "There are no friendly ships within twenty-four hours," the Marine commander Devereux was told by one of his officers. "Not even submarines?" he asked, receiving the disappointing answer: "Not even them."[75] At 8 am, Devereux walked towards the Japanese line, carrying a white rag tied to a swab handle.[76]

While the US forces surrendered on Wake, Task Force 14 received orders from Pearl Harbor to turn around. The decision was greeted by the members of the relief force with shock, anger—and a rebellious attitude. Some advised Fletcher to disobey the command and head straight for Wake.[77] Fletcher, of course, ignored these recommendations. Had he continued on his mission, he might have scored an early victory for the US Navy, as several of the Japanese vessels that had participated in the invasion were now sitting targets at Wake. It would probably not have turned the tide of the battle, or kept Wake in American hands, but it would have been an early boost to American morale at a time when everything else seemed bleak. This was all in the realm of what might have been. In the real world, Wake did mark the first major US attempt at fighting back against the Japanese juggernaut, but any benefit to the mood at home was counterbalanced by the strategic loss of a vital strongpoint in the vast expanses of the central Pacific.[78]

CHAPTER TWO

Asia Engulfed

Late December 1941

The Japanese pilots flying over the Philippines in the days after Pearl Harbor were experiencing an entirely new form of war. Many of them were veterans from the long conflict in China, where they had been facing Chinese and sometimes Soviet aviators in Russian-built planes. Now, in the midst of the crucial battle for control of the Philippines skies as a prelude to the planned invasion of the islands, they were up against Americans in US-built aircraft. They found to their relief that their own Mitsubishi A6M "Zero" fighter was a more than adequate match for the American P-40, as the Japanese plane outshone its US counterpart in everything except diving acceleration. "The confidence of our fighter pilots continued to grow, nurtured by the absence of effective opposition," wrote Shimada Kōichi, on the staff of the Eleventh Air Fleet, which had the responsibility for air operations over the Philippines.[1]

The Philippines, under the overall command of General Douglas MacArthur, was not Wake. And yet, despite its much larger size and more awe-inspiring defensive potential, it was essentially just another piece of US-held territory that the military planners in Washington had to effectively abandon beforehand. In the tense years prior to the outbreak of war in the Pacific, the US government, faced with the likelihood of being sucked into the ongoing war in Europe, had been forced to allocate desperately scarce military resources elsewhere. "Adequate reinforcements for the Philippines at this time," according to General George C. Marshall, the US Army's chief of staff, "would have left the United States in a position of great peril should there be a break in the defense of Great Britain."[2] What was not clear at the time was the fact that the Japanese were similarly constrained, and that the Japanese high command intended to take the Philippines with the smallest feasible number of troops.

Placed in command of the Japanese 14th Army, which was to conquer the Philippines, was 54-year-old General Homma Masaharu. He incorporated many of the paradoxes of the high-level officers of the Japanese military who oversaw the rapid expansion of Hirohito's empire in the winter of 1941 and 1942. They were men who had set out on their careers respecting and, in many cases, even appreciating the nations of the West. Some developed deep personal attachments. Homma, for one, had been a military student with the East Lancashire Regiment three decades earlier, and during World War I, he had been assigned to serve with the British Second Army headquarters in France.[3] Of course, this paled in comparison to the officer's sense of duty towards the emperor, and once war broke out, his loyalties were not in doubt.

On December 10, about 48 hours after Japanese airplanes had started dropping bombs over the Philippines, the first invasion troops consisting of about 5,000 men disembarked on two locations at the northern end of Luzon, the largest island of the Philippine archipelago.[4] The purpose of the operation was to seize airfields in preparation of a larger invasion planned for later in the month.[5] Despite the heavy blow that the US Army Air Force had received at the outset of the campaign, it was still able to inflict at least a psychological toll on the invaders. For the Japanese troops waiting on ships off the invasion beaches, the scattered US air raids were their baptism of fire, and their commanders requested air support to ward off the threat.[6]

The Japanese landings were limited in scope, as per the overall need to use only the very minimum of troops for each operation, but the mere presence of the enemy created a deep sense of unease. "The rat was in the house, and it was no comfort," said General Jonathan M. Wainwright, the senior US commander in northern Luzon.[7] Nervousness abounded. On the same day as the landings, about 100 miles further south, a single Japanese reconnaissance vessel was detected, setting off a furious barrage from Philippine artillery inland, fired in the belief that an entire invasion force was underway. "It was like dropping a match in a warehouse of Fourth of July fireworks," an American advisor to the Philippine unit wrote.[8]

The American commanders had to husband their resources, and they considered the landings in the north to be a feint ahead of a larger invasion elsewhere.[9] The same was true for their reaction on December 12, when yet another small detachment of about 2,500 Japanese troops landed in Legaspi harbor in the south of Luzon. A story, possibly apocryphal, was later related about the railway stationmaster in the harbor calling US military representatives in Manila to inform them that the Japanese had arrived and were standing in his office. "See what they want," the officer in Manila ordered. The stationmaster replied: "Those Japs want me to give them a train to take them to Manila, sir. What do I do now?" The officer in Manila reacted promptly: "Tell them the next train leaves a week from Sunday. Don't give it to them."[10]

The landings in both north and south of Luzon were only preliminaries to the main Japanese invasion, which the Americans knew was coming. They had to wait exactly ten days for that to take place. At 5:17 am on December 22, the first men of a Japanese landing force numbering more than 34,000 waded ashore at Lingayen Gulf about 100 miles north of Manila. The invasion, carried out by the 14th Army under the command of General Homma, got off to a bad start as the ships missed

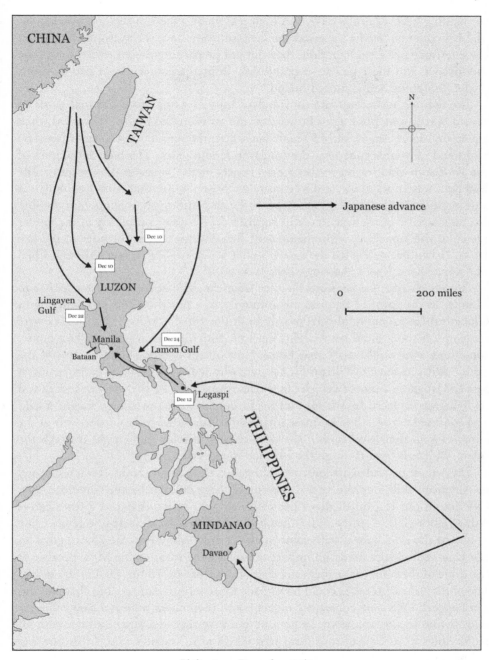

Philippines, December 1941

the landing beaches in the dark, and high seas made a mess of the disembarkation. The US commanders had guessed the invasion zone since the gulf was the natural place to carry out a landing. Still, they did not prepare any major efforts to oppose the invader, and the Japanese, meeting only limited resistance from two divisions of the Philippine Army, moved inland.[11]

The fighting picked up later in the day. The US Army's first armored battle of World War II took place a few hours after the invasion had begun. It erupted when a platoon of five American M3 Stuart tanks attempted to block a force of Japanese tanks and anti-tank guns near the Lingayen landing area. The high silhouettes of the American vehicles made them easy targets of the Japanese 47mm guns. The lead tank was knocked out and its crew taken prisoner. Another American tank was also hit, and the shell tore off the head of the assistant driver, making him the first US tank soldier of the war to die in combat.[12] "We were completely at the tender mercy of the Japanese," wrote Lieutenant Ben Morin, the commander of the five tanks. "I had personally led the first US tank attack of WWII, and although I had not stopped the Japs, I had slowed them down."[13]

Greater success was in store for the American M3s some days later, closer to Manila, in the town of Baliuag, a community of a few thousand people living in a labyrinthine assembly of huts mostly built on stilts.[14] "Most of the houses were built up off the ground some eight, ten feet, and when you went under a house, sometimes you would carry that house built out of bamboo right on top of the tank," said Lieutenant William H. Gentry, who led a company of tanks against a force of Japanese armored vehicles in the narrow streets. As the sun was setting and its light was replaced by the fires set off throughout the town, they fought a wild and confused battle, while Japanese infantrymen fired their rifles ineffectively at the Americans in their steel hulls. "We were chasing the Jap tanks right through the town. We'd run right through the bamboo huts," said Gentry.[15]

The Americans ended up destroying altogether eight enemy tanks. It was testimony to American skill, but also to a technological edge enjoyed by the American side. "We found out real quick that their turret would not traverse, just a few degrees either right or left," Gentry said. "They had to be pretty much facing, so if you came at him at the side, he was vulnerable as all get-out." Moreover, the 75mm guns on the Japanese vehicles made no impact if they hit the front of the M3s, because of the slope of the hulls made them ricochet off. A Japanese 75mm shell in the side of one of the American tanks could have made more serious damage, but that also did not happen. "We were constantly moving, and their tanks were real slow," Gentry said. Before leaving the town, he got out and investigated a Japanese tank with 40 or 50 holes in it. "It had four dead Japs inside of it," Gentry said. "This one was sitting near the town square, and as everybody came by, they didn't know whether it was moving or not, or whether it was able to move, so they just poked another round through it."[16]

This and other shows of bravado could not alter the overall strategic situation. On December 24, two days after the main invasion, a force of about 7,000 Japanese soldiers made yet another landing in Lamon Gulf southeast of Manila.[17] The Japanese were winning, pushing the Americans and their Philippine allies inside a narrowing perimeter around the capital. This was in sharp contrast to MacArthur's expectations. Just prior to the start of the war, in November, he had imposed a plan to stop the Japanese at water's edge. The "MacArthur plan" as it had quickly become known, had been unrealistic from the outset. It would have required vastly larger resources than he had to defend the entire Philippine coastline, and the rapid pace of the Japanese advance since the invasion showed that it was not working. Facing imminent collapse, MacArthur was forced to hastily revert to the original pre-war defense plan, which called for withdrawal of all American and Philippine forces to the Bataan Peninsula opposite Manila. Given the limited resources available, it had been the most logical solution all along, as the peninsula could potentially be held for months. The problem was that, as a result of the "MacArthur plan," vital supplies had been dispersed throughout Luzon, and now that the plan had been abandoned as quickly as it had been adopted, there was a feverish rush to salvage as many resources as possible and return them for the final campaign on Bataan.[18]

Withdrawing to Bataan entailed the difficult decision to give up Manila and abandon its inhabitants to an uncertain fate under Japanese rule. Petty Officer Cecil S. King of the US Navy described how that felt for the ordinary American fighting man. He was ordered to leave the capital, and as he walked through the city's streets, suitcase in hand, he was thronged by worried Filipinos. "Where are you going, sir?" they asked. "Where's the Navy, sir? What's going to happen to us, sir?" King tried to answer as briefly as he could, not having the heart to let them know that he and the rest of the US military were getting out. "I just really felt awful about that," he said later. "I really felt like I was abandoning them myself."[19] Meanwhile, as preparations were made for a lengthy siege on Bataan, goods piled up in Manila harbor—everything from canned cherries to grand pianos still in their crates—soon became the target of frantic looting. "Beggars and priests, children and wrinkled old men preyed on the heaps like flies on a dung hill," wrote a civilian employee with the US authorities.[20]

King was not among the Americans ordered to Bataan, and instead he managed to leave the Philippines aboard the destroyer USS *Peary* in the last days of December. It was a nerve-wracking voyage south. By day, the destroyer would keep near tree-covered islands, camouflaged with branches and leaves to look like part of the jungle. At night, it moved on, sometimes passing close by Japanese vessels, whose crews assumed it was part of *their* navy. As a bitter irony, the destroyer had almost made it out of danger when it was attacked by three Australian twin-engine Lockheed Hudson light bombers, which misidentified the ship as Japanese. King was on the bridge with several other sailors trying to dodge the savage attacks. "We had a string of sandbags up on the flying bridge, and we would get on one side of the sandbags when they came from that direction, and hop on of the other side, and that sort of thing," he recalled later. It worked right until a bomb hit the ship's stern, killing the man right next to King: "A piece of shrapnel from the bomb... came up and took half his head off." After this tragic encounter, it was smooth sailing, and the *Peary* made its way to Australia to fight another day.[21]

Even for the Japanese, the Malayan peninsula was an intensely alien environment, where surviving, let alone fighting, was a tremendous challenge. F. Spencer Chapman, a British soldier, recalled the experience of being caught by a sudden tropical downpour in the Malay jungle: "Within half a minute we were soaked to the skin and having been unbearably hot all day were now equally disconsolate with cold. The rain came down so hard that it actually hurt our bare heads and hands, and we had to take shelter under a grove of coconut palms."[22] Worse perhaps than the actual physical hardship was the mental strain. "To troops unused to it, the jungle is apt to be terrifying and to produce physical and emotional distress which has to be felt to be appreciated," in the words of the British official historian. Even the rubber plantations, where the jungle had been touched by civilization, were deeply unsettling, as their "interminable lines of evenly spaced trees... and gloom, dampness and sound-deadening effect" had a depressing effect on the soldiers' morale.[23]

The peninsula had become a battleground from day one, after Japanese forces disembarked on the border between Malaya and Thailand, quickly establishing a foothold, and started their 450-mile-long march south towards the ultimate prize, Singapore—Britain's Gibraltar of the East. The Malay geography dictated the Japanese plans for reaching Singapore. A mountain range down the middle of the peninsula prompted the Japanese to divide their offensive into one southward thrust along the peninsula's west, and another along its east coast. There was only one way forward, and the troops were pushed with relentless energy: "To the south! To the south!" a Japanese major-general shouted in one of the battles, standing among flying bullets, while urging his troops forward.[24]

This was not at all what the British planners had expected. Singapore was supposed to be an impregnable fortress, and it had been fortified at great expense in the preceding years, with great guns able to blast any invading fleet off the surface of the ocean. This had lulled the British into a false sense of security. For while it was true that Singapore was hard if not impossible to attack from the sea, it was extremely vulnerable to attack via the land route. In this sense, the Singapore fortress was similar to the Maginot Line, which just one and a half years earlier had proven of no value in saving France from German conquest. Indeed, by deterring a frontal German attack, the Maginot fortifications had almost forced the Germans

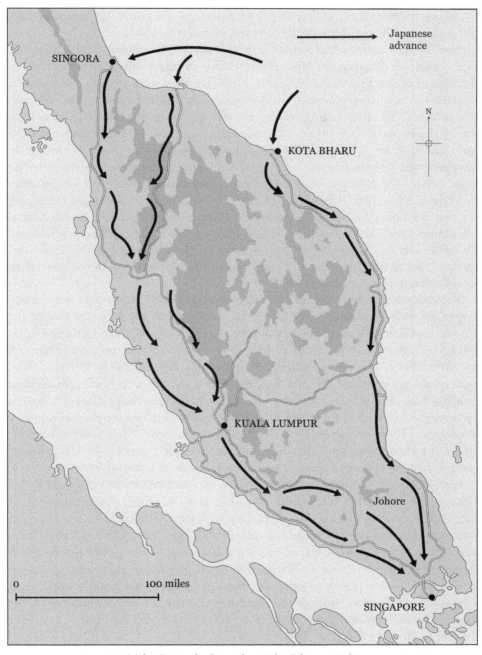

Malay Peninsula, December 1941–February 1942

to choose another strategy, attacking from a different direction. The same was very much true for the approach of the Japanese planners in 1941.

The Western nations had known at least since the Russo-Japanese War nearly four decades earlier that the Japanese were a foe to be reckoned with. Even so, in the course of the first weeks of war in East Asia they were surprised repeatedly, and with deadly consequences, as they gradually realized how much they still had to learn. The British Empire, Japan's old ally from the start of the century, was perhaps particularly guilty of underestimating the Japanese, and even the early loss of *Prince of Wales* and *Repulse* did not do much to shake its arrogance. Nowhere was this more evident than in Malaya, and nowhere was this attitude more costly. The Japanese were tough and committed, as was their commander in Malaya, Yamashita Tomoyuke, 56 years old and known among his colleagues for two personality traits: his extreme capability, and his extreme conservatism. Like Homma in the Philippines, he had been exposed to the Western world and European culture, having spent time both as a student and a diplomat in Germany, Austria, and Switzerland, but old affinities counted for nothing in the new harsh world created after December 7.[25]

The defenders only awakened to this threat little by little, and they were not helped by their commanders. Some of the scorn against the Japanese among the Commonwealth rank and file seemed to be the result of deliberate misinformation spread by officers keen to boost morale in an increasingly desperate situation. A few days after the war had started, soldiers of the 8th Australian Division, who were encamped south of the frontline, received a visit by an officer from division headquarters. The officer claimed to have first-hand knowledge from the battles up north and described the Japanese soldiers as fanatical and tough, but not very intelligent. "They were armed with small-caliber rifles," the officer told the soldiers. "If by any chance you were shot, the bullet only made a small hole which healed quickly, making it unnecessary for the wounded man to leave his unit."[26]

Lesley Gordon Gaffney, an infantryman with the division, was also told by his officers that he and his fellow soldiers had little to fear from the Japanese. Their airplanes, they were informed, were tied up with rope. The Japanese soldiers were short-sighted, and even if by chance their bullets hit their targets, the projectiles were made from rubber. Gaffney was soon disabused of any false notions about the weakness of the Japanese. Shortly after the beginning of the invasion, he was in a car with other passengers that fell into an ambush. He heard a click when a Japanese bullet went through the windshield of the car and hit another of the passengers, an English officer. "It went straight through and hit him… just above the temple through the glass. They weren't made of rubber, I can tell you," Gaffney said later.[27]

In fact, soldiers such as Gaffney were atypical. The first troops which the Japanese encountered when disembarking on the Malay coastline were Indians, and Indian units remained their main opponent throughout the campaign. Britain used one part of its empire to defend another. Out of 31 Commonwealth battalions deployed on the Malay Peninsula, 18 were Indian, six were British, six were Australian, and one was Malay.[28] A large number of Indian troops had originally been earmarked for the Middle East and had undergone training in Australia, specializing in tactics suitable for desert warfare. Now they were in the jungle. "One could argue that the Commonwealth troops in Malaya failed to unlearn the lessons of desert warfare in tropical conditions," Indian military historian Kaushik Roy writes, "and failed to adopt the required tactical techniques for fighting effectively in the different ecological landscape."[29]

The poor preparation of the Commonwealth troops made the preparations carried out by the Japanese seem all the more impressive. As a matter of fact, the Japanese campaign in Malaya was a rush job, planned in less than a year by a small group of dedicated officers operating on a minimal budget, seeking information from whoever in the Japanese Empire might be a good source. An old sea captain who had spent many years plying routes in the areas Japan planned to invade provided details about weather patterns and coastal conditions. The Ishihara Mining Company had useful information about the geography of the Malay Peninsula. Professors at Taiwan University filled the group in on hygiene in the tropics and measures against malaria.[30]

The Japanese, whose main experience with war had been on the Mongolian steppe and the rice fields of China, were no more used to jungle warfare than their Western counterparts, but they went into battle better prepared because of the questions that the planners asked, and found answers to. "What alterations had to be made in the organization of troops and the type of weapons and equipment used on the Siberian and Manchurian battlefields at twenty degrees below zero to meet requirements for fighting in the dense jungles of the tropics?" asked the planners, led by the capable but brutal officer Tsuji Masanobu. "How should tactics and strategy used against the Soviet Union be revised for action against British and American armies, and what comparisons could be made between the tactics, equipment and organization of Soviet, British, and American troops?"[31]

The preparations paid off. The Japanese soldiers landing in Malaya were equipped for quick, decisive movements through terrain where modern roads were only sparse. They had light tanks, light trucks, and first and foremost bicycles. An Australian staff officer, C. B. Dawkins, concluded that the Japanese had, in fact, understood what the Westerners had not: "Jungle, forest and rubber areas are *par excellence* infantry country—every move is screened from air and ground observations, the value of fire of weapons of all natures is very limited, and troops on the offensive can close to within assaulting distance unmolested."[32]

By Christmas, Lieutenant General Arthur Ernest Percival, the overall commander of Commonwealth forces in Malaya, had to revise many previously held views of the Japanese foes, as he explained later: "It was now clear that we were faced by an enemy who had made a special study of bush warfare on a grand scale and whose troops had been specially trained in those tactics. He relied in the main on out-flanking movements and infiltration by small parties into and behind our lines... his infantry had displayed an ability to cross obstacles—rivers, swamps, jungles, etc.—more rapidly than had previously been thought possible."[33]

Faced with a terrifying foe, the Commonwealth defenders went from under-estimating the Japanese foes' quality to overestimating their quantity. "A British soldier is equal to ten Japanese, but unfortunately there are eleven Japanese," an injured Tommy told American correspondent Cecil Brown.[34] The British Army in Malaya could not believe it was being beaten by the Japanese, and its members had to conjure up superior numbers to explain what happened to them. In fact, there were about twice as many British-led soldiers as there were Japanese. In Malaya as in all other major land campaigns that the Japanese waged early in the war, they invariably fielded numerically inferior troops, which nevertheless excelled in all other parameters.[35]

Some Commonwealth soldiers, incredulous at the skill of the Japanese, believed they saw a German or other European hand guiding them. For instance, in an unsuccessful attempt to take the tactically important Batu Pekaka bridge on the west side of the peninsula, the soldiers of one Japanese unit disguised themselves as Malays, and, according to persistent rumors, they were led by a mysterious European in plainclothes, who was killed in the skirmish...[36] Some thought the European, if he ever existed, was a former member of the French Foreign Legion, who had ended up in Japanese captivity during the invasion of Indochina in 1940 and had opted for cooperation rather than prison camp, but most believed he was a German who had somehow ended up thousands of miles from home.[37] The bottom line was that the extent of cooperation among the Axis partners was unknown at the time, giving rise to wild speculation. British pilots flying over Malaya even reported sightings of Messerschmitt 109s and 110s as well as Stukas.[38]

In fact, there were less fantastic explanations for the serial defeats. One of them was betrayal in Commonwealth ranks. Within just three days of the first landings in Malaya, Japanese aircraft had destroyed almost all British planes operating in the north. It turned out that they had been successful partly because they had been guided via radio by a centrally placed spy, New Zealand-born, 31-year-old Captain Patrick Heenan. Apparently, he had been recruited by Japanese intelligence during a lengthy leave from active service spent in Japan in the late 1930s. As early as December 10, Heenan's activities were discovered and he was placed under arrest, but by this time, the damage had already been done.[39]

★ ★ ★

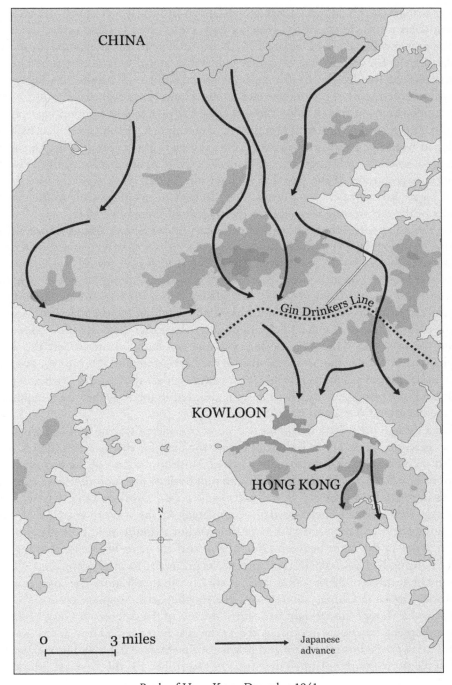

CHINA

Gin Drinkers Line

KOWLOON

HONG KONG

N

0   3 miles   Japanese advance

Battle of Hong Kong, December 1941

Hong Kong, which had been a British possession for nearly a century, had existed precariously on the fringe of the growing Japanese Empire in China since the end of the previous decade, and by late 1941 it paid the price for its exposed location. Militarily, the tiny colony was extremely vulnerable, and as a naval base it had been overshadowed for decades by the Japanese strongpoint on Taiwan.[40] As Japanese forces occupied south China in the late 1930s, Hong Kong eventually found itself surrounded from nearly all sides. Nevertheless, the planners in London repeatedly emphasized the need to defend Hong Kong, arguing first and foremost that its loss to Japan would be a serious blow to British prestige in the region.[41] This put them in a bind, since the only alternative option, to pull out all or most forces from Hong Kong in recognition of the fact that it could not be defended, was considered an even bigger loss of face.[42] As a result, they decided to maintain their soldiers and sailors in the city, setting the stage for the tragedy of December 1941.

At the exact time when the Japanese military unleashed its offensive potential across the region, Japan's 38th Division, reinforced with extra artillery units, marched across the Chinese border into Hong Kong. The British plan for this scenario was clear and followed logically from the colony's geography. Hong Kong island itself was only a small, but relatively easily defendable part of the territory under British control. In addition, the British authorities had leased part of the mainland north of the island, which was much harder to protect. Therefore, there was little question about the priorities. "The main defense was on the island," wrote Robert Brooke-Popham, commander-in-chief of the British Far East Command. "Whilst the enemy were to be delayed as long as possible in any advance over the leased territory on the mainland, the troops had orders to retire if attacked in force, as they were required for the defense of the island itself."[43]

Even though the British defenders had never considered staying on the mainland for an extended period once hostilities began, the fight for that part of Hong Kong ended up being even shorter than anticipated. Within two days of the commencement of hostilities, the British forces had to pull back to the main defensive feature across the mainland territory. It was the so-called Gin Drinkers Line, a system of pillboxes that had only been partially completed. At the western extreme of the line, a Japanese battalion seized the key Shing Mun redoubt, held by a platoon of Royal Scots, in the night between December 9 and 10. Years of intense training in night fighting had paid off for the Japanese, at great cost to their adversaries. "The capture by surprise of this key position," wrote Christopher Maltby, the commander of British troops in China, "directly and gravely affected subsequent events."[44]

Once the Shing Mun redoubt had fallen, the rest of the defenses at Gin Drinkers Line collapsed like a house of cards, and over the next four days, all British-led troops were ferried across from the mainland district of Kowloon to the island proper, leading to phase two of the planned defense. On December 13, the Japanese attackers requested the surrender of Hong Kong island, and were turned down. In response, several days of artillery shelling and bomber attacks followed, knocking out a large number of British positions. On December 17, the Japanese commander sent yet another group of envoys carrying a demand of surrender. "Envoys apparently genuinely surprised and disconcerted when proposal was summarily rejected," Maltby reported to his superiors. "They left with hint that bombardment would be more indiscriminate than hitherto."[45]

The confident British attitude disguised an uncomfortable fact. The battle had not gone well. Partly this was due to flaws in the defense. The British forces had grown soft during years of uneventful garrison service. "Between the two World Wars the British soldiers in Hong Kong had never had it so good," according to historian Tim Carew. Food and beer were plentiful, and although the weekly wage was only 14 shillings, "one shilling and three pence per week purchased the services of a servant."[46] Further lowering their combat readiness, their best officers and NCOs had been sent to the war in Europe. In addition to a locally recruited force of volunteers as old as 65, reinforcements had been dispatched to Hong Kong just before the Japanese invasion, but they were of inconsistent quality. Two Canadian battalions that arrived just on the eve of the battle were trained mainly in internal security functions. Two Indian battalions with tough but woefully ill-prepared junior soldiers known as *jawans* were sent into battle with newly supplied mortars but no training in how to use them.[47]

Partly, and just as importantly, the British debacle was, once again, due to a systematic pre-war underestimation of Japanese military prowess, which now came back to haunt the defenders. Christopher Maltby, whose troops also counted a large number of Canadians and Indians, quickly became impressed with the Japanese ability to move swiftly and stealthily. "All were provided with rubber soled boots that made movement very silent, systematically they used the smallest of paths and avoided all the more obvious lines of advance, and their patrols were very boldly handled," he wrote after the war. "The pace of the advance was surprisingly fast, the troops were lightly equipped and must have been very fit to accomplish the marches undertaken."[48] John Monro, a brigade major, described how the Japanese "pulled a gigantic surprise on us," and as an artilleryman he envied their capacity to immediately provide close support for their infantry. "Before the war we looked down upon him, considering ourselves more than his match both in physique, training and equipment. To our consternation we found him better than ourselves in all respects."[49]

As in Malaya, a major reason for the rapid Japanese advance was solid preparation, including prior espionage and recruitment among locals. "It was obvious from all sources that agents and spies had been placed both on the mainland and the island well beforehand. Spies led the leading elements on the mainland, disguised as innocent laborers or coolies," Maltby wrote. "Their patrols advanced by paths which could have been known only to locals or from detailed reconnaissance.

Armed agents in Kowloon and Hong Kong systematically fired during the hours of darkness on troops, sentries, cars and dispatch riders, but little damage was done thereby beyond straining the nerves of a number of the men."[50] The local auxiliaries seemed to be selling their services not so much because of any particular disdain for the British, and rather because of the remuneration the Japanese offered. This included loot; several British prisoners later reported having their watches, jewelry, and other expensive belongings removed by them.[51]

The Japanese landing on Hong Kong began in the evening of December 18, with a focus on the northeastern part of the island. The brunt of the attack fell on one of the two Indian battalions, which quickly buckled. To quote an Indian historian, once the British officers and NCOs had become casualties, "the illiterate *jawans* could not tackle the fluid battle scenario."[52] Defenses in the invasion area were weak because the British commanders were concerned that landings might also take place in the south of the island and therefore had to allocate troops there too. In some spots the Japanese advance from the coastal area was alleviated by the local fifth columnists, who had cut holes in the barbed wire along the beaches, and in the course of the dark hours, they secured a solid foothold on the island.[53]

The defenders were pushed back along the entire front, and it was questionable how much longer they could hold up. "The troops had now been in action for eleven days with no respite," Maltby wrote. "Owing to the shortage of hot food and sleep, and the impossibility of providing reliefs because of the lack of troops, signs of strain were beginning to appear."[54] In the course of the following week, the Japanese forces gradually pushed their way west towards the most developed part of Hong Kong island. Although the final outcome was not in doubt, the Japanese attackers admitted to the trouble they were encountering in a later account: "The enemy fire from these positions was so heavy that not only was the advance balked, but our troops were thrown into confusion... Furthermore, the terrain in this area was so rugged and separated by interlocking ravines that our contact with the advance units was at one time entirely broken."[55] Maltby attempted an ultimately futile counterattack on December 20, but it was marred by flawed execution. When an Indian officer was ordered to disengage from the enemy prior to the counterstrike, he misunderstood the message and took it to mean that the fight had to be abandoned altogether, leading him to destroy his howitzers.[56]

The Japanese air force came as an unpleasant surprise to the Hong Kong garrison, who had also succumbed to the widespread propaganda about Japanese inferiority. High-level bombing was crushingly efficient, just as low-flying attack planes put on a display of skill and boldness that, once again, caused many British defenders to believe they must be led by Germans.[57] In addition, Japanese infantry units carried armor-piercing ammunition, turning out to be highly useful against the steel shutters of the British bunkers and pillboxes.[58] Maltby, too, was impressed by the Japanese mortar units: "The Japanese handling of mortars was extremely good. They were quick into action, were quickly ranged, and accurate concentrations were put down at short notice at ranges of 1,500 yards."[59]

Meanwhile, Hong Kong was turned into a city under siege. One of the most noticeable changes was the breakdown of all reserve in a society that had traditionally prided itself on the tradition of the stiff upper lip. American author Wenzell Brown recorded this strange transformation: "Englishmen whom I had seen a few times before raised their hands in greeting and laughed as they passed or stopped to ask if I was all right and if there was anything they could do for me. Men who I had no idea knew me called me by name and sometimes stopped to chat. The comradeship which a common danger engenders sprang up and never abated during the siege."[60]

The new-found solidarity among Hong Kong's Western residents did little to counteract the general eeriness of approaching doom. The stench was the worst, as the smell of sewage spilling out of broken mains combined with that of the dead who had been rotting in the sun. "Exhausted soldiers slept... and buried their faces in their arms in order to keep out the stench of death, excreta and putrefaction," Brown wrote. At night, he felt as if he was walking the streets of a dead city, where the sounds of war moved ever nearer and mixed with other, quite unrelated sounds of a millennium-old Chinese culture that seemed to live its own life apart from the ongoing conflict: "The thin, monotonous wail of Chinese musical instruments could be heard through darkened, barred doors of Chinese shops."[61]

Churchill emphasized in a telegram to the beleaguered garrison that surrender was not an option: "The enemy should be compelled to expend the utmost life and equipment. There must be vigorous fighting in the inner defences, and, if need be, from house to house."[62] By Christmas, however, it was abundantly clear that further resistance served no purpose. On December 25, Maltby asked one of his regimental commanders how much longer he could hold out. The reply was, "One hour." At a quarter past three in the afternoon, he advised the colony's governor that no further useful military resistance was possible. "I ordered all the Commanding Officers to break off the fighting and to capitulate to the nearest Japanese Commander, as and when the enemy advanced and opportunity offered," he wrote later.[63]

During the battle of Hong Kong, the Japanese put on display concepts of honor that to their Western foes came across as being archaic or downright alien. During fierce fighting on Hong Kong island on December 19, Brigadier J. K. Lawson's headquarters was overrun by the Japanese, who were shooting into the shelters at pointblank range. Lawson reported to General Maltby that he would destroy anything of value to the enemy and then walk outside "to fight it out."[64] This was the last anyone heard from him alive. The Japanese found his body where he had been killed and treated it with great respect. "I ordered the temporary burial of the officer on the battleground on which he had died so heroically," a Japanese colonel wrote in a post-war account. The body was wrapped in a blanket belonging to the Japanese officer who had led the final storm on Lawson's position.[65]

This was in sharp contrast to Japanese conduct elsewhere during the battle. At St. Stephens College, which had been turned into a military hospital, Japanese soldiers broke in on Christmas morning, stabbing the patients in their beds. "I clearly saw the intention of the Japanese troops who had reached the hospital and had already commenced bayoneting every bed they encountered," one of the patients later said. He and his wife, who was a nurse, hid under his bed, escaping the fate of the others.[66] This atrocity appears to have been carried out without the sanction of higher-level officers, and there is some evidence to suggest that the Japanese Army itself executed soldiers found guilty of having committed the outrages.[67] Elsewhere, it often seemed as if senior officers condoned the excesses. Personnel at an advanced dressing station at Shau Kei Wan, in the northeast of Hong Kong island, surrendered to the Japanese and were executed almost immediately afterwards. Some were bayoneted, and others were decapitated. Corporal Norman Leath survived a Japanese officer's attempt at killing him with his sword: "I [...] felt a terrific blow on the back of my neck. The blow shot me into the air, spun me completely round and I fell to the ground face downwards. I lay in this position with blood pouring into my eyes, ears and mouth."[68]

CHAPTER THREE

"A Clockwork of Gears and Cogwheels"

January 1942

During the first four days of 1942, Chinese and Japanese troops were locked in a desperate struggle on the outskirts of the city of Changsha. Fighting was particularly intense in the areas around the southern and eastern gates of the ancient city walls and see-saw battles raged over positions of special tactical value. A mound known as "Graveyard Hill" changed hands 11 times in the course of 72 hours.[1] It was the third time in little more than two years that Chinese and Japanese soldiers were fighting for the city, and with good reason. It was the key to China's most important rice-producing provinces, which supplied food for populous areas around the city of Chongqing, the nation's wartime capital deep in the country's southwest. That made it one of just a handful of positions that the Chinese could not afford to lose, no matter how much pressure was applied on them on other fronts.[2]

Changsha was the capital of Hunan province, but it was also considered the unofficial "capital" of the local Chinese commander, Xue Yue, a 45-year-old fiery southerner who was nicknamed the "Tiger of Changsha" because of his history of organizing a highly successful defense of the city during earlier Japanese offensives. Xue pushed himself as hard as his men, getting up at half past three every morning,[3] and unlike many other senior military men in China, he had been appointed mainly because of his professional capabilities, not because of his personal connections. Indeed, he had a history of rivalry with Chiang Kai-shek, China's overall leader, but now when the nation was involved in a life-and-death struggle against the Japanese invader, past grudges sometimes mattered less. After days of fighting in early January 1942, Chiang even sent a telegram to Xue Yue and his troops: "If you persevere, you will be able to destroy the enemy and achieve everlasting glory."[4]

The most recent battle of Changsha was triggered by the Japanese. General Anami Korechika, the commander of Japan's 11th Army, which was responsible for operations in Central China, had launched an offensive in the direction of the city in December, hoping to support the invasion of Hong Kong by diverting part of the Chinese attention away from the south.[5] It could have worked if it had taken place simultaneously with the Hong Kong battle. Instead, it only really got underway at a time when the fighting over the British colony was already over, defeating the entire point of dividing the enemy's attention.[6] More seriously, the Japanese had prepared a swift attack by light forces, supported by a slender supply route. The Chinese took note and used the Japanese's own tactics against them.[7]

The Chinese managed to lure them into a trap. While the Japanese infantry was fighting for Changsha, Chinese troops cut their supply lines in the rear, forcing them to beat a humiliating retreat and killing large numbers of troops along the way.[8] Surprisingly, Xue Yue had succeeded in preparing a ruse virtually identical to one he had used during the previous battle of Changsha, only a few months earlier, in the fall of 1941. Both then and now, a strong Japanese force had penetrated south deep into Chinese-held territory, aiming for Changsha. And both then and now, they had failed to protect their supply lines to the rear, with fatal consequences to themselves.[9] "The withdrawal was carried out under considerable hardship," according to a post-war Japanese account. "Not only did the Japanese forces have to fight off persistent assaults from large enemy forces... but they had also been compelled to escort a large number of casualties and rear service units."[10] Indeed, the Japanese troops might have been annihilated entirely, had they not enjoyed nearly complete air superiority, the official Chinese history of the war commented.[11]

Apart from the advantage in the form of tactical air support, the Japanese were in an unfavorable situation in ways that took them by surprise. They had been accustomed to having better and more abundant materiel in most previous battles with the Chinese, but now suddenly found themselves out of supply in terms of both ammunition and provisions. In some regiments, soldiers had only 10-15 bullets, and several platoons were supplied with just one or two hand grenades to share among their soldiers. Under these circumstances, they were forced to fight with swords and bayonets.[12] Japanese soldiers taken prisoner by the Chinese reported having gone into battle carrying five days of rations, but not having eaten for entire days prior to their capture, since it was impossible to cook rice due to the incessant fighting that took place both night and day.[13]

Even though the Japanese had made grave mistakes, victory did not come easily to the Chinese. Casualties were massive and beyond anything that a Western army would accept, but in the Chinese context, a high death toll seemed almost to be a point in itself. Discipline was Draconian in the Chinese Army, and life was cheap, even among officers. A company commander left the frontline just before a Japanese attack, ostensibly to ask for instructions from division headquarters. The divisional commander did not bother to listen to a single word that his officer had planned to utter but ordered him executed on the spot for dereliction of duty. "On the spot" meant what it said. The officer was put against a wall and shot moments later.[14] Given the high risk of meeting a sinister fate, most Chinese soldiers remained in their positions, and ended up paying the ultimate price anyway. One regiment was down to just 58 survivors after several days of fighting.[15]

Changsha was the only place where the Japanese Army was suffering defeat in early 1942. At a time of rapid advances everywhere else, the battle was a reminder that China remained a major liability to Japan. Preparations for the offensive in the Pacific had confronted Japanese planners with one of their main strategic conundrums. Ultimately, the war with America and the other Western powers had been unleashed over China, but at the same time, China was a major reason why the Japanese Army could not allocate all its resources to the vital task of beating the new enemy into submission in the crucial first months of the campaign. Large numbers of troops were required to carry out garrison duty in China and keep the Chinese military at bay, and in the north sizable forces were required to remain idle in a passive wait for a Soviet invasion that might never happen, but then again could happen at every moment. Therefore, only limited numbers of troops could be detached from duty in China for service in the Pacific.[16]

After four years of war, Japan was forced to acknowledge the inherent toughness and unending patience of the Chinese foe. Japanese from all walks of life who came into contact with the Chinese reluctantly came to admire their perseverance. A Japanese factory manager in northern Manchukuo, a puppet state established on the territory of three former Chinese provinces, was impressed by the endurance of his manual workers, giving him "a mysterious feeling" that they were "not human."[17] During the last days before Hong Kong's occupation, Westerners accidentally watched a telling scene. A group of civilian Chinese were made to walk through a barricade guarded by Japanese gendarmes, when one of them suddenly hurled an insult at the Japanese. A gendarme walked down the line of Chinese, and picked one of them at random, striking him furiously over the head and torso with a heavy stick. The other Chinese were watching in silence, but once the gendarme turned his back to them, they laughed out loudly. Even the man who had been beaten up joined in. "Monkey man," he said with glee in his voice, even as he was wiping blood from his face, "very, very stupid. He beat wrong man." One of the Westerners who had watched the entire brutal scene asked a friend of his: "How can the Japanese win against a people like that?"[18]

China's willingness to hurl millions of its own people into a long, bloody war was a major asset to its new American and British allies. "The stubborn resistance of the Chinese," a US State Department memorandum declared, "destroys Japan's claim that she comes to emancipate either China or Asia!"[19] At the same time, a track record of having stood up to Japan for more than four years prior to Pearl Harbor gave China new confidence. This was in evidence shortly after the outbreak of the Pacific war when Archibald Wavell, the commander-in-chief of British forces in India, visited Chiang Kai-shek in Chongqing, carrying only news of endless defeats and setbacks. "You and your people have no idea how to fight the Japanese," Chiang told his British guest in language that was only slightly mitigated by the nervous translator. "Resisting the Japanese is not like suppressing colonial rebellions... For this kind of job, you British are incompetent, and you should learn from the Chinese how to fight against the Japanese."[20]

★ ★ ★

China was a prominent issue dividing the United States and Britain from the outset. Churchill and Roosevelt did not see eye to eye. On his trip across the Atlantic for the Arcadia Conference, the first summit on British-American strategy after the US entry into the war, the British prime minister later said, "If I can epitomize in one word the lesson I learned in the United States, it was 'China'."[21] Britain's lukewarm attitude towards the Chinese friend was a mirror image of its denigration of the Japanese foe, partly borne out of more than a century as a colonial power in Asia, which had led to an ingrained feeling of cultural and even racial superiority. In conversations with Roosevelt in Washington DC, Churchill stretched as far as he thought he could on the issue, which was not much: "I said I would of course always be helpful and polite to the Chinese, whom I admired and liked as a race and pitied for their endless misgovernment, but that he must not expect me to adopt what I felt was a wholly unreal standard of values."[22]

The two leaders and their governments had entirely different views on the value of China as an alliance partner. United States envisaged a major role for China in the war in East Asia and expected it to become one of the predominant Allies setting the tone for the entire effort to defeat Japan. Britain, on the other hand, expected little from China and often treated it as something in between an annoyance and a strategic competitor. When China offered to send two armies to the British colony of Burma, which had up to then largely escaped Japanese aggression, Britain initially turned down the offer. This was based on the belief that Japan was too tied up elsewhere to attempt a major offensive onto Burmese territory. In this perspective, a Chinese presence on British-controlled soil was a price not worth paying considering expectation of only meager payoff.[23]

In spite of the British reservations, Sino-American cooperation was beginning to materialize in a small way, even as Roosevelt, Churchill, and their aides were talking in the US capital. For Claire Chennault, the flamboyant former Army aviator who now headed a group of American volunteer pilots in China, the time had now come to put his men into action. One morning a few weeks after Pearl Harbor, staff at his airbase near the city of Kunming in southwest China received reports from a network of Chinese observers on the ground that ten unescorted Japanese bombers were heading in his direction. He ordered one squadron of P-40 planes in the air to intercept the approaching aircraft. "This was the decisive moment I had been awaiting for more than four years," Chennault wrote in his memoirs. "American pilots in American fighting planes aided by Chinese ground warning net about to tackle a formation of the Imperial Japanese Air Force, which was then sweeping the Pacific skies victorious everywhere."[24]

Chennault listened tensely to the radio as the American fighters started their search. "There they are," one metallic voice crackled over the wireless. "No, no, they can't be Japs," another voice replied, triggering a quick retort: "Look at those red balls." A disorganized battle followed, in which the American pilots closed in on the bombers, shooting wildly. There was no coordination, and it was mere luck that no US plane was shot down by friendly fire. Three Japanese bombers went down in flames, and smoke was tracing several others when they abandoned their mission and steered for the horizon. Back home at the base, Chennault was standing ready, and even though it was the first time his pilots had seen battle since the United States had entered into the war, he had less-than-encouraging words for them: "It was a good job, but not good enough. Next time get them all."[25]

There would be many more opportunities to face the Japanese in the air in the weeks that followed, as the Americans operated not just over China, but also over neighboring Burma and Thailand, where the air war would soon be raging despite the absence of action on the ground. David Lee Hill, a pilot from Texas, had his first combat mission around New Year and found himself chasing a Japanese fighter. "I just pulled right up behind him, fired my machine guns, and he blew up. Simultaneously, someone had made an overhead pass on me and shot 33 holes in my airplane. I'm turning into this second guy coming head-on. I shot him down," Hill said. Despite the damage done to his airplane, he made it back to his base.[26] The exploits of the American volunteer pilots, soon known as the "Flying Tigers," was one of the few bright spots at a time when the Western powers were forced into the defensive everywhere. In a telegram to Churchill, the British governor of Burma, Sir Reginald Hugh Dorman-Smith, wrote: "The victories of these Americans over the rice paddies of Burma are comparable in character, if not in scope, with those won by the Royal Air Force over the hop fields of Kent in the Battle of Britain."[27]

The "Flying Tigers" were also a major boon for morale at home in the United States, but the small band of mercenary aviators could only do so much in the Chinese theater of war, which was essentially continental in mere geographical extent. In light of its view of China as a pivotal battleground, the US government wished to signal its commitment to its new Asian ally in the clearest way possible. A much wider commitment of men and materiel was needed, just as coordination with Chiang Kai-shek at the highest level was required. Chiang wanted an American officer with the rank of at least lieutenant general to serve as his chief of staff, and Washington was ready to give him what he wanted. The question was who.[28]

After some discussion, the War Department nominated Major General Joseph W. Stilwell. It was an obvious choice. Stilwell's numerous tours on the Asian mainland, adding up to a decade spent in China, had made him extremely knowledgeable about the Chinese Army, and his ability to speak and read Chinese was an added advantage. However, he was lukewarm about the position, since he had already been tentatively selected to a much more visible job as commander of the Allied invasion of North Africa. On January 14, he got a first inkling that he was in fact going to China. "More and more, the finger of destiny is pointing at you," Secretary of War Henry L. Stimson told Stilwell after inviting him to his home. Stilwell's reply was brief and unenthusiastic: "I'll go where I'm sent."[29]

On January 1, MacArthur estimated in a message to Washington that his forces in the Philippines could hold out for no longer than three more months, arguing that reinforcement was essential for the future of the United States in that part of the world. "The yielding of the Philippines by default and without a major effort would mark the end of white prestige and influence in the east," he warned. "In view of the Filippinos effort the United States must move strongly to their support and promptly or withdraw in shame from the Orient."[30] General Marshall replied in a non-committal way, stating only that "every day of time you gain is vital to the concentration of the overwhelming power necessary for our purpose."[31] How overwhelming that power would have to be was highlighted in a study that war planners were completing while Marshall was writing to MacArthur. In order to realistically relieve the beleaguered forces in the Philippines, it would be necessary to undertake "an entirely unjustifiable diversion of forces from the principal theater—the Atlantic."[32] In other words, MacArthur and his men were on their own.

As if to underline the dwindling hope in the Philippines, the Japanese Army under General Homma entered Manila on January 2. American and British civilians residing in the city were ordered to stay at home, awaiting registration as enemy aliens. "Enemy alien! That was a queer thing for an American to be in the Philippines," wrote Margaret Utinsky, a nurse who had lived in the country for the better part of a decade.[33] The Japanese residents of Manila, many of whom had been incarcerated since the start of hostilities nearly a month earlier, were enthusiastic at what they saw as liberation. The tables had been turned. "The joyful voices of the Japanese residents were overwhelming," said General Morioka Susumu, commander of the troops marching into the conquered city.[34]

Meanwhile, the reversal of the "MacArthur plan" continued in the first days of January, as long columns of American and Philippine soldiers streamed into Bataan, while their comrades manned thin defense lines in an attempt to keep a corridor open against Japanese attacks from both north and south. The withdrawal was a "sickening" experience, and the soldiers filing into the peninsula were a "pathetic lot," according to Wainwright, who witnessed how many of his Filipino soldiers were now barefoot after having seen their sneakers cut to pieces from days of fighting in razor-sharp jungle grass. "Some came in silent, blacked-out busses," he said in his memoirs. "But most of them came stumbling down the main highway from San Fernando, heavy with weariness and steeped in the knowledge that they were walking into little more than a trap."[35]

The American-led forces which now took up position in Bataan were decimated and worn down, but at the same time, and without knowing it, they faced a weakened Japanese force. On the same day that General Homma's troops moved into Manila, he received a message that his 48th Division, by far the best unit under his command, was to move to the Dutch East Indies. This left the task of completing the Philippine campaign to the 16th Division, considered below average in fighting capabilities, and the 65th Brigade, which had recently been shipped in from Formosa and was, even in the assessment of its own commander, "absolutely unfit for combat duty."[36]

The American troops on Bataan made a fighting retreat, pulling back to successive defensive lines prepared in advance across the peninsula. Somewhat symbolically, while the previous month had seen the first US armor battle of World War II, this month saw the last cavalry charge in American military history. On January 16, First Lieutenant Edwin Ramsey led a platoon of mounted soldiers into the streets of Morong village, located near a river in northwestern Bataan, attacking a Japanese force head-on in a fashion reminiscent of the American Civil War eight decades earlier. "Bent nearly prone across the horses' necks, we flung ourselves at the Japanese advance, pistols firing full into their startled faces," Ramsey wrote in his memoirs. "A few returned our fire but most fled in confusion, some wading back into the river, others running madly for the swamps. To them we must have seemed a vision from another century, wild-eyed horses pounding headlong; cheering, whooping men firing from the saddles."[37]

While American and Filipino soldiers were fighting and dying, MacArthur's senior staff received a donation of 650,000 dollars by presidential order number one of 1942 by Manuel Quezon, the Philippine head of state. Of this amount, 500,000 dollars went to the general himself. "God, I would like to be a general," Master Sergeant Paul P. Rogers, a stenographer attached to the American staff, thought to himself as he typed up the order.[38] While there was nothing illegal about the payment, it was highly unusual. "Seldom, if ever, have American military officers received such evidence of high esteem," commented historian Carol Morris Petillo, who first found evidence of the presidential generosity .[39] It is one of the most controversial aspects of MacArthur's legacy, even though historians have pointed out that the payment was made at a time when he and his closest family, surrounded on all sides by Japanese forces, believed they were facing either death or at best lengthy captivity. "He accepted the money with poor prospects of ever getting to spend it," one of his biographers commented.[40]

★ ★ ★

The virtual impossibility of relieving MacArthur's forces in the Philippines reflected the overall strategic situation in early 1942. The Western nations, who for more than a century had been the masters of the Asia Pacific, were forced into playing a reactive game in the weeks and months after Pearl Harbor. "The Japanese, taking full advantage of surprise, not to mention treachery, have succeeded in isolating, for the moment, the region of the Far East in which they wish to operate," John Kennedy, a senior officer in the British War Office, wrote in a note. "The possibility of serious interference with their plans by either the British or the American fleet must be ruled out for a very considerable period."[41]

The best the Allies could do in the face of a determined and well-prepared adversary was to pool their resources and ensure that their forces in Asia were operating in a coordinated manner. Among the senior officers, who retained painful memories of the costly lessons of the previous war against Imperial Germany, there was widespread agreement about the need to cooperate. "It was not until 1918 that it was accomplished and much valuable time, blood, and treasure had been needlessly sacrificed," General Marshall argued, speaking on behalf of many of his much-tried cohort, not just in the United States but also in Britain and the Commonwealth.[42]

ABDA Command was established on January 2, 1942, unifying American, British, Dutch, and Australian troops fighting in Southeast Asia into a hastily built multinational force. There was little rivalry among the involved nations to fill the position of ABDA commander, since most of the territory he would be ordered to defend was all but certain to fall soon to the Japanese. Unsurprisingly, America suggested a British general at the head, and the day after the formation of ABDA, Archibald Wavell, the commander of British forces in India, was appointed to the job.[43] Churchill was lukewarm towards the arrangement, but decided there was no way around bowing to the US wishes. "We are no longer single, but married," the British prime minister said, arguing for the need to compromise.[44]

There was no doubt that Wavell was assuming a crushing burden. The instructions to ABDA Command, sounding weirdly out of touch in the middle of defeat everywhere, and unlikely to reflect any notions of what could realistically be done, were to "maintain as many key positions as possible, but to take the offensive at the earliest opportunity and ultimately to conduct an all-out offensive against Japan."[45] In practice, what was expected of Wavell in the early stages of the war was to hold onto the Malay Barrier,[46] defined as a line cutting down the Malay Peninsula, Sumatra, Java, and eastwards towards Australia.[47] Even that was a tall order, and Wavell, keeping within the matrimonial terminology used by Churchill, exclaimed: "I had been handed not just a baby but quadruplets."[48]

★ ★ ★

One of Wavell's first acts as ABDA commander was to inspect the defenses in Malaya. During a hectic few hours in the frontline, he visited a number of field units and had frank discussions with two brigade commanders, who had spent exhausting weeks with their Indian troops in a failing bid to stem the Japanese onslaught. "I have never seen two men look so tired," Wavell's assistant Alexander Reid Scott wrote in his diary.[49] Returning to Singapore, Wavell penned his impressions in a report. "These divisions have now been fighting for over [a] month without rest and retreating continuously under most trying conditions," he wrote, adding tersely: "Retreat does not bring out [the] best qualities of Indian troops and [the] men are utterly weary and completely bewildered by Japanese rapid encirclement tactics, by enemy air bombing (though this has luckily been only intermittent) and by lack of our own air support."[50]

Shortly afterwards, Wavell ordered the troops in Malaya to retreat to Johore, the territory forming the southernmost part of the peninsula, to prepare a more solid defense there. By this time, however, the psychological war was already lost. As the Japanese were moving rapidly towards the ultimate objective of Singapore, the initial sense of superiority that many Commonwealth soldiers had felt towards the Japanese had been replaced by an incipient feeling of inferiority. The frequent use of attacks after dark, a tactic mastered by the Japanese, gave them an edge. In one instance, a group of Japanese soldiers took advantage of the dark to penetrate deep into British-held territory and attack the headquarters of a brigade, killing every officer except the brigadier himself.[51] "The night is one million reinforcements," was one of the mottoes used by the Japanese Army when training its soldiers.[52]

Winston Mathews, a British soldier, spoke for many when he argued that the British lacked the necessary training for warfare in a jungle. "I can remember the sergeants telling me who came from England, there is a gorge here and a hedge here—fiddlesticks, there is no hedge in the blooming jungle," he said "You needed what the Japanese had, rubber shoes and a bicycle. And that's how you got on. They advanced at a rate of knots per hour, and here we were fiddling around with army boots and packs and all that sort of thing. You don't do that in a jungle."[53] He also noticed that the ordinary Japanese soldier carried his own food—a little bag of uncooked rice and small amounts of dried and salted food. "We had great big containers with stew and vegetable and potatoes and all that kind of thing, and then you had to go to each soldier and give it to him," he said. "We didn't have a clue as to how to train our people."[54]

National differences came out more clearly in the harsh jungle. The stiff pecking orders of the British military were maintained even in the primitive conditions, whereas the flat hierarchies of the Australians appeared to some observers more suited for the new strange environment. "The Australian Army is undoubtedly the world's most democratic, and the troops in Malaya prove it," wrote American correspondent F. Tillman Durdin, reporting how the salute resembled a "Hi, there" gesture. "An Australian officer can command his men only if he proves himself as good a man as any of his unit."[55]

Given the nature of the fighting, and the fact that much of it took place at night, the belligerents rarely got to see each other up close. A group of British soldiers operating behind enemy lines were able to observe the enemy from a distance, hidden by the dense jungle vegetation. They were surprised by what they saw: "Some of them were actually wearing football jerseys; they seemed to have no standard uniform or equipment and were traveling as light as they possibly could. Some were green, others gray, khaki or even dirty white. The majority had trousers hanging loose or enclosed in high boots or puttees; some had tight breeches, and others shorts and rubber boots or gym shoes. Their hats showed the greatest variety: a few tin hats, topees of all shapes, wide-brimmed terai or ordinary felt hats, high-peaked jockey hats, little caps with eye-shades or even a piece of cloth tied round the head and hanging down behind."[56]

The Japanese forces might have come across as a juggernaut to their shocked enemy, but in fact they were spread extremely thin during the offensive operations taking up the first months after Pearl Harbor. As the official Japanese history put it, "the units concerned had to move as an elaborate clockwork of gears and cogwheels."[57] This was the reason why the 48th Division was removed from the Philippines in early January. It was not that its services were no longer needed in Bataan, but it was needed even more desperately in the Netherlands East Indies. The Dutch colonies were the ultimate objective of the entire Japanese offensive, but they could only be approached now, about a month into the Japanese offensive, once control of the "steppingstones" on the road towards the Netherlands empire—the Philippines and Malaya—were within grasp.

By mid-January, the timing was right, and the Japanese invasion of key islands in the Dutch East Indies commenced. The Japanese offensive proceeded along three major axes, of which the central thrust was directed at the island of Borneo and its major oil fields. A landing on the oil-producing island of Tarakan had been expected to take place in pitch black, but the Dutch had set fire to their oilfields, and the raging flames burned the sky an ominous red, against which the island was put in stark silhouette.[58] The Dutch defenders found that local troops under their command quickly switched loyalties. Indonesian soldiers who were taken prisoner willingly gave up Dutch positions to their Japanese captors.[59]

Nearly 3,000 miles to the east, Japan was looking towards strengthening the eastern boundary of its much-expanded empire. Rabaul was a strategically located harbor, originally established by Germans prior to World War I as part of the Kaiser's fledgling Pacific empire. Possession of Rabaul was a major benefit to the Japanese war machine, as it put it closer to cutting off the vital supply line from the US West Coast to Australia. It also offered a base for both navy and air force operations extending southeast towards the Solomon Islands and west towards New Guinea. Ostensibly, therefore, the seizure of Rabaul was an offensive move, but essentially it had a defensive purpose. From the airfields at Rabaul, the Allies could bomb Truk, a lagoon in the Caroline Islands which had been in Japan's possession since the end of World War I and was its largest naval base outside the home islands.[60]

A Japanese landing force disembarked at Rabaul on January 23. An Australian observer remarked on the almost causal way in which the first Japanese soldiers hit the beach, as if expecting no opposition at all: "As they landed the Japanese were laughing, talking and striking matches… one of them even shone a torch."[61] Despite the somewhat amateurish performance of the Japanese vanguard, the Australians were hopelessly outnumbered and stood no chance. Within hours, the strategic harbor had fallen into Japanese hands, while the defenders disappeared into the surrounding jungle.[62]

The need to save resources led the Japanese into a great deal of improvisation, which in turn caused logistical chaos on several occasions. Colonel Ueno Shigeru, who was stationed at Shipping Transport Command in Saigon, recalled how a decision to speed up deployment of troops decided at his command was not communicated with sufficient clarity to commanders in charge of dispatching vessels from Japan and China. Ships that left Japanese and Chinese harbors received conflicting demands from Saigon and Tokyo. "Although it was just for one or two days, the whole shipping situation was thrown into total confusion," the colonel wrote.[63] The situation was only brought under control when the Shipping Transport Command issued a classified telegram, unifying all transportation under its command: "From now on, all ships involved in the southern operation shall be operated under the orders of Saigon."[64]

It was mid-morning on January 27, 1942, roughly 200 nautical miles west of Midway Island, when submerged American submarine USS *Gudgeon* finally spotted the enemy. It was a Japanese sub, *I-73*, homebound after weeks of combat patrol along the coast of California. Unlike its American counterpart, the *I-73* was traveling on the surface, as if its crew were unable to imagine any danger lurking in the deep. Through his periscope, the USS *Gudgeon*'s skipper, Lieutenant Commander Joe Grenfell, could see Japanese sailors on deck, enjoying the tropical breezes of the central Pacific.[65]

The encounter was not a coincidence. It was a carefully planned ambush. American code breakers had obtained information about the *I-73*'s approximate location and course, and they had promptly passed the intelligence on to Grenfell. For the 56 men on board the USS *Gudgeon*, this was the chance they had been waiting for. Weeks of cruising off the Japanese home islands had brought meager returns, and the American submarine had sent only one Japanese freighter to the bottom of the ocean. This morning's target was entirely different. It was a vessel of the Imperial Japanese Navy, which had dealt such a devastating and humiliating blow to the United States at Pearl Harbor. Revenge was in the air. "We wanted to get them sons-of-bitches. That's all we talked about," recalled Chuck Ver Vallin, one of the sailors on board the USS *Gudgeon*. "We were going to get them boogers. We had a brand-new boat and we had a good crew and we had real experienced guys."

Grenfell ordered the forward torpedoes to be prepared. Long months of monotonous and grueling training had paid off. Each member of his crew was able to carry out his job with swift robot-like efficiency, and the few minutes between identification of the target and the final attack proceeded with the confident routine of true professionals. Everything was in place when Grenfell gave the order for the release of three deadly torpedoes against the Japanese submarine, now at a distance of 1,800 yards: "Fire One. Fire Two. Fire Three." Grenfell stared intently at the Japanese target through his periscope but lost sight at the crucial moment when the torpedoes impacted. Instead, he and his crew heard a pair of muffled thuds, followed by the sound of explosions, telling them that at least two of the torpedoes had hit the objective. Grenfell would have liked to surface to inspect the wreckage, but there might have been other Japanese vessels in the area, so instead he searched the horizon with his periscope. The *I-73* was nowhere to be seen. It had gone down. Wild cheering filled the submerged hull of the USS *Gudgeon*.

The triumphant mood was even more warranted than the sailors could have known that January morning less than two months into the war. It later turned out that the *I-73* was the first military vessel to be sunk by any unit of the US Navy after the start of hostilities. In this as well as in other ways, the USS *Gudgeon* was a pioneer. It had left Pearl Harbor on its first wartime patrol as early as on December 11, while dead bodies were still floating in the water of the wrecked naval port. Its objective had been to sail to the Bungo Channel, separating the Japanese islands of Kyushu and Shikoku, in search of enemy merchant and military vessels.

In other words, just four days after the surprise attack on the US Pacific Fleet, not only was the US Navy on the attack, but it was taking the war halfway across the Pacific to Japan's inland waters. The green light had been given on December 7, 1941, at 5:52 pm Washington time, while it was early afternoon in Hawaii, and American sailors and soldiers were still struggling in the mayhem left behind by Japanese planes at Pearl Harbor. At that moment, Admiral Harold Stark, the US Chief of Naval Operations, had issued a sparsely worded, but fateful order:

EXECUTE AGAINST JAPAN UNRESTRICED SUBMARINE AND AIR WARFARE.

If any service was able to strike back immediately, it was the American submarines. Their crews had been carefully selected and rigorously trained, their sleeves proudly sporting the dolphin that signaled their status as the elite beneath the waves. All vessels of the service had escaped unscathed from the Pearl Harbor attack and needed no extra time to recover from the shock of the attacks. They were able to undertake operations within just days. It meant that the United States was, in a sense, on the offensive from day one of the war in the Pacific, even as American forces were being pressured and pushed back everywhere else.

It also implied that the United States had abandoned the principle of freedom of the seas which had otherwise formed the bedrock of American international behavior for generations. More seriously, perhaps, it was in breach of the London Naval Treaty of 1930, signed by both the United States and Japan as well as other major naval powers. The treaty had banned unrestricted submarine warfare against merchant shipping, and it had laid out a series of rules, which, in retrospect, seemed hopelessly unrealistic. For example, the treaty's Article 22 had called for the crew and passengers of unarmed merchant vessels to be taken to safe locations before the ships were sunk.[66]

What began with the USS *Gudgeon*'s daring mission would eventually develop into one of only three strategic submarine campaigns carried out in the history of warfare. The other two campaigns were the ones conducted by Germany against the United Kingdom in the First and Second World Wars, and in contrast to the German efforts, which both failed in their objective of strangling the British economy, the US campaign against Japan's merchant marine was a crushing success. It would turn out to be one of the most important—and at the same time least acknowledged—factors behind the eventual defeat of the Japanese Empire.

In the Atlantic, the German submarines faced a resourceful Allied enemy who gradually developed a system of convoys sailing under heavy escort. The Japanese had none of this, and as a result their cargo ships, laden with soldiers or strategic materials, were easy prey for the American submarines. The Japanese Navy, despite its status at the start of the war as one of the strongest naval forces in the world, failed almost entirely to protect civilian shipping. The Naval planners had focused on developing a large surface force with the battleship as the all-important center, and as a result the Japanese Navy had at its disposal only a tiny number of slow escort vessels at the start of the Pacific War. "All Japanese merchant vessels were absolutely unprotected from the enemy's attacks," a Japanese official stated later.[67]

This was a failure with a long history. As early as during the 1904–1905 war with Czarist Russia, Japan had lost merchant shipping to attacks by enemy surface vessels, and the intervening decades had brought little improvement, even while the emergence of the submarine as a fully functional weapon made the oceans more treacherous than ever.[68] Led astray by an almost inexplicable complacency, the Japanese decision-makers simply failed to see the potential danger posed by the US submarine fleet. "The number of submarines possessed by the United States is of no concern to the Japanese," Foreign Minister Shidehara Kijūrō had exclaimed in the 1930s, "inasmuch as Japan can never be attacked by American submarines."[69]

While Japan's Navy offered only haphazard protection to merchant ships plying routes near the home islands, it made no plans whatsoever to protect ships in the South China Sea, the South Pacific, and more distant waters. It was a fatal flaw in the entire Japanese war effort, since the whole reason for attacking the United States and going to war with the world's strongest power had been to gain access to the riches of Southeast Asia and make those resources benefit Japan's economy. As one of the few clear-sighted Japanese officials commented, "the issue was not getting the oil out of the Indies, but getting it back to Japan."[70]

Even so, it would be months and years before the Americans started sinking Japanese ships in significant numbers. Their submarines were beset by problems in the early part of the war, mostly technological. The Mark 14 torpedo, which was standard issue at the start of hostilities, was hampered by serious flaws. These flaws had not been sufficiently appreciated during peacetime maneuvers, and the devastating consequences only became clear once the submarines entered into real action. The torpedoes ran too deep and therefore often missed the hull of the target ship. They also had a tendency to veer off course and were occasionally reported to make a full circular motion and come back to endanger the submarines that had fired them.

Most frustratingly to the submarine crews, even torpedoes that had been fired correctly and were heading straight at their targets often failed to cause any damage. They were known to hit the hulls without detonating. Torpedoes with magnetic mines—developed in utmost secrecy prior to the war and designed to detonate when triggered by the magnetic field of the target ship—exploded prematurely, at too large a distance. Lucius Chappell, the skipper of the US submarine USS *Sculpin*, had the frustrating experience of attacking three Japanese freighters in the course of a six-day period, firing three torpedoes at each, without a single one of them scoring a hit. Chappel was "so demoralized and disheartened from repeated misses he had little stomach for further action until an analysis could be made."[71] These were teething problems, but as long as they were not corrected, the "silent service" would not be able to develop its full potential.

CHAPTER FOUR

Graveyard of Empires

February–March 1942

The city of Moulmein had been in British possession since 1826, and it had been the first capital of colonial Burma. The newspaper *The Maulmain Chronicle*, which had introduced modern journalism to Burma, had been published in Moulmein, and Eric Arthur Blair, later known under his pen name of George Orwell, had been a police officer there. In his "barrack-room ballad" *Mandalay*, the poet of empire Rudyard Kipling had written dreamily about the Burma girl "by the old Moulmein pagoda," celebrating the both mystical and carnal bond between the common British soldier and the seductive Orient. On February 1, 1942, all that was history. Moulmein had fallen to the Japanese Army, and along with it, the surrounding region of Tenasserim. The battle for the city had been drawn out over four days and had highlighted the disadvantages faced by a European army when fighting in an alien environment. In one instance, a group of Japanese soldiers had dressed up like Burmese civilians and had suddenly turned up among a battery of British artillerymen, stabbing them to death.[1] "In spite of effort to gain contact and delay [the] enemy he attacked Moulmein yesterday from all directions," General Thomas Hutton, the commander of the Burma Army, wrote to Wavell. "Divisional commander has decided on evacuation while still possible."[2]

During its initial campaigns, the Japanese Army had largely left Burma for later. The only exception was a series of bombing raids carried out in December, combined with the capture in the south of the colony of two airfields deemed necessary for securing the rear of the forces operating in Malaya. Still, it had been an integral part all along of Japanese planning to eventually take Burma. It was a vital station in the British supply lines to Malaya and Singapore, just as the port of Rangoon, the Burmese capital, was key to any Western supply effort aimed at the beleaguered Chinese government in Chongqing. The full-blown invasion into Burma got underway in the middle of January. Unsurprisingly, the Japanese Army went into action with the bare minimum of forces necessary for the job, in this case two understrength divisions, the 33rd and the 55th.

Following the fall of Moulmein, the Japanese proceeded with the aim of taking over control of all of southern Burma. The decisive battle was for the only bridge across the Sittang River, and thus the only direct route to Rangoon. The river had a swift current and broadened both above and below the bridge. Its possession would mean an immense advantage to the advancing Japanese. In two fierce days of combat the mixed British-Indian 17th Division struggled to hold on the eastern end of the bridge against forces from the 33rd Japanese Division. By February 23, it was clear that the Japanese were having the upper hand, leaving the British commander, Brigadier John George Smyth, in a painful dilemma. "He had to decide whether to risk the bridge falling intact into the enemy's hands, when they could sweep on to Rangoon, or to blow it up, leaving a large part of his force cut off on the other side," wrote General William Slim, soon to be made commander of the Burma Corps.[3]

Smyth decided to blow the bridge. Among the thousands abandoned on the other side of the treacherous river was Neville Hogan, an officer with the Burma Auxiliary Force. He later described how the soldiers were organized into parties of 30 to 40 men and ordered to swim across the river: "Coming down a swift flowing river is something. It's frightening. You look at water, it's so beautiful, but once you get there, underneath, oh it's frightening. Boots around my neck, a 4.5 pistol with its big web belt, a big broad web belt choking you. Tin hat, which I lost immediately I got into the water, a pair of shorts and that's it." About halfway across he felt a thud in his thigh and thought he had perhaps touched someone struggling underwater. Only when he reached the other side did he realize he had been hit by a piece of shrapnel. That was also when he found out he was one of just ten survivors.[4]

Blowing the bridge had been costly but, some said, necessary. "It is easy to criticize the decision," wrote William Slim in his post-war memoirs. "It is not easy to make such a decision."[5] It served the purpose of slowing down the Japanese advance. There now was a lull in the fighting while the Japanese brought up bridging material, and it was not until early March that Japanese forces began crossing the Sittang River. In the meantime, the British had given up hope of reinforcing Rangoon with any significant numbers of new troops and instead flew in General Harold Alexander, recently appointed commander-in-chief of British forces in Burma, to command the beleaguered garrison. Once there, Alexander realized the situation was hopeless, and ordered a retreat combined with destruction of the capital's oil refineries and other important installations.[6]

A Japanese regiment had been ordered to form a roadblock north of Rangoon, while the Japanese Army's 33rd Division formed an encircling operation in order to be able to attack the capital from the west. Once the division was in place and ready to carry out the storm of the city, the regiment believed it had completed its duty and lifted the roadblock. As a result, Alexander and his troops were able to walk north unhindered, and the Japanese missed out on killing or capturing a general who would later become one of the chief British commanders in North Africa and the Mediterranean.[7] Alexander was known to live a charmed life, but even for him this was special. "Alex," said Thomas Hutton, the Burma Army commander, "never had a greater stroke of luck in his life."[8]

The Commonwealth forces in Burma made the same discovery that they had made in Malaya. The Japanese, carrying only the bare minimum of equipment, were able to move through jungle which on the face of it was impenetrable. "Our British, Indian and Gurkha troops were a match for the Japanese in a stand-up fight but, invariably, this being tied to a road proved our undoing," Slim wrote later. "It made us fight on a narrow front, while the enemy, moving wide through the jungle, encircled us and placed a force behind us across the only road. The Japanese had developed the art of the road-block to perfection; we seemed to have no answer to it. If we stood and fought where we were, unless the road were re-opened, we starved. So invariably we had turned back to clear the road-block, breaking through it usually at the cost of vehicles, and in any case making another withdrawal."[9] Adding to the problems on the ground, the Japanese soon had command of the air, ranging seemingly unopposed over all of Burma, and bombing many of the larger towns. "In these raids, the towns were almost completely destroyed, either by bombs or, as these buildings were almost entirely made of wood, by the resultant fires," a British officer wrote. "In the absence of any allied air power, they were able also to strafe at will railway installations, trains and river steamers."[10]

Just as the Dutch had found to their chagrin in the East Indies, the loyalties of the local communities in Burma were fickle, too. The majority may have felt a strange detachment from the struggle taking place on their doorsteps, and some might have felt that life under one occupying force would not differ significantly from life under another. Yet others opted to bet on one or the other side winning in the end. "The hill tribes were almost all actively loyal," wrote Slim, "but the Burman of the plains, where the bulk of the fighting would take place, was, generally speaking, apathetic and out to avoid getting involved on either side. A small minority was actively hostile under Japanese officers or agents."[11]

Accompanied by his wife Song Meiling, China's leader Generalissimo Chiang Kai-shek flew to India in February 1942. His purpose was to seek to persuade the British authorities to grant their colonial subjects a greater measure of freedom so that India would commit itself and its enormous resources fully to the war against Japan.[12] Chiang's anti-imperialist credentials were widely known, and the possible consequences of his visit, during which he also hoped to see pro-independence leader Mahatma Gandhi, caused trepidation in London. The British authorities were prepared to accept a meeting between the two but feared that an encounter at Gandhi's residence at the town of Sevagram in central India would deliver a wrong message to the Indian public. Eventually, Churchill sent a personal secret telegram to Chiang, warning him that unless the venue was changed, it could endanger efforts to rally India for the war against Japan. "It might well have the unintended effect of emphasizing communal differences at a moment when unity is imperative," the British prime minister argued.[13]

Chiang heeded the advice, and he met Gandhi in Calcutta on February 18. The Chiang couple were eager to see the world-famous Indian and they went to visit him at Birla Park, a residential estate, within an hour of his arrival. Still, the five-hour-long encounter did not go well. It was a clash of world views, which proved irreconcilable. Gandhi assured Chiang that if they were to occupy India, "Japan or Germany would be confronted with fierce non-co-operation or civil resistance." Chiang, whose rise to power and subsequent battles with Chinese warlords and invading Japanese had cost the lives of millions, was unimpressed: "Your civil resistance is not mere passivity, I am sure," he told Gandhi. "But these foes may not listen to active civil resistance, and may even make the preaching of non-violence impossible." After three conversations interrupted by brief breaks in between, the two leaders parted, promising to meet again. After all, Song Meiling noted, Calcutta was only 12 hours by plane from Chongqing.[14] It was all courtesy, and neither side felt an urgent need to see each other again. Gandhi considered the meeting with Chiang an exercise in futility. "He came empty-handed and left empty-handed. He amused himself and entertained me," the Indian leader wrote one week later in a letter to an acquaintance. "But I cannot say that I learned anything."[15]

In a public and widely disseminated address just before his departure, Chiang urged the British empire to loosen the reins: "I sincerely hope and confidently believe that our ally, Great Britain, without waiting for any demands on the part of the people of India, will as speedily as possible give them real political power." In this way, the war against Japan could become "a turning point in their struggle for India's freedom."[16] The Chinese government was clearly aware of the controversial nature of the remarks, and at the same time its spokesman in Chongqing, Jiang Tingfu, published comments in the *Ta Kung Pao* newspaper which expressed hope that the British and Indian people would find a way out of their differences, and argued that Britain was India's best bet: "If once Japanese power gets rooted in India, then India's freedom or self-government is inconceivable. After all, England is the cradle of freedom, while Japan is the destroyer of freedom."[17]

Just days after Chiang had left India, his future chief of staff Joseph Stilwell arrived in the British colony. True to his impatient temper, the American general moved on to China after quickly stopping over in Calcutta to shop for a sun hat and a sleeping bag.[18] Once in China, he found his position complicated almost as if by design. In the words of an official American historian: "As US Army Representative he was under the Secretary of War. As supervisor and controller of lend-lease he was under the President. As Chief of Staff of the Generalissimo's Joint Staff he was under the

Generalissimo."[19] It was a delicate position where tact and discretion were everything, but unfortunately, according to an American historian, "undisciplined in tongue, Stilwell was totally lacking in the art of diplomatic finesse."[20]

Stilwell sympathized with the ordinary Chinese soldier, and admired his skill in the battlefield, but he had mostly only scorn for the senior officers surrounding Chiang, considering them to embody an unfortunate mixture of sycophancy and incompetence. "The Chinese commanders are up and down—highly optimistic one minute; in the depths of gloom the next. They feel, of course, the urgent necessity of pleasing the Generalissimo, and if my suggestions or orders run counter to what they think he wants they offer endless objections," he wrote, venting his anger at procrastination bordering on disobedience. He described his frustration in his trademark hard-hitting fashion: "I can't shoot them; I can't relieve them; and just talking to them does no good."[21]

Stilwell got his chance to work with Chinese foot soldiers when Chiang Kai-shek overcame British reluctance against a Chinese presence on Burmese soil and was able to send his 5th and 6th Armies into the British colony. Stilwell believed optimistically that Rangoon could be taken back from the Japanese. This provided the impetus for the first of what was to become a long succession of arguments with Chiang. Still, he received permission from Chiang to command three Chinese divisions on the frontline in Burma and was himself surprised that it was at all possible. "In all fairness, it must have been a severe strain on him to put a foreigner in command of regular Chinese troops in action at all. It had never been done before, and he was trying it on short acquaintance with a man he knew little about," Stilwell wrote in a report shortly afterwards.[22]

Stilwell used his new-won authority with greater audacity than Chiang had expected, sending two Chinese divisions south in preparation for a counter-offensive against the Japanese. "I wanted to fight as far forward as possible, after concentrating all available forces there," Stilwell wrote in a report.[23] Chiang, by contrast, wanted a more cautious approach, preferring to keep his troops in the center of Burma, near the city of Mandalay, which was a key transportation hub. This way he might even be able to lure the Japanese in deep and then cut them off, in an operation similar to the recent battles over Changsha. In the end, Chiang seemed to be right. Stilwell was forced to pull back, losing men and materiel for no obvious gain. "If my original plan had been followed and the main body had been concentrated in the highlands Northeast of Old Mandalay, today's defeat would not have happened," Chiang wrote regretfully.[24]

To the British officers, the Chinese units in Burma presented a somewhat chaotic spectacle, with organizational structures shifting on a daily basis, and local commanders afraid to make any major decisions before referring back to Chiang Kai-shek first. In addition, the Chinese forces had a habit of shooting at any Burmese on sight, perhaps believing them to be Japanese.[25] "It is difficult to put any definite estimate on how much or how little effect the Chinese Armies had on the campaign," wrote a British officer in his memoirs. "There is no doubt that without them… the Japanese would have overrun the whole of Burma in a matter of weeks or even days, rather than months. On the other hand, had the Chinese Commanders co-operated to the full, both with the British forces and with each other, and had they obeyed the orders given by their own High Command, with reasonable promptitude, the Japanese could well have been dealt severe blows."[26]

For American and Philippine troops on the Bataan peninsula in early spring of 1942, life was a fight not just against the enemy, but also against hunger and disease. Adding to the anguish, Japanese radio was mocking the worn-down soldiers with a sinister sense of humor, sending a special greeting to the "rats of Bataan" as it played a song called "Ships That Never Come In."[27] The Americans holed up in the tropical nightmare dismissed this as unreliable propaganda. Many were convinced that the rescue was on its way, just beyond the horizon. "No one will do that to Uncle Sam and get away with it," said one soldier. Another added: "Wait 'til the Navy moves in and clears the path."[28]

The fact was that no help was even contemplated, apart from a few US submarines that made it to Bataan with supplies which, given their extremely limited storage room, added up to virtually nothing. There was no question that morale was boosted by false hopes that the United States might actually be able to relieve the beleaguered American garrison, but some in the know considered it a cruel form of deception. President Quezon expressed his concern about the plight of the Philippine Army in a memorandum to MacArthur on February 7. "I wonder if those men knew that help is not coming within a reasonable time and that they are only being used to gain time in other fronts," he wrote, "I wonder, I repeat, how long their morale and will to fight would last."[29]

MacArthur was told that immediate assistance was impossible, and that help could only be sent once the US Navy had restored its strength in the Pacific. "It was as if," according to American historian Forrest C. Pogue, "a man dying of thirst were told that he must wait for a drink of water until a well could be dug and a water main laid."[30] Yet, for all the hardship involved and for all the essential hopelessness of the situation, MacArthur was probably having the time of his life, his former aide Dwight D. Eisenhower wrote in his diary, monitoring the situation in the Philippines from a great distance in the United States: "Bataan is made to order for him. It's in the public eye; it has made him a public hero; it has all the essentials of drama; and he is the acknowledged king on the spot."[31]

MacArthur was located, Alamo-style, in the tunnels of the fortified island of Corregidor at the entrance of Manila Bay. The island, somewhat larger than

New York's Central Park, was occupied by a mixed band of Marines, soldiers and sailors and was frequently exposed to Japanese shelling. While the men and women on Corregidor awaited the almost inevitable fall of the bastion, there was a surprisingly limited number of nervous breakdowns, and life was lived as intensely as possible.[32] Helped by home-made liquor, some soldiers whiled away time with gambling, using their accumulated and useless pay to bet ever bigger amounts of money.[33] "Jam sessions attracted great crowds which gathered in the dark and hummed softly or tapped feet to the nostalgic swing of the organ, a haunting guitar, or a low moaning trombone. Sometimes a nurse and her boyfriend of the evening would melt into a dance," in the words of Maude R. Williams, a hospital assistant. "The eyes of the onlookers would grow soft and thoughtful, while other couples would steal out into the perilous night."[34]

The question to Washington was what to do with MacArthur, who was accompanied by his wife and five-year-old son on Corregidor. Eisenhower, for one, was not sure of the wisdom of evacuating the general, worrying that it was tantamount to pandering to public opinion rather than conforming with any military logic: "He is doing a good job where he is, but I'm doubtful that he'd do so well in more complicated situations," he wrote in his diary. "If brought out, public opinion will force him into a position where his love of the limelight may ruin him."[35] As MacArthur indicated he wanted to fight to the last on Bataan and then on Corregidor, Washington was alarmed at the prospect that the general, by now a national hero at home, rather than being killed might be captured by the Japanese, which would deal a blow to American morale. The general was eventually persuaded to leave Corregidor on board a patrol torpedo boat, which took him to the southern Philippine island of Mindanao. From there, he went on to Australia, where, upon arrival, he told waiting reporters, "I came through and I shall return."[36]

At Singapore, the drama that had played out in Hong Kong was almost replicated. The Commonwealth forces that had been ordered by Wavell to withdraw into Johore soon found it necessary to retreat further onto Singapore island, awaiting the final Japanese assault there. While pre-war planning had been based on the assumption that the Japanese would storm the fortress from the sea, it was now clear that the main assault would come overland, and in this unforeseen situation desperate measure were called for. Commonwealth forces blew up a causeway linking Singapore island to the mainland on January 31, delaying the Japanese plans, but the first troops started crossing over on February 8, soon causing the defending lines to crumble.

Singapore city was descending into chaos. Large numbers of Commonwealth soldiers deserted and were desperate to find ways to escape from the beleaguered city. Some sought to make their way aboard transport vessels meant to evacuate women and children, and a few even tried to climb up the mooring ropes in a frantic attempt to avoid a sinister fate.[37] "Personally I do not feel that there is much hope of saving Singapore," Alan Brooke, chief of the Imperial General Staff, had written in his diary as early as mid-December the previous year.[38] On February 11, when the fall of the city was imminent, he added: "I have during the last ten years had an unpleasant feeling that the British Empire was decaying and that we were on a slippery decline. I wonder if I was right?"[39]

The fall of Singapore came faster than anyone had expected. Tsuji Masanobu, a Japanese staff officer, was in the frontline on February 15 and was concerned to see that the artillery shells brought up by the Japanese forces were almost depleted, while the British artillery seemed to maintain most of its bite. Just as Japanese infantry got out of their trenches to carry out a storm of a key position, the British artillery built up to a fearful crescendo, exploding among the exposed men. Arms and legs were flying through the air, and detached heads were scattered all over the place. Next to Tsuji, a Japanese soldier was decapitated by shell fragments, splattering blood on the men who had been standing next to him. On his way back, Tsuji was dejected. "If the enemy resists in this manner he probably contemplates fighting from house to house," he thought.[40] Without endless amounts of ammunition, the Japanese side had to devise a new plan. There seemed to be no end to the campaign. And then suddenly, after returning to his headquarters, he received a call from a colleague: "The enemy has surrendered! [He] has surrendered!"[41]

What had happened was that the British commander, Lieutenant General Percival, running out of supplies and, most crucially, water, had received Wavell's permission to surrender. Facing a stern Yamashita, who refused to discuss any terms, he was forced into signing an unconditional surrender. The Japanese soldiers now swarmed into the allegedly impregnable fortress, rounding up prisoners. "Can't one of the officers do something?" one of the scared British soldiers said, as they were kicked and beaten outside their barracks, while Japanese infantrymen went up and down the ranks, stealing watches, cigarette lighters, and other valuables. He received an abrupt answer from the man next to him: "Just keep your mouth shut. There's nothing to be done. We're at their mercy now."[42]

Even some of those who had managed to escape from Singapore prior to its capture eventually fell victim to the Japanese and their indiscriminate vengeance. The yacht *Vyner Brooke* left Singapore on February 12, carrying a number of civilians as well as nurses and injured soldiers. Two days later, the vessel was attacked by Japanese aircraft off Sumatra, and the survivors climbed into rescue boats, ending up on the beaches of nearby Banka Island. There, on February 16, about 100 injured soldiers and 22 nurses fell into Japanese hands. The soldiers were summarily shot. The nurses were raped and then forced to walk out into the surf. "Chin up, girls. I'm proud of you and I love you all," said the head nurse Irene Drummond.

One of the doomed women commented with dry humor: "There are two things I hate in life, the Japs and the sea, and today I've got both."[43] They knew they were going to die. "We stood waiting. There were no protests," said Vivien Bullwinkel, the only survivor of the carnage that followed when the Japanese soldiers shot down the defenseless women.[44]

Meanwhile, in Singapore, members of the ethnic Chinese community were being rounded up and placed in camp-like conditions in an operation led by the Kempeitai, Japan's feared military police. Among the prisoners were the young girl Elizabeth Choy, her parents, and five siblings. Choy was screened but apparently not considered dangerous and was let go with a stamp to show she had been approved. Most of her family were released in similar fashion. The problems began when her father, who was over 50, was about to leave the camp along with her 18-year-old brother. Decades later Elizabeth Choy recounted the incident: "Father was walking out with him and the Kempeitai, the soldiers, said, 'No, you go. Leave your son behind.' And my poor brother said, 'Daddy what's going to happen to me? Why can't I come with you?' or something. So the soldier said, 'You just stay behind.'" The family never saw the teenage boy again.[45]

Countless other families among Singapore's Chinese lost male members—sons, fathers, and brothers. The sinister truth was that they were taken to remote places and killed. Major Onishi Satoru, an officer with the Kempeitai, reported having received instructions from General Headquarters: "Due to the fact that the army is advancing fast and in order to preserve peace behind us it is essential to massacre as many Chinese as possible who appear in any way to have anti-Japanese feelings."[46] The Japanese soldiers in Singapore were given a quota of 50,000 Chinese that needed to be killed within five days, and having become used to mass brutality during the war in China, they went about the task with no objections. The methods available to the Japanese—shooting, machine-gunning, stabbing or bludgeoning—proved inadequate, and it was impossible to meet the number of kills required. Even so, the final death toll is believed to have been at least 25,000, perhaps more.[47]

Among the Commonwealth defenders, the sudden surrender of Singapore came as an enormous shock. For Wavell, in what seemed an attempt to place at least part of the blame with the rank and file, it was a sign that the British soldier had lost his hardness and fighting spirit. "Until we have again soldiers capable of marching twenty to thirty miles a day for a number of days running, and missing their full ration every second or third day, and whose first idea is to push forward and to get to grips with the enemy on any and every occasion and whatever the difficulties and odds, we shall not recover our morale or reputation," he wrote.[48] The assessment was universal that the loss of Singapore was a disaster. "The importance of Singapore to the war in the Far East and to the World War could not be exaggerated," British and American officers meeting immediately after Pearl Harbor had concluded. "Its loss would probably be followed by that of the Netherlands East Indies." This now proved almost prophetic.[49]

★★★.

Shortly before noon on February 14, a group of Japanese Ki-56 transport planes—Lockheed 14s built on license acquired from the Americans before the war—were approaching southern Sumatra. On board were 390 men of the 2nd Parachute Raiding Regiment on a mission that they had been told could decide the entire war: to capture the oil fields near the city of Palembang. The action around Palembang was the main focus in the westernmost portion of a three-pronged attack that the Japanese Army and Navy directed against the Dutch East Indies in February. In the central part of this advance, a battalion of the Sakaguchi Detachment had attacked and seized Bandjermasin, in an oil-producing region in southern Borneo on February 10. In the east, the Sasebo Combined Landing Force had disembarked in southern Celebes on February 9, and on February 19, the island of Bali fell. On February 20, the 228th Regiment landed on Timor.

Palembang, however, was paramount. "It is no exaggeration to say that the Greater East Asian War was launched for the oil in Palembang," according to the official Japanese history of the war. "It was one of the main missions of the Southern Army to occupy Palembang at an early stage before [the facilities] were destroyed by the allied forces."[50] The need for prompt action preventing the Dutch forces from blowing up the oil wells had dictated the tactics. Conventional troops could only reach Palembang by entering Musi River and sail 40 miles upstream, in an operation that would be far too slow and eliminate the element of surprise. Palembang had to be taken from the air.

Airborne troops were an arm of the Japanese military that had only come into existence very recently, and it was not until the German successes in the Low Countries and Crete that development of their capabilities had been expanded to a level where they could be of true operational use.[51] One of the first times ever that Japanese troops carried out a combat drop into enemy territory had been just three days earlier, on February 11, in the northern part of Celebes island, and their success on the battlefield had been kept secret until now lest the much more important operations at Palembang be compromised.[52] Aside from the oil fields, the area was also valuable due to the presence of two airstrips, which were key to the control of southern Sumatra as well as the large island of Java to the east.

The personnel on the airfields were a mixture of Dutch, Indonesian, and Commonwealth troops. The Royal Air Force had gradually moved more and more bombers and fighters to the area, as ever larger portions of Malaya and Singapore were lost to the Japanese, and along with the planes came ground personnel. However, most of the ground staff had been forced to hand over their rifles upon

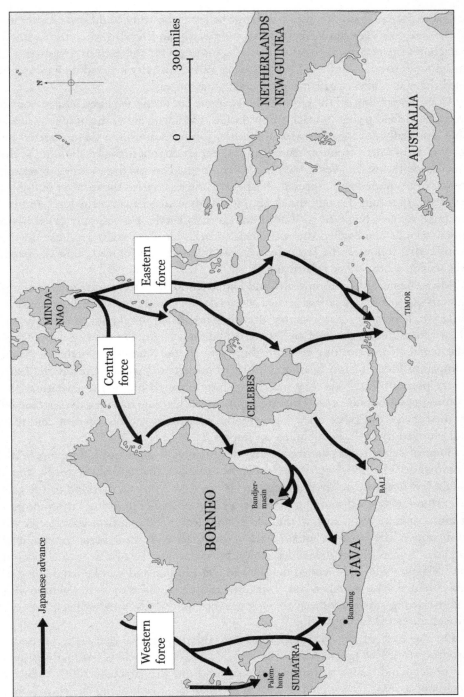

Invasion of Dutch East Indies, January–March, 1942

arrival in Sumatra, as the officers in charge believed the army could make better use of the weapons. As a result, the airfields were partly undefended when the Japanese parachutes opened up in the sky above. To make up for this lack in firepower, the anti-aircraft batteries at the airfield closest to Palembang city lowered their guns and used them as artillery against the Japanese paratroopers.[53]

Upon assembling on the ground, the Japanese cut telephone lines, and personnel from the airfield trying to reach troops inside Palembang along the only road available repeatedly ran into Japanese ambushes. Johnny Johnson, a driver, steered his lorry straight into a Japanese roadblock. He ended up in a firefight, shooting at the Japanese with his .38 Webley revolver. When he had ceased fire in order to reload, he was overpowered and captured. A Japanese officer wrestled the revolver out of his hand and shot him through the thigh. He was then stood against the lorry and the Japanese soldiers prepared to shoot him, execution-style. He was only saved when a new vehicle approached the roadblock and the Japanese again got busy. In the combat that followed, the Japanese unit was defeated, and Johnson, now liberated, was sent to a hospital at Pelambang.[54]

Mixed bands of Commonwealth and Dutch troops milled around in the countryside, trying to evade Japanese troops. Most aviators found themselves in an unusual situation, having to act as infantry after they had failed to take off in their planes. "I am no soldier or woodsman," wrote Rhodesian Flight Officer Graham "Ting" Macnamara, "and pushing through those woods, not knowing whether I would bump into friend or foe, hearing all sorts of noises, etc., was not, to say the least, a very pleasant job."[55] As they made their way through the dense vegetation, the Commonwealth soldiers saw Japanese paratroopers hanging from the trees, strangled by their own strings. For other Japanese, the parachutes had not opened, and they had plunged to earth, being killed on impact.

Some of the defenders survived merely due to deception and quick thinking. Wing Commander Harold Maguire was inside the airfield at the time of the attack, when after a few hours he believed a Dutch relief force had arrived. Walking to the gate he encountered, at a distance of 50 yards, a Japanese soldier pointing a machine gun at him. Maguire walked up to the soldier and demanded in a firm voice to see his commander. The Japanese soldier fetched an officer with some basic command of English. "I immediately demanded surrender, saying that I had a large force behind me," Maguire said. "He replied that he had a large force and that he would give us safe conduct if we marched out." Maguire said he would discuss the matter with a non-existing superior officer, turning around and briskly walking back into the airfield, probably saving his life.[56]

On day two of the Japanese attack on Palembang, February 15, yet more airborne troops were landed on the airfield, and the attackers gradually gained the upper hand. Later the same day, soldiers from the Japanese 229th Infantry Regiment arrived in the city, having made their approach along the slow route, in boats up the Musi River, bringing the battle to an end. "The manner of the Japanese advance resembled the insidious yet irresistible clutching of multiple tentacles," the US Navy's official historian wrote. "Like some vast octopus it relied on strangling many small points rather than concentration on a vital organ. No one arm attempted to meet the entire strength of the ABDA fleet. Each fastened on a small portion of the enemy and, by crippling him locally, finished by killing the entire animal."[57]

By late winter 1942, the multi-tentacled Japanese offensive had reached Australia. On February 19, a total of 242 carrier- and land-based aircraft attacked the northern port city of Darwin, sinking 11 vessels and damaging many more, while also destroying several aircraft. A total of more than 200 soldiers, sailors, and civilians were killed. T. Minto, chief officer on the Australian hospital ship *Manunda*, watched the American destroyer *Peary*, which had narrowly escaped from Manila less than two months earlier, "a solid mass of flame with burning oil all round her and what was left of the crew jumping into the burning oil. We manned our motor life-boat with four of a crew and went to their rescue and eventually picked up over thirty badly burnt and wounded men."[58]

The raid strengthened fears in Australia that a Japanese invasion was imminent. This was not part of the initial Japanese thrust south, but at the very time when Darwin was under attack, the Japanese high command was discussing the merits of extending the offensive to Australia. Somewhat vague proposals were put forward for how a few divisions could seize control of the southern continent, but fears in the Army of a war of attrition, perhaps inspired by the situation in China, caused the plans to be canceled.[59] The Navy, too, believed it could do without Australia. "We didn't want to go to Australia. The Navy was very rich with ships so we only planned to set up a protective wall extending from Singapore through the East Indies, Solomons, and the Marshall group to Kiska [west of Alaska]," Watanabe Yasuji, an officer on Yamamoto's staff, said after the war.[60]

Soon after the invasion plans were definitively abandoned, Australia started receiving significant reinforcements from abroad. Three Australian divisions had been sent to the Middle East to fight for the British Empire and were now speedily extricated and returned to the Far East to face the threat from Japan. The Japanese military, worried about what this might mean to its fortunes in Asia, resorted to rough generalizations about the quality of the Australian soldier. "Based on their military achievements in the Near East, and due to their national trait of adventurousness and determination, they will demonstrate considerable bravery," according to an official Japanese assessment. It added, "They are known for their lack of military discipline and public morals."[61]

Some civilian Australians might actually have been inclined to agree with this latter characterization. American officer Elliott Thorpe described the warm welcome given in Melbourne to "the rats of Tobruk," Australian soldiers arriving from North Africa en route to Southeast Asia: "Many of the local girls sought to show their appreciation of the warriors' efforts by bestowing their favors on them in rather public places. For a short time, it got so one could not walk through the parks on the banks of the Yarra [river] without being in danger of tripping over a couple engaged in what is usually regarded as an indoor activity."[62]

The main rationale for the raid on Darwin had been to destroy facilities which the Allies might have used in order to prevent Japan from completing its conquest of the Dutch East Indies. For this, the crowning achievement in the long offensive across Asia and the Pacific, everything now seemed in place. By the end of February, a potent Japanese force was preparing to attack the main island of Java. The Allies knew what was afoot, and an ABDA fleet consisting of five cruisers and 11 destroyers under the command of Dutch Admiral Karel Doorman set out to intercept the invasion convoy, focusing their efforts on Japanese warships shielding the landing force. The encounter that resulted on February 27, later known as the Battle of the Java Sea, was yet another disaster for the Allies, brought about by a lack of ability to communicate, made worse by successful Japanese endeavors to jam the radios.

Unlike the carrier and submarine operations about to change the face of war elsewhere, the Battle of the Java Sea was a traditional affair, with opposing surface fleets meeting and exchanging shots. As the shells were approaching the Japanese ships, the sailors could do nothing but wait, helpless and counting on mere luck to save them. In this sense, it was reminiscent of 18th-century land warfare, in which rows of infantrymen were fully exposed to the deadly volleys of the other side. "We stood there, stiff, silent, nervous," Ensign Candidate Kimura Hachiro said.[63] "A near miss dashed water on my face. My knees shook and my arms trembled at the time," Hara Tameichi, captain of destroyer *Amatsukaze*, wrote in his memoirs. "I was not worried about being a coward, but was concerned that my cool judgment might vanish, being under the fire of enemy ships for the first time."[64]

However, far more Allied than Japanese ships were sent to the bottom. One of them was the destroyer HMS *Electra*. The ship's First Lieutenant, the 27-year-old Richard Jenner-Fust, was strolling on the bridge, "generally behaving with the greatest good humor, as though the whole episode was a social event," according to one of his fellow officers, remarking in an off-hand manner matching his cold-blooded demeanor: "Rather looks as though we've had it."[65] On the morning after the battle the surface was filled with flotsam, and surviving Allied sailors. "Large numbers of white and black sailors were floating on rafts," said Masuda Reiji, an apprentice engineer in the Japanese merchant marine, who was on board a freighter headed for Java. "We sailed on without stopping—we had to put our force ashore—but I heard they were later picked up by our subchasers."[66]

The following day, Admiral Arthur Palliser, the Royal Navy's chief representative in the Netherlands East Indies, went to see Conrad Helfrich, the Dutch commander of all ABDA naval forces, telling him that he was about to withdraw all British ships from Java. The Dutch admiral was suitably vexed at this act of mutiny. "You realize that you are under my orders?" he asked. "I do of course. But in this vital matter I cannot do other than my duty as I see it," Palliser replied. Understanding that there was nothing to be done to alter the British officer's decision, Helfrich inquired if he could at least wait one hour, while he saw the Dutch governor general and informed him about the new turn of events. Palliser was adamant: "I cannot delay longer. Every minute counts now."[67]

From here on, the main battles moved onto dry land. Johannes Vandenbroek was a Dutch soldier taking part in the defense of a valley near the city of Bandung in western Java in early March 1942. After dark, stragglers from the forested no-man's-land in front of the Japanese positions made it back to the Dutch lines, and Vandenbroek's unit, which had started out numbering 100 soldiers, soon grew to 200. However, there were still Dutch soldiers in the dark, some of them crying out for help. The officer in charge of the position refused to give permission to go out and assist. "It is too dangerous," he said, "the place is crawling with Japanese." In the end he relented, and Vandenbroek was among the soldiers who slipped out into the surrounding hills, guided by the miserable cries. "I found one man who was wounded in the hip," he said later. "He was heavy, but we got him down to the truck and with other wounded, he was driven to the hospital in Bandung."[68]

Individual acts of heroism did not amount to much. The battle for Java lasted a week, and the Dutch colonial authorities decided to surrender on March 9. Abruptly, 339 years after Dutch merchants first established a trading post on Java, the Netherlands East Indies had come to an end. A sense of doom descended over the Dutch community. Barend A. van Nooten, a boy of barely ten, and his two siblings received a shocking message from their mother when the Japanese approached: "You know that I have a gun. I will shoot all three of you in the back of the head and then kill myself." They were saved from this sinister fate. When the Japanese did arrive, local mobs stood ready to loot the homes of the Dutch colonizers. Thinking quickly, his mother prepared a sumptuous meal for two Japanese officers who paid back the favor by declaring the house under Japanese protection, threatening with drawn swords that anyone defying the order would be beheaded.[69]

Other Dutch civilians were struck by disaster even after they thought they had escaped to safety. Some had made it out by flying boat in early March, reaching the town of Broome, a refueling stop in Western Australia. Shortly after arriving, they were resting inside the aircraft anchored in the harbor when they got caught up in a Japanese air raid. Dozens were killed, including women and children. The dead were fished out of the water and placed on an old locomotive, which transported them downtown, where recently arrived US soldiers were garrisoned. "Many of the American troops remember the funeral train; but the sight of it seemed to produce a curious apathy among the Dutch... A spark seemed to have been extinguished," according to a contemporary account. "They refused to help bury the dead, and the work had to be turned over to the local Home Guard who burned the rest of the bodies."[70] One Dutch civilian was completely distraught, tearing his hair from his scalp and muttering to people passing by. "You still have everything, you understand, everything. But I have nothing left! My wife, my children are gone. They are dead, all dead!"[71]

★ ★ ★

Both the US and Japanese Navies were bent on keeping their opponents on their toes, launching a series of raids in early 1942, which at the same time served as training for later more important engagements and an antidote against lethargy setting in while forces were being prepared for major operations. Admiral Chester W. Nimitz, a Texan of German descent who was named commander-in-chief of the US Pacific Fleet after Pearl Harbor, carried out a series of early strikes with carrier task forces against Japanese possessions in the Pacific, including Marshall and Gilbert Islands on February 1 and Wake on February 24. Marcus Island was attacked on March 4.

More ambitious in scope and planning was the Japanese Navy's Indian Ocean raid carried out in March and April. The Japanese Navy was under pressure to keep up the offensive momentum and decided for a raid westward into the Indian Ocean. The immediate aim of the five-carrier fleet, commanded by Admiral Nagumo Chūichi, was to assault air and naval bases in Ceylon and, more importantly, track down and destroy Britain's Eastern Fleet. Some planners hoped that a successful foray could be the first step towards the Middle East, linking up there with successful units of German General Erwin Rommel's Afrika Korps.[72]

Planes from the Japanese task force attacked the Ceylon port of Colombo on Easter Sunday, April 5. While some aircraft swooped down to as low as fifty feet and strafed ground targets, bombers dropped their load on the harbor from a high altitude. British airplanes, including 36 Hurricanes, were able to take off before the raid began and engaged the attackers, but came under severe fire from Japanese fighters acting as escort. Fifteen of the Hurricanes, or nearly half, were lost in the battle. On the other hand, the loss of civilian life on the ground was small, primarily because the holiday had kept most people at home rather than commuting to work. Still, the attack came as a shock to Colombo's population, and in the time that followed some fled as far away as the Indian mainland, causing a serious labor shortage.[73]

As Nagumo was preparing aircraft for a second strike against Colombo, he was alerted to the presence of a British cruiser force in the vicinity. He then ordered the aircraft, which were being armed with high-explosive bombs, to be rearmed with torpedo bombs suitable for targets at sea. "Under the best circumstances, it took from 1.5 to 2.5 hours to change armament for a squadron of eighteen aircraft in the limited space available in our hangars. It is during that critical time that an aircraft carrier loses its fighting strength and is most vulnerable," ace pilot Abe Zenji wrote in his memoirs. It was a lesson the Japanese could have taken advantage of—but did not—two months later at Midway.[74]

All in all, the raid was a Japanese success, but the Naval command decided to pull back the aircraft carriers into the Pacific for much-needed maintenance. A peculiar episode in the history of the Imperial Japanese Navy was at an end. In postwar accounts, the raid has often been described as a sideshow, but according to the historian H. P. Willmott, much had been at stake. "Had the Japanese risked everything on a major military and naval effort in the Indian Ocean, then both Britain and the USSR might have been forced out of the war."[75] This would, however, require an offensive mindset which had already begun eluding the Japanese command by mid-spring 1942.

Hirohito, the man in whose name the war was being waged, had conflicted feelings. In some moments he seemed beside himself with joy at the seemingly never-ending string of victories. "The Emperor was beaming like a child," his aide Kido Kōichi wrote in his diary after one of the early triumphs. "The fruits of war, he said, 'are tumbling into our mouths almost too quickly'."[76] At other times, the divine ruler appeared much more realistic in his appreciation of the enormous risk Japan had taken. "I presume," he said sternly to Prime Minister Tōjō Hideki at an audience, "that you are paying full attention so as not to miss the opportunity to terminate the war. It is not desirable for the sake of humanity and peace to have the war drag on needlessly, extending the ravages wrought by it. The longer the war goes on, the worse the troops will become in quality."[77]

Even in the early heady days, when triumph followed upon triumph, Hirohito had kept a sober mind, realizing that a short war would be in Japan's best interest. The Japanese resources were already stretched to the limit, and even though the gain of the Southeast Asian raw materials provided some respite, a conflict that was drawn out for long would mean that the Western Allies would sooner or later recover and strike back with a vengeance.[78] Even while the Japanese military was at its most triumphant, clear-headed politicians at home understood that the Allies would fight back very shortly. Konoe Fumimaro, the former prime minister, told Prince Higashikuni, a distant relative of Hirohito's, that the war must end as soon as possible, as a prolonged conflict would entail the growing risk of a communist rebellion at home in Japan.[79]

Despite its successes, the Japanese Army was unenthusiastic, too. It had been dragged away from its traditional preoccupation with the Russian threat and was therefore happy with leaving the initiative as much as possible in the hands of the Navy. Army officers were intensely suspicious about sending troops on dubious assignments into the Pacific vastness, as they could ill afford another open-ended adventure to match the endless war in China. "If we send small numbers of troops to faraway isolated islands, command and control as well as resupply will be extremely difficult," Army Vice Chief of Staff Tsukada Osamu said even before the war. "It's like sowing salt in the sea."[80]

CHAPTER FIVE

Turning Points

April–June 1942

On the morning of April 18, 1942, Jacob Eierman, staff sergeant of the US Army Air Force, was curled up inside his B-25 bomber on the deck of aircraft carrier USS *Hornet* in the western Pacific, ready for take-off against Japan. The raid on the Japanese home islands, the first ever by American aviators, had been moved up one day after the fleet assembled for the purpose had been spotted by a Japanese vessel. It was not nearly close enough to ensure that the aircraft would be able to overfly Japan, drop their bombs, and land safely in unoccupied China as foreseen in the carefully laid plan, but there was no other choice, now that the secret mission had been detected. There was now a very real possibility that the bombers would not reach the Chinese mainland and instead make emergency landings somewhere in the ocean west of Japan. To make matters worse, the sea was at its most violent, and the rolling and pitching that shook the *Hornet* meant more than a dozen men had to keep each of the 16 participating planes steady before take-off. "If anyone wants to withdraw, he can do it now," the pilot on Eierman's plane had said. "It's your right." No one had taken him up on the offer.[1]

The origin of the hazardous mission lay several months in the past, during the bleak weeks of December, filled with shock and anger after Pearl Harbor. President Roosevelt had wanted to take the war to Japanese shores, not for the actual military advantages such a strike would bring, but because the American people, not used to being on the defensive, was in desperate need of good news.[2] That was also clear to Lieutenant Colonel James Doolittle, the aviator who was picked to head the mission. "An attack on the Japanese homeland would cause confusion in the minds of the Japanese people and sow doubt about the reliability of their leaders. There was a second, and equally important, psychological reason for this attack. America and its allies had suffered one defeat after another," he wrote later. "Americans badly needed a morale boost."[3] Different ways of bringing bombers within striking distance had been under consideration, but in the end, transporting them across the ocean onboard an aircraft carrier had emerged as the most feasible alternative.

Preparations for the daring raid took place in an atmosphere of rushed secrecy. Technologies had to be adapted in order to enable the planes to carry enough fuel to fly 2,400 miles with a 2,000-pound bomb load. Everything that could possibly be stripped away was removed from the aircraft, including the lower turret. In order to deter Japanese fighter planes, two painted wooden sticks were placed in the rear, to look like .50-caliber machine guns. The advanced Norden bombsight was removed from the planes lest the sophisticated technology fall into enemy hands, and it was substituted with a simpler device nicknamed "Mark Twain" by its designer. Meanwhile, the pilots were put on an expedited training regimen to learn the techniques of shortened take-offs.[4]

A fleet consisting of USS *Hornet* and several support vessels passed through San Francisco's Golden Gate Bridge on April 2, heading west. North of the island of Midway, it rendezvoused with a second fleet led by the aircraft carrier USS *Enterprise*. By now half the US Navy's carrier strength in the Pacific was devoted to this one mission.[5] The challenge, in a sort of reverse Pearl Harbor attack, was for this large force to approach all the way to the enemy's doorstep undetected. By the morning of April 18, the mission's luck was up. The ships were spotted by the 70-ton patrol craft *Nittō Maru*, which was duly sunk, but not before it had radioed a warning to Japan. Doolittle and his staff decided to launch the planes immediately, even though the distance to the targets was still too long to ensure a safe landing in China.

Doolittle himself was first to launch his heavy plane down the *Hornet*'s short flight deck. As his aircraft gathered speed, carefully avoiding the carrier's bridge, the other pilots were watching intently. If Doolittle couldn't do it, how would they ever be able to? After a few tense seconds, he became airborne, with even a few yards of runway to spare, and a cheer went through the crowd. One after the other, the remaining planes took off, each starting out on their lone missions immediately, as there was not fuel enough to linger near the carrier and fly in formation. Earl Richard, an electrician's mate on board the heavy cruiser USS *Vincennes*, stood on a crowded deck, counting the planes. "We were just going to show them. Do a little damage," he said later, "just to let them know we could do it."[6]

The planes were heading for various Japanese cities. Lieutenant Ted Lawson, whose plane *The Ruptured Duck* had been assigned to targets in Tokyo, was surprised to find the Japanese capital a sprawling city resembling Los Angeles. There were no enemy planes, but the anti-aircraft guns opened up at once, and the exploding shells created ominous dark puffs all around the plane. "A black cloud appeared about 100 yards or so in front of us and rushed past at great speed. Two more appeared ahead of us, on about the line of our wingtips, and they too swept past," Lawson wrote in an account shortly afterwards. "They had our altitude perfectly, but they were leading us too much."[7] He identified his targets, and within 30 seconds he had dropped his four bombs, managing to get a glimpse of the destruction wrought by the attack: "I got a quick, indelible vision of one of our 500-pounders as it hit our steel-smelter target. The plant seemed to puff out its walls and then subside and dissolve in a black-and-red cloud."[8]

The bomber crews caught the Japanese people completely by surprise, appearing over the horizon as they were engaged in their daily activities. A cleaning lady came out of her building, shaking a mop at one of the bombers. On board a plane attacking the city of Nagoya, the pilot suddenly called out: "Look, they've got a ballgame on over there. I wonder what the score is." "It was a baseball game, sure enough, and a big crowd was in a wild scramble getting out of there fast."[9] US diplomat Robert A. Fearey, interned but enjoying relative freedom in Tokyo, was playing golf with Assistant Army Attaché Stanton Babcock when they both heard explosions in the distance. They looked up and saw a large airplane fly low over the Japanese parliamentary building. "Babcock said that he was sure it that it was an American bomber, but that he had no idea how it could have got to Tokyo," Fearey remembered later.[10] US envoy Joseph C. Grew was equally mystified, but for the Western embassy people, unsure when they could get home, it was a welcome visit from the outside world. "The British told us later that they drank toasts all day to the American fliers," he wrote in his diary.[11]

Fifteen of the 16 planes reached east China but were short on fuel, and the crews were forced to either bail out or crash-land. Two of the crews were subsequently caught by Japanese forces, and some were executed on trumped-up charges of war crimes, while others spent the rest of the war incarcerated. One aircraft landed near Vladivostok and the Soviet authorities, concerned about disturbing its precarious peace with Japan, detained the crew. All bombers used in the operation were lost, one way or the other. More seriously, from a strategic point of view, it removed from the pool of available vessels the two carriers *Hornet* and *Enterprise* at a time when the struggle with the Japanese Navy in the South Pacific was heating up. Besides, it caused a period of tension in the relationship with China. Chiang Kai-shek was dissatisfied because he had not been given a full advance briefing of the plans, even though the bombers were to land on airfields controlled by his forces.[12]

It was a steep price compared with the actual toll inflicted on the Japanese: 12 killed and about 100 injured. Still, that was not the main point. Morale, boosting one's own and shaking that of the enemy, was at the heart of the Doolittle raid, and it succeeded immensely in lifting the spirit of the American public. "The Tokyo raid was a hypodermic to the morale of the United States, which had suffered the worst series of military reverses in its history," according to the official air force history.[13] Claims by the *New York Times* that the raid had caused "tremendous moral damage"[14] were somewhat more hyperbolic. The Japanese authorities sought to minimize the impact of the raid, while also exaggerating the successes of the anti-aircraft effort. The evening papers carried images of nine bombers having been brought down, but the military staff at the US Embassy concluded that the photos were of the same downed plane, taken from different angles.[15]

Still, Japanese whose job was to protect the empire from assault were affected, if not shocked, by the daring raid. "This is more than regrettable, because this shattered my firm determination never to let the enemy attack Tokyo or the mainland," Admiral Ugaki Matome, chief of staff of the Combined Fleet, wrote in his diary. "This is one up to the enemy today."[16] Pilot Abe Zenji reluctantly acknowledged that the entire operation had required a type of ingenuity that the Japanese Army or Navy would not be able to produce. "Although we were certainly incensed by this intrusion upon our soil, the Americans' bravery was praiseworthy and much admired," he wrote later.[17]

Other members of the Japanese military reacted with more than just admiration. In China, the army of occupation panicked, worrying that airfields in the country's eastern provinces could be used as a base for bombing raids against their home islands. This was, in fact, not entirely unfounded. As early as 1937, Chinese bombers had succeeded in launching a bombing raid against Japan. In reaction, local commanders now unleashed a vicious campaign in the eastern provinces, occupying all airfields where the Doolittle bombers had been intended to land.[18] At the same time, Japanese troops swept through towns and villages, killing anyone in possession of American items, including small souvenirs that Doolittle pilots had left behind as tokens of gratitude for help they had received upon landing or bailing out. At least 10,000 civilians died in the reign of terror that unfolded. "Jap soldiers would be standing on bridges being used by refugees streaming into the interior," according to an eyewitness. "As the aged Chinese would pass by, Jap soldiers would push them off the bridge and into the water. Those who could not swim, of course, drowned; those who could swim afforded tragic targets for Jap riflemen."[19]

At the missionary station in the town of Yihuang, a priest by the name of Father Verdini had shielded orphans and elderly. The Japanese killed them all. "In a pond, in the garden, we found Father Verdini's body," according to a fellow missionary. "Nearby were the bones of the orphans and the aged men and women. Few met the merciful death of a bullet." Two had been burned to death as "human candles."[20] In the city of Nancheng, Japanese soldiers carried out a massacre, which in its ferocity was comparable to the Rape of Nanjing four years earlier. "For one month the Japanese remained in Nancheng, roaming the rubble-filled streets in loin clothes much of the time, drunk a good part of the time and always on the lookout for women," wrote the Reverend Frederick McGuire. "The women and children who did not escape from Nancheng will long remember the Japanese—the women and girls because they were raped time after time by Japan's imperial troops and are now

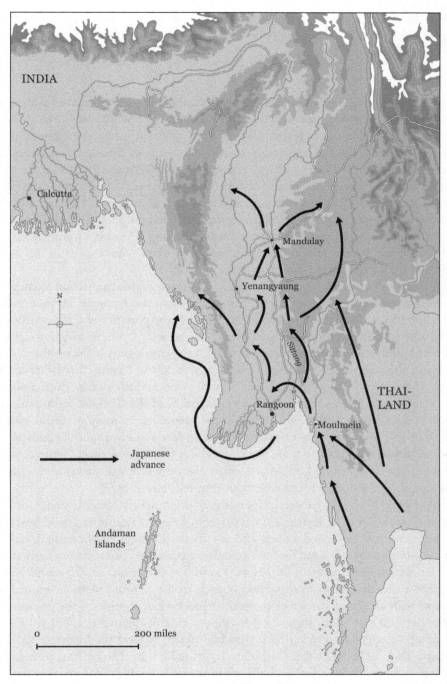

Burma, January–May 1942

ravaged by venereal disease, the children because they mourn their fathers who were slain in cold blood for the sake of the 'new order' in East Asia."[21]

At the exact time when the Doolittle bombers landed in various parts of China, at the other end of the continent-sized nation Chinese troops were involved in desperate battle with Japanese forces. China's 38th Division under the command of General Sun Liren was fighting at the oil fields at the city of Yenangyaung in central Burma. General Sun, 41 years of age, impressed most Western officers that he met. "He was a slight but well-proportioned, good-looking man... alert, energetic, and direct," Slim wrote. "I found him a good tactician, cool in action, very aggressively minded, and, in my dealings with him, completely straightforward."[22] Unlike most other Chinese generals, he spoke fluent English, having attended Virginia Military Institute in the 1920s. The institute, according to Slim, "could be proud of Sun; he would have been a good commander in any army."[23]

Since the fall of Rangoon in early March, Commonwealth troops had attempted to make a stand further up north in Burma and stem the Japanese advance. Even though the British had given up their opposition to the presence of Chinese troops, it did not stop the gradual loss of Burma. In the east, Chinese troops fought a series of bloody engagements, but even though the contingent included the 200th Division, the only fully mechanized outfit of this size in China, this failed to do more than merely delay the Japanese. Stilwell, who had arrived in Burma along with the Chinese troops, had already been skeptical of the Chinese regime during previous stays in the nation, and he was now becoming thoroughly disillusioned. "The Chinese government is a structure based on fear and favor, in the hands of an ignorant, arbitrary, stubborn man," he wrote about Chiang Kai-shek. "Only outside influence can do anything for China—either enemy action will smash her or some regenerative idea must be formed and put into effect at once."[24]

Stilwell was one among several Americans who felt deeply about China. Gordon Seagrave was another. A Burmese-born surgeon, he was working in a field hospital on the border of China and Burma and witnessed the huge sacrifices the Chinese were making. One busy April day, the ambulance brought a particularly grizzly case: a soldier with a shell fragment in the brain as well as shell wounds all over his body. Seagrave asked the nurses to carry him outside to die in peace while he tended to patients with an actual chance of survival. When he had completed the operations of the day and was about to take off his gloves, one of the nurses asked if he was not going to operate on the patient they had placed behind the kitchen. "Golly," Seagrave said, "is he still alive? Gosh darn it, bring him in." It took him an hour to perform surgery. "I don't believe he is going to die, after all," Seagrave wrote with a clear note of satisfaction in his diary.[25]

Burma's second largest city Mandalay fell on May 1. This set in motion a general retreat to India of Commonwealth divisions, as well as those Chinese units unable to return home to China. The withdrawal out of Burma was grueling, according to Shi Linxian, chief of staff of the Chinese 64th Regiment, but there were advantages to making up the rear: "Trekking through the mountains was very tough; long after the lead regiment had passed a point, we would take a very long time before reaching the same spot. Shanties were erected along the roads through our campgrounds... There were countless bodies along the way; some had already decomposed, while some had drawn their last breath not so long ago. Most of those who had given up were lying inside the shanties. Some were unconscious. Others, having lost all hope, had hanged themselves in the trees. A truly unbearable sight!"[26]

The retreat often verged on chaos. Panic tended to break out for no good reason. Survivors reported how the sound of irrigation canals could be mistaken for approaching Japanese tanks, causing stampedes along narrow, muddy roads.[27] Friction emerged between Chinese and Western troops. "They obstinately refused to obey any instructions given to them by the railway authorities," a British officer said about the Chinese being transported by train. "Their habit of utterly disregarding warnings of trains coming in the opposite direction to theirs, finally brought all rail movement to a halt, as it was impossible to repair the damage caused by the inevitable accidents."[28]

The retreat out of Burma into India was a race against time, as it had to be completed before the onset of the monsoon. The troops made it, just. The last stage of the British withdrawal was bogged down by torrential rains, which began in May. Pearl "Prue" Brewis, a British nurse, was on a train that managed to travel 65 miles in six days, since movement could only take place at night. On the sixth day, while the carriage was sitting idly on the tracks, a senior railway official entered and offered a ride up north on his train. It was crowded, but fast. "Standing room only, you know," Brewis said about the 100-mile ride north. "Actually, we got the last plane to leave Burma because the next day the aerodrome was bombed."[29]

More than a million Indians lived in Burma prior to the war, but most still considered India their home. When the Japanese launched their invasion, there was a mass exodus of Indians, and soon most major Burmese cities were virtually emptied of them.[30] The senior medical officer, Brigadier Short, described the Indians who arrived at the town of Ledo in easternmost India in the summer of 1942: "Complete exhaustion, physical and mental, with a disease superimposed, is the usual picture... all social sense is lost... they suffer from bad nightmares and their delirium is a babble of rivers and crossings, of mud and corpses... Emaciation and loss of weight are universal."[31] Slim watched how an Indian woman died from smallpox, leaving behind her small son. He and his staff bribed an Indian family to take the boy with them. "I hope he got through all right and did not give smallpox to his new family," Slim wrote in his memoirs.[32]

In the manner of Dunkirk, the defeat in Burma was in a way turned into a victory by the British. "The Army in Burma," the official British history says, "without once losing its cohesion had retreated nearly one thousand miles in some three and a half months—the longest retreat ever carried out by a British Army."[33] The American assessment of the British record was less kind: "Though there were cases of individual heroism and desperate fights by small isolated forces, the main body of the British made little or no efforts to stand and give battle," an official US military report on the Burma campaign said. "The piecemeal defense was a piece of stupidity which resulted in tens of thousands of casualties to the troops, the complete destruction of every town and city in Burma, and the loss to both the Chinese and the British of a vast amount of irreplaceable installations and equipment."[34]

The American and Philippine forces holding out on Bataan surrendered on April 9. Starvation, partly caused by the disastrous supply situation brought about by the MacArthur plan to spread assets across Luzon, had reduced the daily intake of calories to 1,000. It was a level at which the body stopped functioning properly and cognitive abilities were lagging, too. "It wasn't the enemy that licked us; it was disease and absence of food that really licked us," said Harold K. Johnson, a lieutenant in the 57th Infantry Regiment.[35] With the defeat on Bataan, a total of 76,000 men, including 12,000 Americans, fell prisoner to the Japanese. They were soon to become victims of the gravest war crime committed during the entire Philippine campaign.

Within hours of throwing down their arms, the American and Philippine captives were put on a forced march of over 60 miles to central Luzon and their destination, Camp O'Donnell, a military barracks that the Japanese had recently converted into a POW camp. The treatment of the prisoners became progressively worse during the march and ended in horrendous cases of brutality. An American prisoner was forced at bayonet point by the Japanese to bury Filipinos who had broken down during the march. Some were dead, others were merely dying. "The worst time," he later testified, "was once when a Filipino with about six inches of earth over him suddenly regained consciousness and clawed his way out until he was almost sitting upright. Then I learned to what lengths a man will go… to hang onto his own life. The bayonets began to prod me in the side, and I was forced to bash the Filipino over the head with the shovel and then finish burying him."[36]

More horrors awaited the prisoners along the road. Leaning against a few strands of barbed wire, they saw the body of a Filipino soldier. "The abdomen had been slashed open, and the bowels ripped therefrom, and hung on the wire!" one of the eyewitnesses said. "The reason for this barbarity was merely the Japanese way of telling everyone to be good!"[37] Clearly, the Japanese would deal savagely with any attempt at resistance, and still there were Filipino civilians who risked everything to help the prisoners. "They were very sympathetic, noting our misery. They risked death, by covertly throwing raw turnips to us," a US prisoner said.[38] These acts of kindness were too few to make any difference. The result of what was soon to be known as the Bataan Death March was horrifying. Estimates vary of how many prisoners died while being forced along the slightly more than 60 miles. According to one count between 5,000 and 11,000 lost their lives, the vast majority Filipinos.[39]

While this ordeal was still going on, a few thousand soldiers and sailors under General Wainwright maintained a last stand on the island of Corregidor. Now that the Japanese could focus all their attention on this tiny spot, they rolled up their artillery on the tip of Bataan and exposed Corregidor to merciless shelling for weeks, while air raids continued in unabated fashion. Seventy Filipinos were buried when the cave where they were seeking shelter collapsed.[40] War correspondent Clark Lee described digging out 35 young Americans whose shelter had received a direct hit. "The bomb explosion didn't kill them," he wrote, "but it blew their mouths and noses and lungs full of dirt and suffocated them."[41]

On May 6, the Japanese launched the long-awaited amphibious assault on Corregidor. A Japanese journalist was watching from Bataan as the boats approached the island, and suddenly were met by fierce fire from the American batteries: "It was a spectacle that confounded the imagination, surpassing in grim horror anything we had ever seen before. An area of not less than a mile square was a solid mass of red-hot, flying steel. And somewhere inside that ring of death was a tiny remnant of those 'human bullets' who had so shortly before left this shore." Only about 30 percent of the soldiers in the first attack wave reached the shore alive, and among these, many were lying heads down at water's edge, playing dead.[42]

Despite the carnage, the Japanese kept coming, and after hours of increasingly desperate fighting, Wainwright decided to put an end to a hopeless struggle. "There is a limit of human endurance and that limit has long since been past," he wrote in his last message to Roosevelt. "Without prospect of relief I feel it is my duty to my country and to my gallant troops to end this useless effusion of blood and human sacrifice."[43] Five months after Pearl Harbor, the last American bastion in the western Pacific had fallen. It was a setback, but a fully anticipated one. And just when it happened, America was on the way to its first significant strategic gain, in an area thousands of miles away: the South Pacific.

During the first days of April, Allied intelligence units noticed an emerging pattern in Japanese radio communications. The signs were mounting that the enemy was preparing a major move out of his newly conquered strongpoint at Rabaul. On April 7, the US Navy's signals monitoring unit in Hawaii, Hypo Station, reported "numerous indications which point to impending offensive from Rabaul base."[44]

The question was what objective these planned Japanese operations were targeted at. A dispatch issued a few days later by British intelligence in Ceylon provided a possible answer: "Part or whole of First Air Fleet appears to be connected with an operation against RZP (identified as Port Moresby). Date and details uncertain."[45]

It was guesswork more than anything else, but the Allied code breakers were exactly right. Since January, the Japanese Navy had been planning an operation to seize Port Moresby, the main city on the south side of the Australian-controlled territory of Papua. The Japanese Naval planners had both defensive and offensive reasons for contemplating the operation. On the one hand, they wished to prevent the Allies from carrying out air attacks on Japanese ports and airfields at Rabaul. On the other hand, once they controlled Port Moresby, the Japanese themselves would be able to carry out air strikes against northern Australia. At the same time, along with a plan to seize the island of Tulagi in the Solomon chain of islands, it was part of a more ambitious strike south towards Fiji, Samoa, and New Caledonia, with the ultimate objective of isolating Australia and cutting off supply lines from the United States.[46]

The Japanese were playing to their own strengths. MacArthur, the new supreme commander of Allied forces in the Southwest Pacific, was worried about the

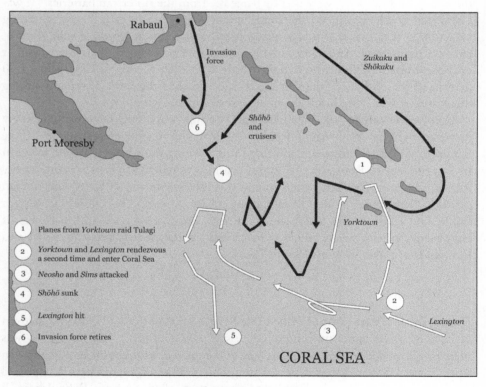

Coral Sea, May 4–8, 1942

preponderance of Japanese Naval power in the Pacific and the American unwillingness to divert Naval assets from the Atlantic Ocean. He advocated a concentration of forces to decisively challenge the Japanese Navy. Otherwise, he said, ominously, "the United States itself will face a series of such disasters and a crisis of such proportions as had never been faced in the long years of her existence."[47] The fog of war was dense. Finding the enemy was often the biggest challenge even for the Americans, despite having cracked the Japanese codes. Admiral Nimitz was dumbfounded when he realized that his chief intelligence officer had no idea where the Japanese carriers were. "For all you know, they could be coming around Diamond Head and you wouldn't know it?" Nimitz exclaimed, referring to one of Hawaii's main features, the volcanic cone visible from most of Honolulu.[48]

Nonetheless, by the middle of April Allied intelligence suggested that a Japanese task force consisting of transports and the light carrier *Shōhō* was about to enter the Coral Sea northeast of Australia. It was also believed that the two carriers *Shōkaku* and *Zuikaku* were in the area. This prompted Nimitz to hastily organize a response in the form of Task Force 17, consisting of the aircraft carrier *Yorktown* and other vessels under the command of Rear Admiral Frank Jack Fletcher. Rear Admiral Aubrey Fitch was ordered to head to the Coral Sea with a small fleet centered on carrier *Lexington*. A motley assembly of American and Australian ships under the command of Royal Navy Rear Admiral John Crace was added to this force. Nimitz and his staff were worried that it was not enough to meet the Japanese challenge, but it was all that could be spared, since part of the Pacific fleet had been allocated to the Doolittle raid. "CinCPac will probably be unable to send enough forces to be sure of stopping the Jap offensive," the CinCPac Command Summary said in a sobering assessment on April 18.[49]

While the Americans were at a slight disadvantage in terms of forces deployed, they had one major factor going for them. There was a marked contrast between the two command styles: a Japanese style where the entire operation was planned down to the most minute detail, as opposed to an American one where only the broad outline of what was to be accomplished was decided beforehand. The overly elaborate Japanese approach might just possibly succeed in a training exercise, but it ran a high risk of failure in real-life conditions, filled with unforeseen contingencies. By contrast, Nimitz's order to Fletcher was so simple as to be almost devoid of content: "Your task [is to] assist in checking further advance by enemy... by seizing favorable opportunities to destroy ship... and aircraft."[50] This allowed for a much higher degree of flexibility, but at the same time placed a considerable burden on the shoulders of the American commander to think quickly and exploit whatever unexpected advantages emerged.

The *Yorktown* and *Lexington* groups rendezvoused off the New Hebrides on the edge of the Coral Sea on May 1. While the *Lexington* group was still refueling, Fletcher's *Yorktown* group departed for reconnaissance of the Japanese task force.

Only hours afterwards, he received reports about the Japanese landing taking place on Tulagi. Fletcher, eager to engage the enemy, sailed north in order to intercept the landing force. On May 4, the *Yorktown* launched a total of four waves of air attacks on the Japanese force disembarking on the island. The actual payoff was limited, with 87 Japanese killed and 126 injured. One destroyer, two patrol boats, and a transport were also sunk.[51] All in all, it was a costly diversion, and wasted the element of surprise, since the Japanese were now alerted to the presence of US carriers in the area.[52]

Fletcher turned around and joined forces with the *Lexington*, and in the following two days, the vessels of both opposing navies were searching for each other. Even though both sides were assisted by land-based planes, in the vastness of the ocean, it was a game very much relying on luck. Early on May 7, Japanese aircraft spotted two American vessels, the destroyer *Sims* and the oiler *Neosho*, erroneously identifying them as a carrier and a cruiser. Believing it was big prey, the Japanese commanders launched a massive air attack which severely damaged the *Neosho* and sent the *Sims* to the bottom after scoring a direct hit. "The last I saw of the Commanding Officer he was standing on the bridge when the ship was blown up by the explosion," said Robert J. Dicken, chief signalman on board the destroyer.[53]

Only minutes later, American pilots sighted an enemy vessel, the light carrier *Shōhō*. Like the Japanese, they thought they had hit on a much more valuable target—the *Shōkaku* or the *Zuikaku*—than they really had, and Fletcher sent a large number of aircraft, which went on to attack the *Shōhō* mercilessly. "I tried to count the bomb hits, but there were too many," said Joe Taylor, a torpedo plane pilot from the *Yorktown*. "Every time a bomb would hit, flames would come licking out both ends of the hangar deck. That bombing was so damned beautiful it was an inspiration to us."[54]

The Japanese carrier disappeared under the waves less than seven minutes after the first bomb hit. "She went straight ahead," said diver bomber William O. Burch, "sinking as she went."[55] In the meantime, the officers on the American carriers were passing the time in almost unbearably anxiety, since they were out of communication with the pilots most of the time during the attack. The painful wait was soon over. Once Robert E. Dixon, one of the pilots who had taken part in the attack on the carrier, could get a message through on radio, he announced in triumphant shorthand style, "Scratch one flattop."[56]

On the Japanese side, the loss of the *Shōhō* came as a shock, and it made the entire operation grind to a halt. Already earlier the same day, the invasion force headed for Port Moresby had been ordered not to enter the Coral Sea but await the situation.[57] "A dream of great success has been shattered," Admiral Ugaki Matome wrote in his diary in the evening of May 7. "Two enemy carriers still remain… It will be risky to carry out an invasion attempt before destroying them."[58] Lieutenant Commander Paul D. Stroop, flag tactical officer on board the *Lexington*, later regretted that too many bombs and torpedoes were spent on just the *Shōhō*, and that it had not been spread among more Japanese ships. "But this being our first battle of any kind, why, everybody went after the big prize, and they sank this rather soft carrier very quickly," he said later.[59]

At dusk, the Japanese sent out 27 bombers and torpedo planes to attack the American carrier force. Searching for almost 300 miles, they found nothing and jettisoned their bombs and torpedoes. "While returning they passed over the American carrier at night," said Captain Yamaoka Mineo, operations officer of the Fifth Air Flotilla. "Some planes mistook the American force for the Japanese carriers, turned on their lights and tried to land before they realized their mistake."[60] Stroop, the tactical officer, was standing on the *Lexington* when this happened: "One of the things that struck me as odd was that the red color of the port running light was different from the shade of running lights that we had on our planes. They had a sort of bluish tint, red-blue tint to it."[61] After some initial confusion, when many of the men on board the American vessels mistook the Japanese for friendly aircraft, the antiaircraft gunners let loose a deadly hail against the planes, shooting down several. Others got lost in the dark ocean, and less than half made it back to their own carrier.

The evening of May 7 passed in tense anticipation of what everyone believed would be the following day's decisive battle. Even though the Americans had no precise idea about the location of the Japanese enemy after dark, it was clear that he was close by. American intelligence personnel could clearly hear radio communication between the Japanese pilots and their carriers.[62] The men who would be putting their lives on the line within the next few hours also prepared mentally. On board the *Yorktown*, dive bomber pilot John J. Powers told his roommate before going to sleep: "I'm going to get a hit tomorrow if I have to lay it on their flight deck."[63]

Early on May 8, the pilots of the opposing fleets found each other. US aviators spotted the *Shōkaku*, while the *Zuikaku* managed to stay undetected under the cover of clouds. The American pilots went on the attack at about 11 am but found conditions less than ideal. Some experienced their sights fogging up and they had to stick their heads outside the cockpit to see the target.[64] John J. Powers was among them and made good on his promise from the night before, releasing his bomb just a few hundred feet from his target and going so near that it cost him his life. "It was believed that his plane was destroyed by the blast of his own missile," US naval intelligence said in its after-action report.[65] The damage done to the *Shōkaku* was, however, non-fatal. "The torpedoes were launched at too great a range permitting both carriers to avoid them," said Captain Yamaoka. "Slow torpedoes and long range. We could turn and run away from them."[66] While the battle was still raging, the carrier began its journey home to Japan.

Almost simultaneously with the US attack on the *Shōkaku*, the *Lexington*'s radars spotted Japanese planes approaching. Twenty minutes later, they emerged in the sky and began their attack.[67] It was a coordinated assault of dive-bombers and torpedo planes. Lieutenant Commander Shimazaki Shigekazu reported flying into "a virtual wall of antiaircraft fire," before approaching the carrier at such a low altitude that the wings of his plane were inches from touching the ocean. "I was so low that I almost struck the bow of the ship, for I was flying below the level of the flight deck, he said. "I could see the crewmen on the ship staring at my plane as it rushed by."[68] On board the *Lexington*, Stroop and the other ranking officers could only watch: "At this point in time—as far as the senior people were concerned—you were completely helpless. You were depending on the training that had been given to the pilots in the air, and you were dependent on the training and practice the gunners had had."[69] Torpedoes hit the carrier at both ends, and dive bombers also scored hits.

Noel Gayler, a pilot from the *Lexington*, returned shortly after the Japanese planes had left and was not initially aware of the attack that had just taken place, but noticed the odd welcome he received when he climbed out of his aircraft. "Nobody paid any attention, and I looked around and some of the faces were looking sort of strange. Then I saw flecks of fire-fighting foam all over the deck, and I knew she had been hit," he said. "There was a lot of things going on, explosions in the ship. One main plane elevator went up on a column of fire and turned over and landed on the deck with a clang."[70]

The *Lexington* headed back towards Brisbane, but between 2 and 2:30 pm the crew heard a large underwater explosion. Many thought the carrier had been hit by a torpedo from a Japanese submarine, but it was in fact the gasoline fuel that had been ignited.[71] The wounded men as well as the air personnel were ordered to abandon ship first, while the rest attempted to fight the fire. It was an impossible task. Stroop explained: "On the hangar deck, apparently torpedo warheads were going off from the storage back aft. You could hear an explosion towards the fantail on the hangar deck, and it sounded like a freight train rumbling up the hangar deck. Actually, it was a rushing wall of flame, you see, which would erupt around the perimeter of the elevator. These flames would shoot up two or three feet, and these were occurring with increasing frequency."[72]

The *Lexington* was lost, but it could have ended up much worse. A total of 150 men were killed in the battle, but very few lost their lives while abandoning ship.[73] There was little panic, and the almost leisurely atmosphere was emphasized when, during evacuation, it became apparent that the ship's service ice cream plant, located in the extreme port quarter, was still functioning. "While they were abandoning ship, sailors were lining up for free ice cream. Of course, they puked it up as soon as they had been swimming in saltwater a little while," Noel Gayler said.[74]

The sailors munching ice cream had just seen history being made. The Battle of the Coral Sea marked a watershed, as it was the first time two surface fleets met in combat without ever being within sight of each other. It was history's first true carrier battle, in which the opposing forces sought a decision not by shelling each other but by sending off successive waves of bombers targeting each other's main vessels. *Shōhō* was the first Japanese carrier to be sent to the bottom of the Pacific Ocean. Tactically speaking, the battle of the Coral Sea was a tie. Strategically, it was an American victory, as the invasion of Port Moresby was delayed, only to be called off entirely later on. Due to the losses inflicted on the Japanese Navy, it also prevented its admirals from applying their full force to a showdown waiting a few weeks in the future: Midway.

★ ★ ★

In the second half of May, US intelligence personnel who had worked long shifts for the previous half year keeping an eye on the enemy understood that something important was underway. It was clear that the Japanese Navy was organizing carriers, battleships, and destroyers, and senior American officers led by Admiral Ernest King, the chief of naval operations, believed that he was seeing the contours of a task force aimed at a possible second strike against Port Moresby or another high-profile target in the South Pacific.[75] Only after careful analysis of the Japanese radio traffic did it become clear that the Japanese were preparing an offensive in a completely different direction—towards the US-held island of Midway nearly 1,500 miles west of Hawaii. On May 20, Yamamoto, the commander-in-chief of the Combined Fleet, sent out the final operations order, which was intercepted by the Americans. "All I knew was I detected something important that night," said Alva B. Lasswell, a specialist in the Japanese language at Hypo station in Hawaii. "I spent the whole night on it."[76]

Only days earlier the US side had obtained definitive confirmation that the Japanese were indeed heading for Midway. For several months, the code name AF had turned up in Japanese radio traffic, and more recently it had emerged as a major focus of Japanese strategic planning. There was broad consensus among American analysts that the two letters stood for Midway, but the last doubters needed to be convinced that this was indeed the case. In a ruse that has gone down in history as a classic intelligence ploy, US forces on Midway sent out an uncoded message reporting technical problems with a fresh-water evaporator. The message was intercepted by Japanese intelligence on Wake island, which reported back to Tokyo about problems with water on "AF." Its identity as Midway was now firmly established.[77]

Edwin T. Layton, the combat intelligence officer on the Nimitz staff, was key in predicting exactly what the Japanese were going to do, where they would do it, and when. "I want you to be the Admiral Nagumo on my staff," Nimitz had told Layton, with reference to the chief of the Japanese Naval General Staff. "Your every thought, every instinct will be that of Admiral Nagumo's; you are to see the war, their operations, their aims, from the Japanese viewpoint and keep me advised what you, as a Japanese, are thinking about."[78] Layton was of a somewhat cautious nature, which occasionally clashed with Nimitz's need for concrete, actionable intelligence.[79]

With just days to go before the expected attack, and the Japanese armada already on the move across the Pacific, the admiral demanded specific details.

"I have a difficult time being specific," Layton told Nimitz.

"I want you to be specific," the admiral replied. "After all, that is the job I have given you—to be the admiral commanding the Japanese forces and tell us what you're going to do."

"All right then, Admiral," Layton said. "I've previously given you the intelligence that the carriers will probably attack Midway on the morning of the 4th of June, so we'll pick the 4th of June for the day. They'll come in from the northwest on bearing 325 degrees and they will be sighted at about 175 miles from Midway, and the time will be about 0600 Midway time."[80]

Layton was remarkably correct in his prediction. The Japanese had made elaborate plans for capturing the island of Midway, lining up an array of landing boats. "We had plenty of equipment for a three month's occupation without help," said Toyama Yasumi, the chief of staff of the 2nd destroyer squadron.[81] However, the primary objective of the Japanese fleet heading for Midway under the command of Admiral Nagumo Chūichi was not so much possession of Midway—and island of 2.4 square miles—as an attempt to lure the US Navy out into the open, where it

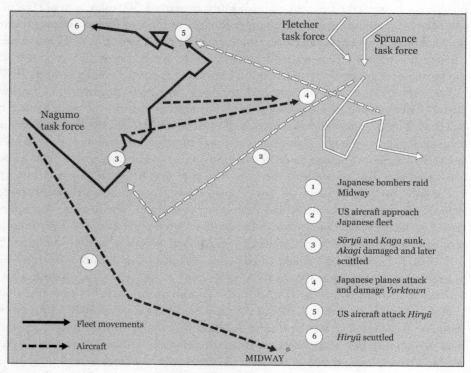

Battle of Midway, June 4–5, 1942

would expose its key vessels in an all-out battle with its Japanese counterpart. Or at least this was the plan.

In reality, it was a case of Japanese hubris, reflecting underestimation of the American foe combined with overestimation of Japan's own capabilities. Due to the recent action in the Coral Sea, the carriers *Shōkaku* and *Zuikaku* were not available for the operation, meaning the Japanese could deploy only four fleet carriers, *Kaga*, *Akagi*, *Hiryū*, and *Sōryū*. Moreover, the plan was a giant construction of moving parts, with task forces scattered over a huge area. Much could go wrong, but it was not encouraged in the upper echelons of the Japanese military establishment to utter dissenting views. Yamamoto pushed through the plans for an offensive at Midway in much the same way that the previous year he had succeeded in gaining acceptance for his daring plan to attack Pearl Harbor—by threatening to resign. In the words of the foremost historians of the Midway battle, he showed himself as a leader "who ruled through intimidation rather than reason and who was not prepared to accept criticism."[82]

Nimitz, for his part, was convinced that a decisive encounter was in the offing and he deployed everything he could possibly spare, including the *Yorktown*, which was in drydock after the Coral Sea battle with damage enough for months of repairs, but was hauled out to sea again after just days. The chief of the US carrier fleet, Admiral William F. Halsey, was hospitalized, and he was temporarily replaced with Admiral Raymond A. Spruance, an aloof but competent commander. Intensive scouting was carried out by planes and submarines, and on June 3, the crew of Catalina flying boat detected the Midway invasion fleet, initially reported in error as being the "main body" of the Japanese attack force. The great showdown would happen the following day.[83]

Early on June 4, Admiral Nagumo sent off the first wave of attack planes, a total of 108 aircraft, to raid Midway island. The defenders were alerted by radar to the approach of the enemy, and while the American aircraft did little damage to the attackers, anti-aircraft fire on the island proved devastating, shooting down 11 planes while damaging 43 others. Nagumo, whose fleet was now beginning to come under attack from waves of US planes, received a message from an observer plane to the effect that a second raid of the island was necessary. He now proceeded to re-arm aircraft set aside for attack on enemy ships, ordering their ammunition to be changed for bombs suitable for land targets. While the time-consuming re-arming was going on, a new sighting was reported to Nagumo, suggesting that the US carriers were close by. At this point, Nagumo ordered his crews to pause the re-arming until the situation had become clearer.

At this particular moment, the American attacks came in rapid succession. Three waves of torpedo bombers approached the Japanese fleet, and most were shot down, while registering no hits themselves. Lieutenant George Gay, a torpedo bomber pilot, was in the first squadron that took off from the *Hornet* and participated in the attack on the Japanese aircraft carrier *Sōryū*. He watched all his comrades be taken out by Japanese "Zeros" swooping down at them, and himself felt horribly exposed to the anti-aircraft guns on the *Sōryū*: "If I had had some machine guns to shoot back at them, I might not have been able to silence those guns, but I could have made the gunners a little nervous. As it was, they were just sitting there shooting at me and I wasn't shooting back at them."[84] Gay later remembered "the little Jap captain up there jumping up and down raising hell, and I thought about wishing that I had a .45 so that I could take a pot shot at him. I couldn't hit him, but, if nothing else, thrown the gun at him, just something." In the same moments, he thought for a split second about crashing into the planes on the deck of the carrier: "It's when a fellow is just gone and knows it, it is just crash into the ship or crash into the sea, and you have enough control to do a little bit more damage, why you crash into the ship."[85]

The torpedo bombers were nearly all sacrificed, but it was not in vain, since it had the effect of attracting the attention of the Japanese gunners and combat air patrols. As a result, when American dive bombers arrived a few minutes later, they met with limited opposition. On the US side there was a mood of elation. "There is no question that all of us knew we were 'on' in the world's center ring that day," said Lieutenant James S. Gray. "Seeing the white feathers of ships' wakes at high speed at the far edge of the overcast, and realizing that there for the first time in plain sight were the Japanese who had been knocking hell out of us for seven months was a sensation not many men know in a lifetime."[86] It was the kind of attack the Japanese feared the most, making them feel much more exposed than either torpedo attacks or bombing from high altitude. "The worst is dive-bombing," said Captain Kawaguchi Susumu, air officer on the *Hiryū*. "You can't avoid it, but you can avoid torpedoes dropped at long range."[87] Tokuno Horishi, assistant gunnery officer on the battleship *Kirishima*, agreed: "We did not like the dive-bombers because they came in at such a high angle they were very hard to hit. We could dodge torpedoes and horizontal-bombers."[88]

John S. Thach, leader of F4F Wildcat fighters protecting the attacking formations of torpedo planes and dive bombers, nearly despaired at the number of Zeros in the air near the Japanese vessels. Both because of their numbers and their superior performance, they seemed an insurmountable obstacle. "Well," he then told himself, "we're going to take a lot of them with us if they're going to get us all."[89] A confused chaos ensued. "When Jap fighter planes attack our dive bombers or torpedo planes, the rear gunner usually has a chance to give the Jap a burst or two," a pilot reminisced. "Then, without watching to see what happens to that Jap, he usually has another one to take care of."[90] Noel Gayler, one of the US Navy's aces, described a typical dogfight: "It was just such an incredibly confusing, mixed-up, screwed-up situation. Poor visibility and people yelling on the radio. Clouds all over the place. I can't give you any coherent description of it."[91]

Out of this confused free-for-all, American victory emerged. Within just minutes, three Japanese carriers were lost. The *Sōryū* and the *Kaga* were ablaze, while the *Akagi* had been seriously damaged.[92] After the loss of the carriers, Japanese planes landed on the surface of the sea near friendly warships. One after the other, the aircraft slowly sank into the ocean.[93] Meanwhile, the Japanese were trying to hit back at the American carriers. As their aviators fiercely attacked the *Yorktown*, its crew was firing back frantically. One of their 5-inch shells struck the stack of the USS *Benham*, killing one crew member and injuring four others. "There's no way to dodge that kind of thing. I think it's one of those acts of battle you can't help," said John Muse Worthington, commanding officer of the *Benham*.[94]

Joseph P. Pollard, a medical officer on board the USS *Yorktown*, was overwhelmed with work, as new wounded were brought in by the minute. "Some men had one foot or leg off, others had both off; some were dying—some dead. Everywhere there was need for morphine, tourniquets, blankets and first aid," he remembered later. "Water hoses were dragged into the passageway in an attempt to control a fire somewhere forward in the island. The hose had been perforated by shrapnel and sprayed water all over the deck and on some of my wounded who were lying in the passageway." Later he went up to the flight deck and was confronted with the gruesome sight of a gun mount that had received a hit. "A pair of legs attached to the hips sat in the trainer's seat. A stub of spinal column was hanging over backwards. There was nothing else remaining." Word came over the speaker, "Prepare to abandon ship." A man with one foot shot clean off and a severe chest wound turned his head towards Pollard and asked, "What does this mean for us?" and turned his head away.[95]

Even as the *Yorktown* was sinking beneath the waves, a mood of despair spread among the Japanese. The *Hiryū* was detected by the Americans late in the afternoon and had received damage that it was not to recover from, adding it to the list of three carriers that Japan had already lost on that fateful day. Some officers were so dejected they considered group suicide. Kusaka Ryūnosuke, chief of staff of the First Air Fleet under Nagumo, managed to dissuade his fellow officers: "You are just like hysterical women," he said. "First you get excited over easy victories and now you are worked up to commit suicide because of a defeat! This is no time for Japan for you to say such a thing."[96] On the US side, the mood was weary rather than jubilant. Two of Spruance's officers were talking casually about a gruesome murder in the United States which had been featured in the news. The two officers mused about how only a sick mind could commit such an unnatural thing as killing another human being. Spruance overheard the conversation and remarked drily, "What do you think I have been doing all afternoon?"[97]

At home in Japan, the defeat at Midway only sank in slowly, partly because of reluctance to lose face, and partly because of continued problems with communication and cooperation among the different services. "I did not hear of the Midway defeat till more than a month after it occurred," Prime Minister Tōjō said after the war.[98] Hirohito, by contrast, was informed immediately about the disastrous defeat, including the loss of the four aircraft carriers.[99] With access to more unbiased information than perhaps any other person in his empire, he was the only one to receive reports from the chiefs of staff of both the Army and the Navy, whereas the services were usually careful not to volunteer information to each other.[100] This placed Hirohito in his own private tragedy: fully aware of how desperate the situation was becoming, but unable to do much about it.

Admiral Ugaki, in a diary entry written on 8 June, 1942, summarizing the battle, concluded by writing, "Thus the distressing day of 5 June came to an end. Don't let another day like this come to us during the course of this war! Let this day be the only one of the greatest failure of my life!" The Japanese, by their own admission, were overconfident and committed huge errors of omission. "Because we had suffered so little at Pearl Harbor at the beginning of the war, we thought we would get away with the same thing at Midway," said Aoki Taijiro, the commanding officer of the *Akagi*, in post-war interrogations.[101] Added Captain Tsuda Hiroaki, also talking after the war: "The Battle of Midway was the beginning of the Japanese failure in the war. I do not mean that this was the decisive battle of the war, but the loss of our carriers and some of our best pilots and officers affected us throughout the war."[102]

Midway has gone down in history as the turning point of the War in the Pacific. It has also been remembered as a rare occasion when the US side got the chance to play the underdog. Both claims are exaggerations, if not entirely untrue. The United States actually had more planes than the Japanese at Midway and was not the underdog except, occasionally, in terms of pilot skill and aircraft technology. On the plus side, the US commanders were effectively in possession of four carriers—three actual carriers, plus a virtual one in the form of the island of Midway. For the Japanese, the long-term consequences of the debacle were grave, and the Japanese Navy never recovered from the loss of four carriers and 322 planes. However, it would be an exaggeration to state that the Japanese naval air corps was almost annihilated at Midway. It had enough fighting power left in it for nearly three more years of war.

CHAPTER SIX

Guadalcanal Gambit

July–September 1942

The seas were rough, and the tropical rain was pouring down when the Marine raiders disembarked from the submarines *Nautilus* and *Argonaut* off Japanese-held Makin atoll in the central Pacific just before dawn on August 17, 1942. The Marines were from the newly formed 2nd Raider Battalion. They were highly trained and had prepared intensely for the mission, one of the first American raids of the war. Commanding the Marines was Lieutenant Colonel Evans F. Carlson, a maverick in uniform who had developed an interest in guerrilla-style warfare during a stint as a military observer with Communist Chinese rebels in the late 1930s. His executive officer was James Roosevelt, son of the American president.[1]

The poor weather conditions caused the plans to go awry from the start. Approaching the atoll in rubber boats, the soldiers reached the shore amid great confusion. One platoon even landed behind enemy lines. Topping off the bad luck, a Marine accidentally fired his weapon, alerting the Japanese on the atoll. The Japanese reacted immediately, launching two suicide-style Banzai attacks. Both assaults were clear tactical victories for the Americans, and the Japanese were wiped out nearly to the last man. As a result, by noon on the day of the landing, Makin was essentially in American hands. However, Carlson did not have the full picture and thought his situation was critical, ordering a withdrawal. The Marines attempted to paddle back to the waiting submarines, but only a few made it through the powerful surf. Some capsized, losing valuable equipment. The rest were forced to turn back.

It was now late in the day, and at this point, Carlson completely lost hope. He was unaware that very few Japanese were left on Makin and decided to surrender. Citing the need to keep the president's son safe, he picked two officers to head out into the night to find an enemy to give themselves up to. However, rather than finding the strong and organized enemy force they had expected, the two officers only chanced upon scattered Japanese, many of them unwilling to fight. In the morning on August 18, the two officers returned to Carlson, informing him that everything indicated he had, in fact, won the battle of Makin.

Abandoning his plan to surrender, Carlson also learned that the president's son was among the few who had made it onto a submarine, and the Marine commander now proceeded to organize a more orderly retreat that same evening. This time, he arranged for a rendezvous with the subs inside Makin lagoon, where the surf was weaker. Despite the more careful preparations, even this last chapter of the raid failed to go according to plan. In the scramble to get back on board the two subs, nine Marines were left behind on the atoll, abandoned to a sinister fate. They tried to hide in the jungle, but less than a fortnight later the Japanese captured them. They took them to the island of Kwajalein, where they decapitated them all. It was a steep price to pay for an operation which was, in essence, merely a feint. It served no independent purpose and was meant to divert Japanese attention away from the main Allied operations taking place at the same time on Australia's doorstep.

What next? This was the question weighing on the minds of both Allied and Japanese planners after the surprise outcome at Midway in early June. During a few short hours of intense battle, the fate of the Pacific had hung in the balance, and the encounter had ended, due to a mixture of careful planning, risk-taking, and luck, in a victory for the US side. For the first time in over six months, the Americans were no longer on the run, and the Japanese had seen an unbroken chain of bold and rapid advances come to an abrupt end. In the words of one historian, "with only slight exaggeration, before Midway the Japanese met nothing but victory, and after Midway the Americans commanded only success."[2]

Each in their own way, the two sides were now forced to reevaluate fundamental assumptions underlying their strategic thinking. Intriguingly, although they viewed the situation from diametrically opposed perspectives, both sides ended up drawing very similar conclusions about where the war should be heading. Both were convinced that the Central Pacific was key to victory, but neither could do much about it at the moment. The Japanese had lost crucial naval assets at Midway, and they were unable, at least for the time being, to conduct major offensive operations. The Americans were similarly hampered from undertaking large-scale initiatives at sea, because they had not yet built up the naval resources needed.

Against this backdrop both decided, albeit for different reasons, that the next showdown was to be in the Southwest Pacific. The ultimate prize here was Australia. The southern continent was important, though not in the sense that the Japanese ever nurtured for more than a brief moment any real ambition of occupying it. The troops needed for an operation of that scale, let alone the shipping required to transport and supply them, were simply beyond the capability of the Japanese armed forces at the time. Rather than hoping to hoist the flag of the Rising Sun over Sydney harbor, the Japanese were keen to defuse the danger that attached to Australia as a potential staging ground for an Allied counteroffensive.

This was the exact reason that the US forces prioritized the security of maritime routes to Australia. Its territory was to be the point of departure for a campaign of reconquest that was to proceed north up the islands of New Guinea and Southeast Asia, leading to the recapture of the Philippines and, in due course, the defeat of Japan. What it meant was this: even this early in the war, little more than six months after Pearl Harbor, the Japanese mindset had fundamentally shifted to a defensive mode, while the Americans were already assuming an offensive outlook, actively planning how to take the war into the enemy's camp.

US commanders in both the Army and Navy agreed that the Solomons, a string of jungle-covered islands northwest of Australia, constituted the most obvious first stepping stone in the long haul of taking back the Pacific. As early as March, Admiral King had suggested an offensive in the archipelago, and the area's importance was further reinforced by reports of the Japanese Navy's occupation of the small island of Tulagi. General Douglas MacArthur, from his isolated position in Australia, now made a proposal of characteristic boldness. He wanted to strike hundreds of miles into Japanese-held territory, aiming not just for the Solomons, but far beyond, heading for New Britain and New Ireland in a bid to retake the strategic deep-water port of Rabaul, which was Japan's most important forward anchorage. Admiral King and the Navy basically subscribed to MacArthur's plan, although they insisted on a more gradual approach, focusing on seizing control of the Solomons before moving on to more distant targets.

Despite the overall agreement among the US commanders about the Solomons campaign, preparations got bogged down in turf wars about who was to be in charge. Should overall command be given to Admiral Nimitz or General MacArthur? In other words, was it to be a Navy or an Army affair? MacArthur was intensely suspicious of Navy intentions. "It is quite evident," he wrote at the end of June to his superior, Army Chief of Staff General George C. Marshall, "that the Navy contemplates assuming general command control of all operations in the Pacific theater, the role of the Army being subsidiary and consisting largely of placing its forces at the disposal and under the command of Navy or Marine officers."[3]

It is well-known that military commanders are frequently at war not just with the enemy but also with rival services. This only gets worse when they are equipped with oversized egos, and in the rich gallery of World War II generals, few were as egocentric as MacArthur. An outstanding commander who was clearly a little too aware of his own capabilities, he was equally skilled in the arts of war and of publicity. Carefully managing the information that flowed to the press, he had built up a public persona, complete with an oversized cap, large shades, and a corn cob pipe, that made him one of the most recognizable and beloved US generals of the war, and convinced both the American public and the elite policy makers that he was irreplaceable.

MacArthur was facing a formidable opponent in Admiral King, who was notorious for his intransigence and intensely disliked by many senior Army officers. "One thing that might help win this war," Eisenhower wrote in his diary, "is to get someone to shoot King."[4] In the end, MacArthur's standing gave him considerable leverage, and he did his utmost to use that advantage in his dealings with Washington. The disagreement only ended when Marshall personally intervened and, in a series of meetings, hammered out a compromise with King during a series of conversations and meetings in late June and early July. Nimitz was to get responsibility for the action in the Solomons, while MacArthur would be in charge of future operations in the advance towards Rabaul.[5]

It was not the outcome that MacArthur had been hoping for, and Marshall was concerned that it would be the source of continued bickering. Worried that there was potential for further argument, he ordered MacArthur to tone down his rhetoric towards the Navy: "I wish you to make every conceivable effort to promote a complete accord throughout this affair," he wrote. "There will be difficulties and irritations inevitably but the end in view demands a determination to suppress these manifestations."[6]

Meanwhile, the situation had taken on new momentum, and a sense of urgency was spreading among American commanders. Reconnaissance reports suggested that the Japanese had consolidated their foothold in the Solomons. They had now set their sights on a larger island across a narrow strait from their Tulagi seaplane base and had started building an airfield there. That island was just one of a myriad of exotically named South Sea locations at the time, but it would soon become a household name in America. Although it was only slightly bigger than Rhode Island, it was to become the scene of the first major American offensive of the entire war. Its name was Guadalcanal.

Guadalcanal: "What is that?" someone asked, and another followed up with an equally bewildered question: "Where is that?" The scene was a locked-up room inside a hotel in Wellington, New Zealand's capital, and the assembled men, all officers of the US Marine Corps had just been told where they would be going in order to land the initial blow against the Japanese empire. Guadalcanal was part of the Solomon Islands, they were told, but few were left any the wiser by this piece of information.[7] Most men in the US armed forces, and outside, would have been just as confused. Guadalcanal was in an obscure part of the world, in a place that few had ever visited. For the same reason, maps of the island were rare and imprecise, and waging war in this forbidding area was a leap into the unknown, even with the most meticulous of preparations.

The problem was, there was no time for lengthy preparations. There was hardly time for any preparation at all. The American landing on Guadalcanal and Tulagi was set for August 1, subsequently postponed to August 7. In late July, vessels from the US, British, and Australian Navies converged in the Pacific to form the invasion fleet that was to land the 1st Marine Division, reinforced with one regiment of the 2nd Marine Division, all under the command of General Alexander Vandegrift. Stopping over at the Fijis, the Marines practiced landing operations on the island of Koro, but with somewhat unsettling results. "That was a disaster," said Lieutenant Colonel Edwin Pollock. "We never could get ashore, because the beaches were too rocky, too much coral, too rough."[8] On the last day of the month, the convoy left Koro, and in the night between August 6 and 7, the task force, consisting of 81 vessels of all sizes, arrived at Guadalcanal, still undetected.[9]

At 9 am on August 7, the Fire Support Group consisting of three cruisers and four destroyers began their bombardment of a 3,200-yard-long stretch of beach in northern Guadalcanal. The fire lasted for less than ten minutes, but for Petty Officer 2nd Class Kaneda Sankichi of the Japanese Navy, who had spent the evening downing sake to celebrate the completion of the airfield, it felt like "the beginning of Hell."[10] The day before, locals who had helped build the airfield had suddenly and inexplicably vanished one after the other, and now it was clear they had somehow got wind of the impending attack through ancient tribal networks.[11] "Shocked and horrified, I became aware of incoming naval shell fire, and I found myself instinctively running barefoot through clouds of sand and gunpowder smoke, jumping head-first into an air raid shelter," Kaneda wrote in his memoirs. "Shell bursts blasted fronds off coconut palms and others blew holes in the ground." Once the bombardment was over, the terrified Japanese troops grabbed whatever supplies they could find and hastily moved inland.[12]

The hasty departure of the Japanese meant that when the Marines stepped onto Guadalcanal, expecting to be shot at from all angles, they were in for an anticlimax. "I lay panting on the sand, among the tall coconut trees," Private First Class Robert Leckie wrote. "But there was no fight. The Japanese had run."[13] The only Japanese the Marines saw were soldiers who had fled into the jungle and made a wrong turn and now walked right back into American lines. They were mostly service troops anxious to avoid a fight, and they were promptly taken prisoner. The surrendering Japanese were, however, not completely out of danger yet. Two Japanese who were brought by boat to the transport ship USS *Neville* off Guadalcanal caused an American officer to panic. Having seen the enemy for the first time up close and personal, he wanted to execute them on the spot, and only after much persuasion did the other crew talk him out of it.[14]

Orientation was a major problem for the Marines after they had landed, as the rudimentary maps that had been available at the start of the planning phase had been supplemented with photos taken by reconnaissance planes, often while Guadalcanal had been covered with clouds. "Our maps that we went into Guadalcanal with had big blank spots of clouds on them," a Marine officer commented. "So they weren't

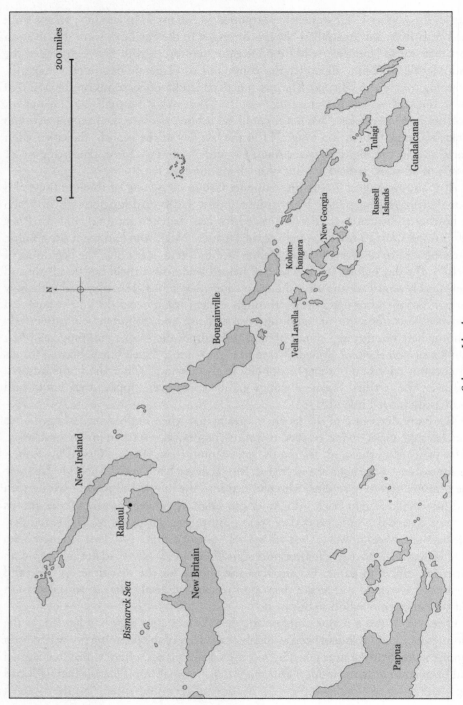

Solomon Islands

really maps."[15] Still, the soldiers moved briskly inland to capture the island's chief asset, the just-completed airfield. Despite the Japanese unwillingness to resist, there was intense, random shooting into the night. Any sound emerging from the darkening jungle was met with frantic volleys. "Whenever you enter battle men do shoot more than there's a need for. They're getting rid of that energy or rather nervousness that they have by firing at anything," said Lewis J. Fields, a Marine major.[16]

On the tiny island of Tulagi, the Marines also disembarked with little more than vague ideas about the geography of the place, having only very simple maps to go by. Lieutenant Colonel Justice Chambers, the commander of Dog Company, reached a tactically important ridge and reported back by radio to his battalion, reaching the executive officer, who, sitting safely on a ship offshore, wanted to know where he was. "I can't tell you very well. All I know is I'm standing under one hell of a big tree on the trail right on the ridge line," Chambers replied. "Will you use code designations and grid?" the officer asked. "If you can figure this out, you're crazy," Justice replied, adding, before signing off: "I haven't got time to fool with this anyway, out."[17]

Unlike the eerily tranquil conditions on Guadalcanal, the Marines on Tulagi encountered determined resistance from Japanese lying ready in tunnels and caves. Savage fights at close quarters developed in the afternoon of August 7. Chambers described how he and his men were attacking a Japanese trench, and how a hand grenade was tossed back and forth in a deadly game that would necessarily end badly for one side or the other: "One of our men threw a grenade in and the Nips threw it right back out at us. We did this a couple of times and then whoever was throwing the grenade let the fuse run before he threw it. I saw this pair of hands come up and catch the grenade again, it went off and we didn't have any more trouble."[18]

The Japanese on Tulagi showed no inclination to surrender, and the battle for the island continued into a second day on August 8. But in the middle of the mayhem there was also room for a touch of civilization. Theodore R. Cummings, a Marine, remembered passing the bombed-out former home of the British resident commissioner of the Solomon Islands. There was a piano, with one leg shot off. A fellow soldier walked up, smiling faintly, and started playing *You May Not Be An Angel*, a tune that had been popular in the previous decade. "I thought to myself," Cummings said later, "the humanity of it with all of that going on, the planes, the ships, the shelling, the action going on ahead of us on the ground."[19]

After more than 24 hours of fighting, the last Japanese resistance on Tulagi was rooted out. About 200 Japanese had been killed. Forty had escaped by swimming to the nearby island of Florida. Three had surrendered. The Marines had lost 36 killed.[20] In the lull that ensued, Cummings's unit was allowed to swim in the ocean. Suddenly a submarine surfaced 100 yards away. "There's one of our subs," one of the bathing soldiers yelled. After a moment of silence, another soldier replied, "Look at the writing." It was Japanese. "I wish somebody had had a camera, taken a picture of us running," Cummings said, "grabbing our clothes and our weapons and making for any shelter whatsoever that we could." A Marine mortar platoon began firing at the submarine, forcing it to hastily submerge and disappear. "It had surfaced and obviously seen that the island was no more occupied by Japanese," Cumming said. "It went away."[21]

While disembarking troops and materiel, in the night between August 8 and 9, the Allied ships off Guadalcanal were surprised by a smaller Japanese force consisting of seven cruisers and one destroyer. The Japanese fleet had departed from Rabaul just hours after being alerted to the American invasion, and immediately upon arrival it commenced its attack. Ohmae Toshikazu, the chief of staff on the Japanese task force, gave a vivid description of the action: "The initial firing range of seven thousand meters closed with amazing swiftness. Every other salvo caused another enemy ship to burst into flames… Second by second… the range decreased, and now we could actually distinguish the shapes of individuals running along the decks of enemy ships."[22]

Within just eight minutes, and despite the uneven odds, the Japanese vessels managed to sink three American and one Australian vessel and damage several others. The heavy cruiser USS *Astoria*, which had only been at Guadalcanal for about a day, was sent to the bottom of the shallow waters. Abe Santos, a sailor in the ship's engineering department, was among the survivors, making it onto the aft deck of the ship after it had been hit. "I could look down into the mess hall that I had just come out of and see a lot of my friends lying there dead. One of them had his head split open like a watermelon," he said. "I found a lifejacket and put it on, but felt something rubbing my neck, so I took it off and found a jawbone with some teeth in it."[23]

Fearing that larger Japanese forces were looming over the horizon, the Allied vessels decided to depart from Guadalcanal, before having offloaded key pieces of heavy equipment that the Marines needed for their continued campaign on the island.[24] The battle of Savo Island, as it was soon to be called, was one of the worst defeats in US Naval History, marking an early setback for the Americans in the struggle for control of Guadalcanal. General Robert L. Eichelberger, an experienced officer who was ordered to the Pacific as corps commander at that exact time, recalled the severe blow to morale caused by the defeat. "It took considerable optimism in those days," he remarked, "to believe we were on the winning side of the fight."[25]

At the very time when the American Marines landed on Guadalcanal, Australian and Japanese soldiers were engaged in intense fighting over the village of Kokoda and its adjacent strategically important airfield in Papua, the jungle-covered peninsula forming the eastern part of New Guinea. The Australians had lost Kokoda several days earlier, and now they were trying to get it back. Three companies set out along separate routes on the morning of August 8, heading towards Kokoda. The central route, which formed the main axis of the attack, was directed straight at the village. When the Australian soldiers moved warily into Kokoda, all they found was four or five surprised Japanese, who immediately fled. The Australians walked on, also finding the airfield unprotected, and dug in for the night.[26]

The lack of resistance in Kokoda was deceptive, and Japanese opposition soon picked up. The other two Australian companies, which moved along parallel axes and covered the flanks, ended up in much heavier fighting. The company occupying the village, too, came under pressure. Soldiers in forward positions in front of the settlements observed Japanese soldiers creeping through the dense vegetation with their faces smeared with mud as primitive camouflage. Some of them reached the Australian lines and cut the soldiers' throats without a sound.[27]

These were just probing attacks, and soon the fighting around Kokoda picked up. A diary that was later recovered from a Japanese officer described the battle as it was experienced by the other side. "Commenced a night attack at 10.20," the diary said. "Advanced stealthily on hands and knees and gradually moved in closer to the enemy. Suddenly encountered enemy guards in the shadow of the large rubber trees. Corporal Hamada killed one of them with the bayonet and engaged the others but the enemy's fire forced us to withdraw. The platoon was scattered and it was impossible to repeat our charge… The night attack ended in failure. No. 1 Platoon also carried out an attack about 0300 but it was unsuccessful. Every day I am losing my men. I could not repress tears of bitterness. Rested waiting for tomorrow, and struggled against cold and bitterness."[28]

On August 10, after three days of battle, the lines had not changed, but it was clear that the Japanese were preparing a major attack. Waiting for a row of howling Japanese to emerge from the jungle at any moment, the Australians suddenly heard a loud, song-like chant emerge from the enemy's position. Then a Japanese, speaking English from his hiding in the thick vegetation, taunted the Australians, "You don't fancy that, do you?" The Australians answered, "Never heard worse."[29] As if upset by the Australians' low opinion of their singing, the Japanese launched a violent attack, the severest so far. It was clear the Australians could not hold the village much longer. During the night and the beginning of the following day, the Australians moved of out Kokoda. They had lost the battle, for now.[30]

Despite their savage skills, the Japanese were as out of place in the wilderness of Kokoda as were the Australians. So why were they there? The Japanese, a unit called the South Seas Force under the command of Lieutenant General Horii Tomitarō, had landed at the town of Gona on the north side of Papua in late July, and had started marching into the interior, facing only weak resistance from a force consisting mainly of militia. The Japanese advance, taking them along narrow, slippery tracks into the inhospitable Owen Stanley Range, might look like an aggressive first step towards invading Australia, but in its essence, it was a defensive move, aimed at creating a barrier to the Allied counterattack which was bound to come sooner or later and was expected to originate in Australia.

The Japanese hoped to control Papua and to establish a series of airfields, as the ability to contest Allied control in the air was a vital precondition for carrying out war on land and at sea. Reaching the south coast and capturing Port Moresby, which had eluded the Japanese since the Battle of the Coral Sea, was an added advantage of a successful offensive, but it was not the main purpose.[31] "We must hold the fronts in eastern New Guinea and Rabaul to the end," Army Chief of Staff Sugiyama Hajime had said on July 11. "If they fall, not only will the Pacific Ocean be in peril, but it will allow the western advance of MacArthur's counterattack through New Guinea and herald the fall of our dominion in the southern area."[32]

After securing their hold on Kokoda, the Japanese started moving south down the 96-mile-long Kokoda Track. It was the kind of daring operation which, had it succeeded, would have merited a place in the annals of military history. However, it was poorly planned and executed. For one, the Japanese had little idea of the kind of terrain they were hoping to negotiate. Lieutenant Colonel Frank Norris of the Australian 7th Division described the track well: "Imagine an area of approximately one hundred miles long. Crumple and fold this into a series of ridges, each rising higher and higher until seven thousand feet is reached, then declining in ridges to three thousand feet. Cover this thickly with jungle, short trees and tall trees, tangled with great, entwining savage vines. Through an oppression of this density, cut a little native track, two or three feet wide, up the ridges, over the spurs, round gorges and down across swiftly-flowing, happy mountain streams. Where the track clambers up the mountain sides, cut steps—big steps, little steps, steep steps—or clear the soil from the tree roots."[33] The Japanese had not expected any of this, and as a consequence of their lack of preparation, they not only had to fight the Australians, but also the elements. "Some of the newly recruited soldiers started saying, 'I cannot walk anymore. Kill me right here, please.' We had to beat them up and force them to walk," Sergeant Kawate Ryōzō said later.[34]

Logistics posed enormous challenges in a terrain radically unsuited for 20th-century armies, and it is questionable if either side could have lasted as long as they did without the assistance of locals accustomed to the extreme conditions since prehistoric times. An Australian eyewitness described the almost tender care which they showered on injured soldiers whom they carried back from the frontline: "With improvised stretchers—one or two blankets lashed with native string to two long poles spread by stout traverse bars—as many as eight or ten native bearers would carry day after day. To watch them descend steep slippery spurs into a mountain stream, along the bed and up the steep ascent, was an object lesson in stretcher bearing. They carry stretchers over seemingly impassable barriers, with the patient reasonably comfortable. The care which they show to the patient is magnificent. Every need which they can fulfil is tended."[35]

While the Japanese were pushing down the Kokoda Track, they landed a battalion-size force on the eastern end of Papua, at Milne Bay, in late August. The purpose was to seize an airfield in the area, which had up until then been protected by a small Australian garrison, and gain an advantage in the battle for the skies. Unbeknownst to the Japanese, the Allies were alerted by signal intelligence to the impending attack and had beefed up their forces. The result was a Japanese debacle, as the landing force encountered much stronger and more determined resistance than expected and was pushed back into the sea. Australians reaching an abandoned Japanese field hospital were exposed to the desperate measures the Japanese were prepared to undertake in defeat. "Here I saw evidence that they'd killed their wounded," a major said. "Several men, neatly laid in a row and naked with bandaged legs and in one case a head wound, had bullet wounds in the vicinity of the heart."[36]

The setback at Milne did not stop the Japanese slog down the Kokoda Track, and by September the exhausted infantrymen had reached so far south that they could actually see the faint outlines of Port Moresby in the distance. The objective that they had fought and died for was almost within reach, and agonizingly this was the point when they were ordered to return. Given the setbacks at Guadalcanal, the Japanese commanders could not find enough supplies to sustain a prolonged campaign in Papua as well. The blow to Japanese confidence was considerable, as was the boost to Australian and Allied morale. "Already," Lieutenant Colonel R. Honner wrote after the war, "there was a bourgeoning confidence born of the first scattered battles which had exploded the myths of Japanese super-soldiers."[37]

On Guadalcanal, the special Japanese warrior code, which prompted nearly all to opt for death in battle over ignominious surrender, gradually dawned on the Americans, but it was a lesson they paid for dearly. In mid-August, the intelligence officer of the 1st Marine Division, Colonel Frank Goettge, acted on reports that the Japanese garrison on Guadalcanal was disintegrating and ripe for surrender. On the night between August 12 and 13, he led a patrol behind enemy lines, hoping to encounter Japanese stragglers willing to give themselves up. Instead, the patrol was attacked immediately, having walked into an ambush. Goettge was killed, along with most of his patrol. Only three survived, escaping individually back to American-held territory.[38] A few days later, an American unit came across the remnants of Goettge's patrol. "The first thing I saw was the severed head of a Marine," one of the soldiers later recorded. "The next thing I noticed was a leg that had been hacked off at the knee... Other chunks of rotting flesh that had once been human body parts were floating in the water and lying on the sand. The smell was overpowering."[39]

The Japanese initially misread the situation on Guadalcanal. The Japanese commanders in the South Pacific underestimated the American presence on the island, believing the operation was a raid undertaken with limited forces and pursuing limited objectives rather than a full-scale invasion. "At that time, we had no means of ascertaining actual facts regarding the extent of the enemy counter-offensive," commented Major General Miyazaki Shuicho, later chief of staff of the 17th Army headquartered at Rabaul.[40] Based on this flawed assumption of enemy means and objective, the Japanese initially committed fewer reinforcements than needed.

On August 19, little more than a week after the Marines had landed on Guadalcanal, Lieutenant Colonel Edwin Pollock, whose men were occupying the banks of Ilu River on the eastern part of the perimeter around the airfield,[41] could hear engines down the coast. When the wind was right, the sound was especially clear.[42] Obviously, the Japanese were up to something. Pollock and his men could not know it, but what they had heard was several hundred Japanese Special Naval Landing Forces disembarking on Guadalcanal. They were from the "Ichiki" Regiment, named after their commander, Colonel Ichiki Kiyonao, and their mission was to retake the airfield.

The Marine positions along the Ilu River were placed astride the route that the Japanese were planning. Initial reconnaissance had left the Japanese with the impression that the Ilu River was only thinly defended, if at all, and when in the early hours of August 21, about 1,000 men of the "Ichiki" Regiment approached the area, they ran into massive Marine gunfire. Large numbers of Japanese were killed by American artillery in the battle that ensued. "We got whole bunches of them. I've never seen so many dead bodies piled up in one area. This was a real massacre," said Major Lewis J. Fields.[43] An even more efficient weapon was provided by a platoon of eight 37-mm guns with canister, cylinders containing large numbers of balls and slugs. Six of the guns fired canister for so long that the barrels eventually melted and were drooping.[44] "[The Japanese] kept throwing them through this one little narrow space, just pushing them through, and that place was piled up with dead so you could hardly see over them," Pollock said. "I never saw so many dead people in all my life."[45]

When daylight broke, the Japanese were piled waist-high across the river in front of each gun. "A lot of them were still living, but the tide came in and drowned most of them," said Marine Captain John Leonard.[46] Individual Japanese who had survived through the night were hunted down the day after. Some who had taken up a position in a coconut grove were crushed under American tanks. "The rear of the tanks," Marine commander Vandegrift wrote, "looked like meat grinders."[47] Pollock searched the other side of the river the following day. They came across a Japanese soldier in the water and motioned him to come out, but he refused. "Colonel, shall I let him have it?" a Marine asked Pollock. Pollock replied, "Let him have it." He shot him and he went down under the water. "If we hadn't shot him he would have shot us," Pollock said years later. "You have to admire the little bastard, really. You have to, because they were courageous, and they just never stopped."[48]

What followed over the next months was a savage struggle back and forth mostly along the perimeter around the airstrip, now named Henderson Field after US Marine Major Lofton Henderson, who had been killed at Midway. Unlike the much larger land campaigns later in the Pacific War, the battle of Guadalcanal was small-scale. The units clashing in the dense tropical jungle were often squads and platoons, companies at most. It was war on an almost intimate scale. "In jungle fighting opposing forces are often only a few yards apart, hidden from each other by a thick, leafy screen," wrote Hanson Baldwin, correspondent for the *New York Times*. "If the enemy sees you before you see him you will probably never know what hit you."[49]

As the true extent of the American presence dawned on the Japanese, they began shipping in reinforcements and supplies in a routine soon dubbed the "Tokyo Express" by American Marines who watched the traffic from their foxholes. Meanwhile, the Americans' own supply lines were unreliable, and the men on Guadalcanal soon teetered on the edge of starvation. "After 2–3 weeks we had no food as the area was controlled by the Japanese Navy," a Marine explained. "Our food consisted a lot of Japanese rice, full of ants and worms. I would not recommend a diet of coconut from experience. It is a very good laxative."[50]

In the meantime, Japanese bombers raided Henderson Airfield on a daily basis. Usually they would come in groups of 18 or 24, protected by agile "Zero" fighters. When they released their load, the men on the ground, huddling and praying in their foxholes, knew what was happening from the sound. The humming of the bombers' engines would be interrupted by the swish-swish-swish of bombs falling through the air: "Then WHAM! (the first one hit) WHAM! (closer) WHAM! (walking right up to your foxhole) WHAAAMM! (Oh Christ!) WHAM! (Thank God, they missed us!) WHAM! (the bombs were walking away) WHAM! (they still shook the earth, and dirt trickled in). WHAM!"[51] The Japanese bombers arrived with such regularity that the Marines thought they could almost set their watches by them. "We got so skilled at it that we could wait till the bomb bays opened and they reached a certain point in the sky before getting into a hole," said Captain Raymond Davis. His job after each raid was to put out grass fires around the airfield before they reached bombs piled up by the American air crews. "I spent many a moment standing on top of a 500-pound bomb beating out a fire around it," he said. "It was a hairy way to spend an afternoon."[52]

Snipers were a serious problem and caused numerous American deaths. One Marine platoon leader was shot in the thigh during a patrol. When he returned to his own lines, a fellow Marine cut his pants open and found a leather string hanging out. It was the string to his locker key. The Japanese bullet had hit the key and pushed it into his thigh, leaving the string sticking out of the wound. Another Marine told him he could knock the lock off with a hammer, but the injured man insisted: "No, I want that key." The medic worked his way around the injury and managed to pull the key out. "So he went away with a nice souvenir," a fellow Marine wrote in his memoirs. "But his key was no good for his locker after that."[53]

Nothing compared with the devastation brought about by naval artillery. "I had the misfortune to be on the receiving end of naval gun-fire," said a Marine about an incident when his unit was shot at with the large-caliber gun of a Japanese battleship in September. "It sounded just like elevated trains going over your head."[54] Marine Louis Ortega was dug in at Henderson Field on October 1942 when a Japanese naval force began bombarding the area. "Let me tell you something," he said later. "You can get a dozen air raids a day but they come and they're gone. A battleship can sit there for hour after hour and throw 14-inch shells. I will never forget those four hours. The next morning when they stopped shelling, there was a haze over the whole area. Five miles of coconut groves were gone! Where the day before you had miles and miles of coconut trees, now 5 square miles were wiped clean. Every tree was gone."[55]

CHAPTER SEVEN

Annus Horribilis

October–December 1942

The village of Kokoda, nested in the New Guinean highlands, fell to the Australian Army for the second time on November 2, and this time it was final. The Japanese soldiers, who had eyed Port Moresby in the distance little more than a month earlier, were now in full, inexorable retreat along the very same jungle trail that had formed their route of advance. Several times during the withdrawal, they attempted to make a stand, but even though they picked natural obstacles that favored defense, they were invariably wiped away by the Australians, now more numerous and better equipped than before. "We will be caught like rats in a trap," a Japanese officer said at one of those obstacles. Many of them were.[1]

It reflected the desperate state of the Japanese Army that now, for the first time since war had broken out, its soldiers felt compelled to abandon their artillery pieces. These were moments of anguish, since many artillery officers felt attached to their guns in a manner similar to the bond between captains and their ships. One company commander begged his superior for permission to disassemble his gun and have his soldiers carry it to the rear. His request was denied. Instead he followed orders and gathered his troops for what almost had the character of a military funeral. The soldiers broke up the gun's breach and proceeded to bury the weapon in the wet mud. The company gave a parting salute and then dispersed. The lieutenant stayed behind, pulled out his gun, and shot himself.[2]

Even while advancing, the poorly prepared Japanese soldiers had been exposed to immense physical hardship, and in retreat that hardship was multiplied. In a verdant rainforest brimming with life, starvation was paradoxically an omnipresent threat, and some soldiers resorted to cannibalism, slicing pieces of flesh from dead enemies. An Australian patrol retrieved several packages of meat, which were subsequently inspected by a medical officer. "I have examined two portions of flesh recovered by one of our patrols," the doctor wrote. "One was the muscle tissue of a large animal, the other similar muscle tissue with a large piece of skin and underlying tissue attached. I consider the last as human."[3]

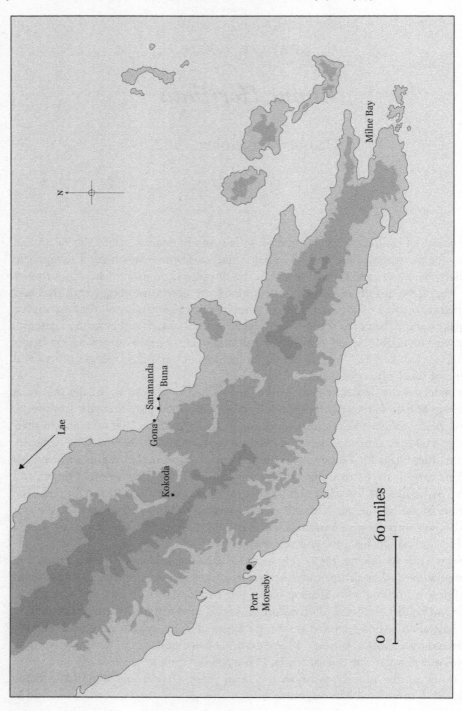

Southeastern New Guinea

The objective of the Japanese retreat was Papua's north coast and, possibly, salvation. The last major obstacle on the way was Kumusi River. Lieutenant General Horii Tomitarō, the commander of the South Seas Force, attempted to flee on a raft down the Kumusi River on November 19. The raft got stuck on a tree one and a half miles downstream, and Horii, along with his chief of staff and an orderly, continued in a native canoe. Taking a rash decision, Horii decided to follow the river out into the sea and proceed along the coastline. To his surprise, a tropical storm struck, and the canoe was tossed among the waves, eventually capsizing six miles offshore. The chief of staff could not swim and drowned almost immediately. Horii and his orderly began the long swim towards the coastline, but after almost three miles of strenuous physical effort, 52-year-old Horii gave up. "I have no strength to swim any further," he told the orderly. "Tell the troops that Horii died here." He lifted both arms above the surface and shouted, "Banzai to the Emperor!" before disappearing beneath the waves.[4]

Things were going in the right direction for the Allies, but the Japanese were still in firm possession of three villages on the north coast of Papua. Two of these, Gona and Sanananda, were left to Australian forces, while the third, Buna, was US Army responsibility. The 32nd US Division, consisting mainly of inexperienced National Guardsmen with minimal training in jungle warfare, arrived south of Buna on November 16. Ahead was a brutal slug, bloody even by Pacific standards. Lieutenant Robert H. Odell described a doomed attack in late December on a section of Japanese defenses outside Buna boosted by several machine gun nests. Odell was told by his superiors the assault could be carried out as a bayonet charge. He knew it was completely unrealistic but felt he had no option but to obey: "Well, off we went, and within a few minutes our rush forward had been definitely and completely halted. Of the 40 men who started with me four had been killed and 18 were lying seriously wounded."[5]

The 32nd Division was getting nowhere, as it lacked the weapons needed to dislodge the Japanese from their positions and was worn down by tropical diseases and lack of food. MacArthur concluded, based on no evidence, that the problem was weak leadership. He wanted a firm hand in charge in Papua, and he decided to send General Robert L. Eichelberger in order to have a capable corps commander in the field. When the two officers met at the end of November, MacArthur's message was clear: get ruthless, or get out. "I want you to remove all officers who won't fight. Relieve regimental and battalion commanders; if necessary, put sergeants in charge of battalions and corporals in charge of companies—anyone who will fight. Time is of the essence; the Japanese may land reinforcements any night." After a pause, MacArthur added with his trademark sense of drama: "I want you to take Buna, or not come back alive."[6]

Eichelberger arrived at the front on December 1. "When the stink of the swamp hit our nostrils, we knew that we, like the troops of the 32nd Division, were prisoners of geography," he wrote in his post-war memoirs. Eichelberger found a demoralized and bewildered force, hungry, and as afraid of crocodiles and snakes as of the Japanese. He immediately halted all operations and spent the next days improving the supply situation, reorganizing, and putting officers with combat experience in the frontline. Crucially, he also ordered systematic reconnaissance to pinpoint the Japanese positions, in order that the GIs were no longer fighting an invisible enemy. On December 5, the attacks resumed, and little by little the Americans began pushing towards Buna. This was a hard-won advance. "It was bought at a substantial price in death, wounds, disease, despair, and human suffering," Eichelberger wrote. "No one who fought there, however hard he tries, will ever forget it."[7]

Pilots were kings in the war between Japan and the Allies. According to the Australian historian Peter Williams, "the Pacific War was first an air war, second a sea war and last, a land war. Regardless of victories on land, armies on Pacific islands eventually starved if denied food coming by sea. The ships carrying supplies would be sunk by aircraft unless the air above them was denied to the enemy."[8] A major reason for Japan's astonishing military advances in the early months of the conflict was the superior performance of many of its planes—the Mitsubishi A6M "Zero" primary among them—and especially the skills of its pilots. A report from US Naval intelligence spoke highly of Japan's pilots in early 1942. "They were seasoned and experienced products of a thorough training program extending over several years… Aggressive and resourceful, they knew the capabilities and advantages of their own aircraft and they flew them with skill and daring. They were quick to change their methods to new situations and to counter successfully the changes, modifications, and designs of Allied aircraft. They were alert and quick to take advantage of any evident weaknesses."[9]

American aviator Jim Morehead flew P-40s over Java and Darwin and was taken aback by the ability of the Japanese enemy, completely at odds with what he had been led to expect: "Before the war officers assured us that American pilots were flying some of the best planes in the world. Everyone underestimated the Japanese and the Zero was a real shock," he told an interviewer later. "I remain bitter that our government, backed by the most advanced economy in the world, would send their men to war in aircraft that were inferior to that of the enemy."[10] Australians who had arrived from Europe tried "Battle of Britain" tactics against Japanese pilots and often paid with their lives when discovering the great maneuverability of the enemy's aircraft. "We told them the basics," an American pilot said later. "Don't think that because you could turn inside a German fighter that you could do the same with a Zero."[11]

This changed with the battle of Midway. Although it was a myth that the elite of Japanese Naval aviation was wiped out in the fateful encounter in June, enough pilots were killed to make it impossible for Japan to ever again recover its greatness in the skies. At the same time, US pilots proved to be quick learners and began showing awe-inspiring ability. A case in point were the "Cactus" pilots on Guadalcanal dubbed after the island's codename. "It is necessary to remember that the Japanese Zero at this stage of the war was regarded with some of the awe in which the atomic bomb came to be held later," according to an early account. "The Cactus fighters made a great contribution to the war by exploding the theory that the Zero was invincible."[12]

US technology also showed its enormous potential. The twin-engine P-38 was not just a piece of state-of-the-art engineering but also entailed a peculiar psychological boost. Since it had two propellers, the pilot could afford to have one engine shot out or otherwise malfunction, and still be able to make it home over hundreds of miles of ocean. This was reassuring for pilots who otherwise would face the prospect of making a forced landing, in which case Japanese patrol boats might not even be the biggest horror. "You look down from the cockpit and you can see schools of sharks swimming around," said George C. Kenney, commander of MacArthur's air forces. "They never look healthy to a man flying over them."[13] All in all, it added up to one thing: towards the end of 1942, the Allies were close to achieving air superiority in key theaters of war in the Pacific. On December 3, a Japanese soldier on Papua wrote jealously in his diary: "They fly above our position as if they own the sky."[14] Even before the first anniversary of the Pearl Harbor attack, when Japanese planes had roamed at will over the vast expanses of Asia and the Pacific, the Allies were winning the war in the air.

★ ★ ★

Guadalcanal was a harbinger of the conditions that awaited American soldiers and Marines during the many more months of battle that lay head in the Pacific. It gave the Marines a taste of Japanese defensive tactics where "fighting to the last man" was more than just a proverb. "Machine gunners fired their weapons until they were killed," according to the official US history about one of the early engagements in the Solomons. "When one gunner fell, another would take his place, a process that continued until all in the position were dead."[15] A US Marine described the outcome of a typical frontal Japanese attack. "Those we did not kill killed themselves right in front of us," he wrote later. "There is a grotesque horror in watching a man activate a grenade and then clutch it to his chest, blowing himself apart before your astonished eyes."[16]

The Japanese were everywhere on Guadalcanal. Marine officer Charles Walker was strolling towards the company kitchen one October morning, when suddenly a Japanese hiding inside a bush in the middle of the camp fired at his head. Walker made a running dive behind a pile of ration boxes, and other Marines alerted to the presence of the Japanese reacted instinctively. "M1 rifles sprang into action; everyone emptied an eight-round clip into the bush. As suddenly as the action had begun, it stopped. The men who had fired from positions of leisure calmly reloaded their weapons as if they had not a care in the world. Finally someone walked over to the bush, then sauntered back. 'He's dead!' the man said laconically."[17] Perhaps because of the ability to sneak up on the Americans undetected, the Japanese had an uncanny understanding of the American positions. A Marine captain remembered seeing a map captured from the Japanese during a patrol: "The maps the Japanese had of our positions were so clear as to startle me. They showed our weak spots all too clearly."[18]

A Marine told American war correspondent John Hersey that the Japanese on Guadalcanal were "full of tricks"; "They hide up in the trees like wildcats. Sometimes when they attack they scream like a bunch of terrified cattle in a slaughter house. Other times they come on so quiet they wouldn't scare a snake... You've probably heard about their using white surrender flags to suck us into traps."[19] Taunting was a form of unsophisticated psychological warfare. A Marine officer was amazed one day to hear Japanese and Americans shouting back and forth at each other: "I heard Franklin Roosevelt and Eleanor vilified by the Japanese, while our troops yelled back, 'Tojo and the Emperor eat shit!' Surprisingly one Japanese soldier spoke fair English."[20]

A form of sadism that was to become a hallmark of combat with the Japanese, but was never seen to the same extent during American campaigns in Europe, was evident on Guadalcanal from the very start. Several Marines later recalled a terrible night when they had been forced to endure the wailing of prisoners being tortured by their Japanese captors. "The sound of someone being worked over out there in the darkness remains with me until this day. The whole battalion could hear their screams," one of them said later.[21] Having been exposed to the brutality of the Japanese, few Americans were inclined to treat their own prisoners with any mildness. Captain John Burden, a language officer, described how a US regimental commander had criticized a unit for bringing in prisoners. "Shoot the sons of bitches," he had ordered. This soon became routine. "On several occasions," Burden wrote in a report after the battle, "word was telephoned in from the front line that a prisoner had been taken, only to find after hours of waiting that the prisoner had 'died' en route to the rear."[22]

The dead were not left alone either. US Marine Robert Leckie described the behavior of a fellow soldier, aptly nicknamed Souvenirs, who "went methodically among the dead armed with a pair of pliers. He had observed that the Japanese have a penchant for gold fillings in their teeth, often for solid gold teeth. He was looting their very mouth."[23] After a particularly vicious night of fighting along the Matanikau river, a group of American soldiers hacked off the heads of three dead enemies and jammed them on poles facing the Japanese side of the river. Shortly afterwards, the regimental commander passed by and was shocked by the scenery: "Jesus, men, what are you doing?" he said. "You are acting like animals." A young soldier replied, "That's right, Colonel, we are animals. We live like animals, we eat and are treated like animals—what the f--- do you expect?"[24]

In the dense jungle, where soldiers could often only see a few yards ahead of themselves, senses other than vision became important. "On several patrols I actually saw Japanese. Sometimes we heard them, and sometimes we smelled them, or any combination of these," said Roy Elrod, a Marine.[25] Western soldiers that were in contact with the Japanese reported a distinct, but indescribable odor. "It was heavy and pungent and compounded of stale cooked rice and sweat and human waste and… Jap," wrote George MacDonald Fraser, who served in Burma.[26] Perhaps it was the smell of the gear the Japanese were using, as the American officer Charles Walker suggested: "Strange to say, Japanese equipment, especially leather belts and goods, had a peculiar, sweetish odor—not an unpleasant scent, but not a familiar odor to Americans. Perhaps it was the tanning process, or was it their perspiration?"[27]

The war in Pacific was one in which the enemy was not the only source of mortal danger, as death could come at the hands of nature itself. "The Terrible Solomons," the author Jack London had called the islands three decades earlier. "It is true," he had written, "that fever and dysentery are perpetually on the walk-about, that loath-some skin diseases abound, that the air is saturated with a poison." Fighting not just the Japanese, but also the elements was a crushing burden, and some could take it, while others could not. Major Raymond L. Murray was a battalion commander at Guadalcanal and experienced war for the first time. "I did discover that I wouldn't break and run under fire, which I suppose most everybody wonders before they ever go into combat, 'Will I really, in truth, be able to stay there and take it?' And you find out that you can, you do."[28]

There was one group of people who suffered just as much as the combatants, if not more. Those were the original inhabitants of Guadalcanal, whose homes had been turned into a battleground. They received very little attention at the time, and their presence was only infrequently acknowledged by the contemporary press. But it was inevitable that the belligerents would come across them. During one of the early battles of the campaign, American soldiers reported the sight of the body of a young local woman lying by the roadside. She had been raped and killed by the Japanese, her torso hacked to pieces.[29]

Sergeant Major Vouza, who only went by one name and was a member of the Native Constabulary, described his treatment at the hands of the Japanese, speaking English with a tinge of the soft tones of the South Pacific: "Well, I was caughted by the Japs and one of the Japanese Naval Officer questioned me but I was refuse to answer & I was bayoneted by a long sword twice on my chest, through my throat, a cutted the side of my tongue & I was got up from the enemies & walked through the American front line... After I wad discharged from the Hospital I wad do my fighting with the Japs & paid back all what they have done with me."[30] This rough treatment earned the Japanese few friends among the local population. Saku, another member of the Constabulary, described a jungle patrol when he and other local constables came across a party of Japanese by a river: "They had piled arms on a rock and were busy getting wild nuts to eat. We cut across the river and took their rifles and hid. When they returned we saw that they were not armed and we closed in on them. They picked up stones to defend themselves, and as we did not want to give things away, we finished them off with axes and spears. They were weak from hunger."[31]

★ ★ ★

The United States retained high hopes for China's potential, and for the overall importance of what was known as the China-Burma-India Theater. From early 1942, large numbers of American personnel were sent to the region, primarily India. Given the conditions, a world at war, moving from one theater to another was a drawn-out affair. The China specialist John Paton Davies Jr, who was assigned as political attaché to Joseph Stilwell, described the 13-day trip from New York to Calcutta: "We flew by one of Pan American's original clippers, a flying boat, to Belém at the mouth of the Amazon—moist, mossed, suffocating, hyper-tropical—then Natal, and across the Atlantic to somnolent Fisherman's Lake in Liberia. The remainder of the trip was by two-engine C-47 transport planes to Kano and then Maidugiri, both in Nigeria, across the scrubby wilderness of Chad to Khartoum dominated by the Nile, up to Cairo, swarming with handsome British staff officers whom the troops called the gabardine swine, over to Tel Aviv, down to Shatt-al-Arab, carrying the mingled waters of the Tigris and the Euphrates, out above the azure-emerald Persian Gulf to Sharjah's desert airstrip manned by an RAF ground crew of a forlorn half dozen and a gazelle, along the desolate, jagged coast of Iran and Baluchistan to Karachi, and finally trans-subcontinentally to teeming, beholy-cowed Calcutta."[32]

The main priority for the United States was to keep China and its vast manpower resources in the war. Since the late 1930s, one of the main routes for keeping China supplied from the outside world had been the Burma Road, linking Burma to Chiang Kai-shek's landlocked government in southwest China. "Though maladministration and corruption had reduced its inherently low capacity," according to the official US history of the China-Burma-India theater, the road had for years "had great symbolic value as China's last tie with freedom."[33] It had been built by hand for more than 700 miles through inhospitable terrain by tens of thousands of workers and had proved an invaluable asset, even though it had been closed briefly in 1940 by the British government, bowing to Japanese pressure.

By the time of the US entry into the war, the Burma Road was again in operation, and it had to be constantly maintained, again with the help of China's most abundant economic resource: manual labor. American pilot John Donovan traveled 200 miles along the road and was stunned by the sight that awaited him. "Seeing thousands upon thousands of coolies," he wrote, "men, women and children; working with their bare hands breaking rocks into small bits like gravel, using nothing more than small hammers, and then spreading these broken bits of rock over the road with their hands... makes one feel so small. How insignificant was the puny amount of work that any one of these coolies could do... The Burma Road is a monumental piece of work considering what they had to work with."[34]

Japan's invasion of Burma in early 1942 eventually resulted in the Burma Road being closed down. The Americans now only had one real choice. They had to airlift supplies into China. Priority was given to flights across the "Hump," from Indian airfields, across the Himalayas into southwest China. September 1942 was a pivotal month. The route claimed its first deaths, when a C-47 transport plane crashed *en route* between Kunming in southwest China and Chabua in easternmost India, killing its crew of two. In the same month, a total of 400 tons of supplies were delivered by air. It was small by most measures, but it was a six-fold increase from just two months earlier and was a powerful sign that the United States was serious about treating China as a key ally.[35]

The "Hump" was stressful in ways other forms of service in the war were not. Not only did the pilots have to deal with the Japanese and extreme natural conditions. They were also haunted by lingering thoughts about the futility of it all: "Combat pilots during and after missions knew they were an essential part of the war. They shot or dropped bombs," according to an official report. "They realized a battle was going on. They saw the damage their bombs did or the enemy plane they shot down. Not so with [a pilot in this theater]. He flew a load of cargo over the Hump. In the majority of cases he did not know what use it would be and sometimes feared, with reason, that most of it would be wasted by the Chinese."[36]

In the autumn of 1942, the USS *Hornet* was the only American carrier left to face the Japanese in the South Pacific. The *Lexington* had been lost in the Coral Sea, and the *Yorktown* at Midway. The *Wasp* had been sunk by a Japanese submarine, and the *Saratoga* and the *Enterprise* were being repaired after extensive battle damage. "Things were pretty grim," said Francis Foley, air operations officer on board the *Hornet*. "As a matter of fact, the general public had no idea what dire straits the Navy was in. We were really hurting in the South Pacific, carrier-wise."[37] For the *Hornet*'s crew it was a source of some pride that they were now holding the fort by themselves. When rumors spread that the Japanese Navy saw the sinking of the *Hornet* as its primary mission, the reaction was characteristic. "The announcement," Foley said, "evoked a resounding defiant cheer from the entire ship's company which could be heard on the bridge!"[38]

At this very moment, help was on the way. The *Enterprise* had completed repairs and was now heading south. "Carrier power varies as the square—two carriers are four times as powerful as one," wrote Admiral Bill Halsey, the newly appointed naval commander for the South Pacific area. "Until the *Enterprise* arrived, our plight had been almost hopeless. Now we had a fighting chance."[39] Halsey himself also improved the American odds, having taken over from the cautious and exhausted Admiral Robert L. Ghormley. Halsey's arrival was felt throughout the ranks. "There was a complete change of momentum and atmosphere," said Major Henry W. Buse, among the Marines on Guadalcanal. "Halsey we felt was going to go with what he had and help us win that thing. It was really noticeable, just like the change of momentum in a ball game."[40] The new commander's recipe for winning the war in the Pacific was simple: "Kill Japs, kills Japs, and keep on killing Japs!"[41]

Just as Halsey wanted a showdown with the Japanese, they too, were spoiling for a fight. The area around the Solomons was frozen in a stalemate, and they wanted to introduce new momentum. A sizeable Japanese fleet, consisting of four aircraft carriers, approached the Solomon Islands in the second half of October. Its mission was to support a land offensive on Guadalcanal aimed at seizing Henderson Field. Although the land offensive failed, the naval task force stayed in the region near the Solomons, hoping to encounter the American adversary. On October 25, US patrol planes reported the sighting of two large Japanese forces heading south. Further reconnaissance yielded no information about the exact location of the Japanese, but Halsey was convinced that a major battle was just hours away, and in a bid to instill an aggressive spirit in his subordinates, he sent out an unequivocal order: "ATTACK REPEAT ATTACK."[42]

In the morning of October 26, waves of planes took off from the *Enterprise* and the *Hornet*, heading for the Japanese fleet. The Japanese, 250 miles away, were doing the same thing, in the opposite direction. Edward L. Feightner, a fighter pilot from USS *Enterprise*, was about 20 miles into his mission and was checking his guns, when somebody yelled over the radio. He looked up. "Zeros were all over us. They had gotten up about two hours before we did, I guess," he said.[43] A brief, confused dogfight erupted, and the Zeros shot down several American planes. "The Zeros made that one pass and went on to our task force, and we headed off on to their task force," Feightner said.[44]

Minutes later, Japanese aircraft attacked the *Hornet*, and within no more than five minutes sealed its fate with bombs and torpedoes. A Japanese torpedo bomber that had been damaged by anti-aircraft fire plowed into the carrier and started a stubborn fire.[45] Meanwhile, the *Enterprise* was only 10 miles away and escaped the first onslaught. It was covered by a rainstorm during the initial Japanese attacks, but later emerged and was exposed to fierce divebombing. Still, the damage was less than on the *Hornet*, mainly because of new anti-aircraft guns that had been installed recently.[46] When Feightner landed on the *Enterprise*, the carrier was still licking its wounds. "I got down to the hangar deck and was wading around in water halfway up to my knees, fuel and dead bodies. Something had burned on the ship; you could smell this all over the place."[47]

Meanwhile on the *Hornet*, air operations officer Francis Foley counted a total of 11 fires. The ship was listing, and there was no power, and all firefighting had to be done with buckets and portable pumps. After abandon ship had been ordered, the life rafts were thrown into the water, but most were carried away by the wind. A fight began among the sailors for a place in the closest of the rafts. As this was happening, the rest of the task force was circling around the *Hornet* "like Indians around a wagon train," Foley recalled. "One destroyer would peel off at a time and come in and pick up survivors and then get back out." While the sailors were in the water, Japanese bombers appeared just above a layer of clouds at 5,000 feet. "Then those bombs came through the clouds. We could see them. Wow, I thought, if we get away with this, we're really going to be lucky. But the bombs, of course, were aimed at the ship, not the people in the water. Some did hit the ship, too. I remember one blew a 5-inch gun maybe 30 feet in the air, a whole gun mount. When the bomb hit the water, I want to tell you, you really felt like you had been hit by a blockbuster."[48]

Lieutenant Commander Okumiya Masatake, a senior aviation officer, was waiting on the deck of aircraft carrier *Junyō* for the return of the attack planes. Only a few made it back, all riddled with bullet holes. "As the pilots climbed wearily from their cramped cockpits, they told of unbelievable opposition, of skies choked with antiaircraft shell bursts and tracers," Okumiya recalled. The only surviving carrier bomber leader was "so shaken that at times he could not speak coherently."[49] The American ability to inflict damage to Japan's previously invincible air force had severe consequences, according to Tanaka Raizō, a senior Japanese Naval officer in the battles around Guadalcanal. "Many reasons may be cited for the failure, but primarily it is attributable to the enemy's aerial superiority," he wrote after the war. "Our movements were watched so closely that the enemy could unleash intercepting operations at a moment's notice."[50]

The upshot of the battle, later known as the Battle of Santa Cruz, was a tactical victory for the Japanese, but a strategic setback, as they lost valuable air personnel who could not be replaced. "Tactically we picked up the dirty end of the stick, but strategically we handed it back," Halsey said.[51] Vice Admiral Komura Keizō, who commanded the cruiser *Chikuma* during the battle agreed about the strategic significance of the battle. "After this action we were never able to reinforce our garrison on Guadalcanal with sufficient strength to recapture it," he said, adding that, by contrast, the Americans could now use Guadalcanal as a base to capture the remainder of the islands. "I think that this was the turning point of the war in that area."[52]

On December 12, Emperor Hirohito went to the Grand Shrine at Ise, a city west of Tokyo. It was one of the holiest places for the official Shintō religion, and a suitable venue for the ruler to consider the position of the nation that saw him not just as a leader but a god, and had already sustained terrible sacrifices in his name. Performing rites going back many generations, he was now staring down into an abyss darker than any of his ancestors ever had to contemplate.[53] The night before, he had spoken with complete candor to his military aide-de-camp, Colonel Ogata Kenichi. The emperor had recounted the numerous battles that had consumed Japan for more than a decade, beginning in Manchuria, then in the rest of China and now all of the Pacific. "It is easy to start a war but hard to end it," the dejected ruler had said.[54]

The fall months, filled with interminable and increasingly hopeless fighting in the deep south far from Japan's own shores, had seen Hirohito subtly change his mind about the war. The setback on the Kokoda Trail had come as a particular shock. "From the time our line along the Stanley Mountain Range in New Guinea was penetrated, I was anxious for peace, but we had a treaty with Germany against concluding a separate peace, and we could not violate an international commitment. This was the dilemma that tormented me," Hirohito told close collaborators after the war.[55] Even small victories could not lighten his mood. After the Santa Cruz battle, in which his warriors had sunk the *Hornet*, he had congratulated them in a statement, which, however, also carried a cautionary note: "We believe the war situation is critical. Officers and men, exert yourselves to even greater efforts."[56]

The start of the year 1942 had seen the Imperial Japanese Army and Navy in triumphant mode. As the months passed, it had begun to take on the form of an *annus horribilis*. However, as his view of the war turned bleaker, Hirohito decided to up the ante. Gamblers come in two categories. There are those who decide to cut their losses when their fortunes fail them, and then there are others who raise the stakes. The Japanese ruler belonged to the latter type. On the last day of the year he met with his senior commanders and agreed that the Guadalcanal operation must be called off. Instead, greater emphasis would be placed on New Guinea.[57] Hirohito was hoping for, if not actively seeking, a big all-or-nothing battle with the Americans that could shock them, and their casualty-averse public, into agreeing to a negotiated end of the war.[58] The year 1943 would put that notion to the test.

The sinking of the HMS *Prince of Wales* and the HMS *Repulse*, photographed from a Japanese aircraft. *Repulse*, near the bottom of the view, has just been hit by one bomb and near-missed by several more. *Prince of Wales* is near the top of the image, generating a considerable amount of smoke. (NH 60566 courtesy of the Naval History and Heritage Command)

Japanese infantry cross the border from China into Hong Kong in December 1941. (Mainichi)

Canadian infantrymen defending Hong Kong await the Japanese advance in hills north of the city. (Canadian Army)

A Chinese soldier and officer in field dress in early 1942, at the time of the battle of Changsha. The M35 helmets are a remnant of earlier close cooperation with Germany in the 1930s. (Office of War Information Photograph)

Japanese prisoners taken by the Chinese during the battle of Changsha in January 1942. (Office of War Information Photograph)

Australian soldiers manning a two-pounder anti-tank gun at a road block in the Malay peninsula. In the background a destroyed Japanese Type 95 Ha-Go medium tank. (Australian War Memorial)

Indian gunners participate in defense of the Malay peninsula. The majority of Commonwealth troops in that theater were from India. (National Museum of the US Navy)

Soldiers of the Argylls and Sutherlanders during patrol in the Malay peninsula, 1942. (Office of War Information Photograph)

Japanese troops advance on a Burmese oil field, 1942. Oil and the other natural riches of Southeast Asia were what set off the Japanese offensive in the first place. (National Army Museum)

Chinese troops advance in single file through Burmese jungle country, March 1942. (Office of War Information Photograph)

Japanese troops cut through barbed wire entanglements under cover of an artillery bombardment during the Bataan campaign, early 1942. (Courtesy of the Naval History and Heritage Command)

A US Marine Sergeant on Corregidor Island explains the use of the Lewis machine gun to a group of Philippine soldiers. (National Archives)

Japanese tank and infantry move into the Bataan jungle, April 1942. In the foreground, the stilts of an elevated house, a common feature in that theater. (NH 73552 courtesy of the Naval History and Heritage Command)

Japanese troops advance on Bataan, during the general attack of April 1942. (NH 73535 courtesy of the Naval History and Heritage Command)

Japanese troops celebrate the capture of an American position during the final offensive on Bataan, April 1942. (NH 73536 courtesy of the Naval History and Heritage Command)

Japanese troops guard American prisoners of war at the beginning of the Bataan Death March, April 1942. A Japanese photographer can be seen in the right foreground. (National Archives)

American B-25 bombers are tied down on the flight deck of aircraft carrier USS *Hornet*, while the carrier is en route to the Doolittle mission's launching point. (NH 53426 courtesy of the Naval History and Heritage Command)

During the Coral Sea Battle, Japanese aircraft carrier *Shōhō* is torpedoed by US Navy carrier aircraft in the late morning of May 7, 1942. (National Archives)

Survivors of USS *Lexington* are pulled aboard a cruiser after the carrier is abandoned at the end of the Coral Sea Battle in the afternoon of May 8, 1942. (National Archives)

Destroyers assemble alongside the USS *Lexington* to assist in the evacuation of the carrier's crew after she has been mortally damaged by fires and explosions during the afternoon of May 8, 1942. (National Archives)

The USS *Yorktown* during the battle of Midway, June 4, 1942, moments after the aircraft carrier has been hit by a series of Japanese bombs. (National Archives)

"Dauntless" dive bombers from USS *Hornet* approach a Japanese heavy cruiser at the end of the battle of Midway. (National Archives)

The hangar deck of the carrier USS *Yorktown*, following a devastating Japanese attack on June 4, 1942. (National Archives)

American prisoners of war mark the 4th of July, 1942, in a Japanese prison camp in the Philippines. Celebrations such as this were strictly prohibited. (United States Army)

US Marines come ashore on Tulagi Island during the landings there on August 7 and 8, 1942. In the first days of the campaign, fighting was considerably heavier here than on Guadalcanal. (National Archives)

US Marines rest in the field on Guadalcanal in late 1942. Most of these Marines are armed with M1903 bolt-action rifles and carry M1905 bayonets and USMC 1941 type packs. (National Archives)

Japanese soldiers killed during fighting along the perimeter of Henderson Field, Guadalcanal, September 1942. (National Archives)

On Guadalcanal in 1942, an Australian major pays a Solomon islander his weekly wage of five shillings for work as a stevedore. Local inhabitants played important supporting roles during the campaign. (USMC)

In the naval battle for Guadalcanal in late 1942, Japanese transports lie burning close to the coastline. (National Archives)

US ships fire at attacking Japanese aircraft during the battle of Santa Cruz, October 1942. (National Archives)

Australian 25-pounder gun is pulled into position during the battle of the Kokoda Trail. (Australian War Memorial)

An injured Australian soldier is brought back by native bearers during the campaign along the Kokoda Trail. (Australian War Memorial)

Japanese transport ship *Heiyu Maru* afire and sinking after she is torpedoed by the submarine USS *Whale* in the central Pacific, January 1943. Photographed through the submarine's periscope. (National Archives)

Members of the submarine USS *Plunger*'s crew display her battle flag. The man seated in the center appears to be wearing a Japanese sailor's hat. The photograph is dated June 21, 1943, following *Plunger*'s sixth war patrol. The image gives an impression of the cramped conditions on board. (National Archives)

American soldiers carry back an injured comrade in subarctic conditions during the battle of Attu island, May 1943. (National Archives)

Indian nationalist leader Subhas Chandra Bose, center, in the summer of 1942 with German dictator Adolf Hitler. On the left, Hitler's translator Paul Schmidt. Bose saw an alliance with the Axis powers as India's best hope of achieving independence from British colonial rule and set up an army recruited among Indians in Japanese POW camps. (German Federal Archives)

American infantrymen on the island of Vella Lavella await the word to advance in pursuit of retreating Japanese forces, September 1943. (National Archives)

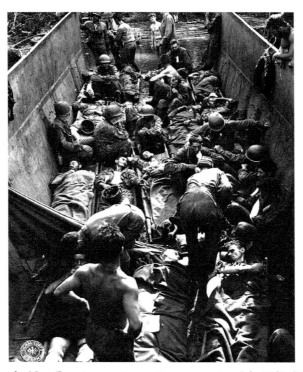

US casualties from the New Georgia campaign await transportation, July 1943. (National Archives)

Man wounded in the face is given first aid during the New Georgia campaign, June 1943. (National Archives)

Cover of magazine showing Japanese and Chinese soldiers smoking together, symbolizing the friendship between the Japanese Empire and the puppet regime in Eastern China. (Private collection)

Chinese officers receive instruction in the use of mortars at US-led training camp in India. (Office of War Information Photograph)

Italian troops in Tianjin, a city near Beijing. Italy had maintained a presence in China since the beginning of the century, and in the first years of the Pacific war, its garrison was tolerated. In September 1943, after Italy defected to the Allies, Japan sought to eliminate the Italian enclaves in Asia, and fighting broke out in both Tianjin and Beijing. (North China Railway Archive)

US Marines have reached the beach of Tarawa in November 1943, but are pinned down by deadly Japanese fire. (National Archives)

Bodies of US Marines on the beach of Tarawa, testifying to the ferocity of the Japanese resistance meeting the men as they waded ashore. (National Archives)

Japanese pillboxes on Tarawa. A US Marine inspects a reveted Japanese tank used as a pillbox. In the foreground, a dead Japanese soldier. (National Archives)

American soldiers wade ashore on the island of Makin. The initial landing went smoothly, but the invading force soon got bogged down in grueling combat with the Japanese defenders. (National Archives)

Chiang Kai-shek at the Cairo Conference in November 1943, along with Franklin D. Roosevelt and Winston Churchill. Chinese First Lady, Song Meiling, is seated with the three leaders. It was the only time during the war that Chiang met his Western counterparts, and he made a generally poor impression. (National Archives)

Chinese soldiers during the battle of Changde, 1943. The battle ended in a Japanese withdrawal but set the stage for major Japanese offensive operations the following year. (National Army Museum)

CHAPTER EIGHT

Starving Continent

January–March 1943

New Year's Day 1943 saw the dwindling number of Japanese soldiers holed up inside Buna Mission Station, on a slim piece of land on the north coast of Papua, in a state of growing despair. Surrounded on three sides by soldiers of the reinvigorated 32nd Division of the US Army, they were defending a shrinking perimeter. The mission, formerly the Australian government center for the area, consisted of three houses and a few dozen native huts.[1] The Japanese had only one way out: they could try to escape by the sea. As the Americans moved ever closer, some Japanese built primitive rafts, while others found logs that they hoped to cling on to while somehow escaping undetected. Yet others vowed to stay and fight to the death.[2]

At dawn on January 2, those who had decided to make a run for it were spotted by observant American eyes as they rushed from the mission station into the blue ocean. Guns and mortars opened up, and soon American planes appeared over the palm trees and strafed the fleeing men caught helplessly in the gentle tropical surf. "I watched the attack on the evacuating Japanese force from vantage points on the beach," *New York Times* correspondent F. Tillman Durdin told his readers. "Handkerchiefs were waved… and some surrendered. Scores must have been killed in the sea."[3]

Shortly after the failed attempt to escape, the Americans began their final assault against the Japanese defenders who had remained inside the mission station. Phosphorous shells exploded among the treetops and set fire to the houses. As the Japanese emerged from the burning buildings, they were cut down by machine-gun fire. The collapse was total, and the two senior Japanese officers at the station committed hara-kiri.[4] When General Eichelberger arrived on the scene, shots could still be heard in the distance as individual Japanese were being hunted down by vengeful GIs. "I saw American troops with their bellies out of the mud and their eyes in the sun," the general wrote in his notes just hours afterwards. "It was one of the grandest sights I have ever seen."[5]

One of the key Japanese bastions in northern Papua was no more. The mirror image of Eichelberger's exhilaration was the distress felt by General Adachi Hatazō, commander of the 18th Army, newly formed to defend New Guinea against Allied landing. Nothing had prepared him for the sight when he arrived at his new command at Lae, a major naval base 180 miles northwest of Buna, in early 1943 and met the few survivors of the recent battles. "For the first time in his career he saw Japanese soldiers in defeat, uniforms in tatters, some propping themselves upright on crudely fashioned bamboo crutches, others being carried by exhausted comrades," according to historian Edward Drea. "Shocked by the sight, Adachi discarded his inspection schedule and instead talked to each man, encouraging and praising them for their efforts and telling them they looked like soldiers."[6]

In Japan, reports of the Buna mission station's fall were added on top of the string of bad news that had hit the nation since the summer. The destruction of the Buna garrison was referred to in the official dispatches with the term of *gyokusai*, meaning "glorious sacrifice," or more literally, "smashing jewels."[7] The crème of Japanese manhood had died on the beaches of Papua. Hirohito's misgivings about the war were now becoming ever more obvious, and he remained attached to the increasingly unrealistic hope of striking a blow so devastating that it would force the Allies to the negotiating table.[8] "The Emperor's will was crystal-clear: he desired peace at the earliest moment," wrote the politician and diplomat Shigemitsu Mamoru, who later became foreign minister. "I constantly conferred with the Emperor on the subject of the war decision and the restoration of peace."[9]

On January 4, the Japanese forces secretly began their evacuation from Guadalcanal, transporting a large number of troops from the island while succeeding in keeping the Americans in the dark about the withdrawal. Ishida Yahachi, a soldier stationed on Bougainville island further up the Solomons chain, was terrified when troops evacuated from Guadalcanal arrived, more dead than alive, the victims of their own commanders' failure to ensure adequate supplies. "Hardly human beings, they were just skin and bone dressed in military uniform, thin as bamboo sticks," he recalled later. "They were so light, it was like carrying infants."[10] Over the following weeks, a total of 13,000 Japanese soldiers were pulled out of Guadalcanal. Organized resistance ended at 4:25 pm on February 7, as units of the 25th Division and the Americal Division linked up at the village of Tenaro.[11]

Despite the retreat from Guadalcanal, the area remained an area of interest to the Japanese. An order issued on January 4, "the Army-Navy Central Agreement on Operations in the South Pacific," called for the continued defense of the Solomon Islands. The Army, which had originally had no desire to become deeply involved in the South Pacific, was now inextricably engaged in the theater, but it remained cautious and wanted the defensive line to be kept as far north as possible, while the Navy wanted it further south, to increase the distance to the important naval base at Rabaul. A compromise solution was found whereby the Navy committed to defending New Georgia and the other central Solomon Islands, while the Army would concentrate its forces on Bougainville in the northern Solomons, and only send a small force to aid the Navy's defense in the central part of the archipelago.[12]

Even so, the setback at Guadalcanal forced the commanders in Tokyo to reevaluate their strategy in the South Pacific. In line with the decision made on the last day of 1942, New Guinea emerged as the main battlefield and the shield against an Allied advance into the East Indies and its resources. On January 7, four thousand Japanese soldiers disembarked at Lae and in the following weeks more troops were landed to reinforce the position there. With a growing Allied presence in the air, this movement of men and materiel across open water entailed considerable risk. "The transports were in great danger from the airplanes," wrote Yoshihara Tsutomu, chief of staff of the 18th Army. "They had no armor-plating, no water-tight bulkheads, but were just small, toy, tinplate ships. If a bomb hit the target, it would immediately catch fire. To maneuver the ships was not quick and easy as with battleships, and this made them all the weaker."[13]

For all Japanese arriving in New Guinea in early 1943, the growing presence of the Allied aircraft was a rude awakening. The diary of Japanese soldier Tamura Yoshikazu reflected this new fact of life at the jungle front: "I could hear the continuous anti-aircraft fire from our troops, but the attack did not have much effect on the enemy planes. They flew around two or three times and dropped bombs. When the bombs exploded with a loud bang, the ground shook. The sky lit up. It was all so close. I did not bother to enter the air-raid shelter but stared at the sky. The bullets and shells that came from the enemy planes and our artillery glowed in the dark beautifully and looked like grand fireworks. Even though our ground artillery fired shells as rapidly as they could, it was unconvincing and none seemed to hit the plane. The plane just seemed to jaywalk across the sky."[14]

Immediately after the loss of Buna, the attention of both Allied and Japanese commanders turned towards the gold-mining town of Wau, which was located inland from Lae and posed a threat to the tenuous Japanese foothold in northern New Guinea. Wau was nearly inaccessible, and almost everything had to be transported in by airplane. "The billiard tables at the hotels were brought in by air," the Australian journalist Osmar White wrote. "Easy chairs, refrigerators, bathtubs, stoves, dynamos, linoleum, carpets, garden statuary, even great mining dredges, bulldozers and power shovels—all were brought in by air." Still, a Japanese reinforced regiment marched out of Lae in January with orders to reach the town overland, hoping to capture it before it was built up to become an Allied stronghold.

What followed in the next weeks was a race between the Allies to fly in reinforcements to Wau, and the Japanese to arrive by foot in sufficient numbers to tilt the balance. The Japanese lost that contest, as their progress was slowed down by inhospitable terrain and scattered Australian resistance, but they came tantalizingly close, reaching the edge of the Wau airstrip. Fighting near Wau was marked by great ferocity. Towards the end of the battle, a forward Australian observer directed mortar fire towards a Japanese field hospital and was able to tell once the fire was precise: "You're right onto them," he radioed back. "I can hear them screaming." The mortars fired 80 rounds into the Japanese position. When the Australians captured the position the next morning, they were met with almost no opposition and saw body parts hanging from the trees. "Christ almighty," one of the Australians said, "the first time I had ever seen the work of a three-inch mortar up close."[15]

The Japanese forces were compelled to withdraw back towards Lae, and only after the war was it made clear to them how close they had been to reaching Wau in time. The commander of the reinforced regiment had been faced with the choice of two routes to Wau, a relatively straightforward route through the Bulolo River valley, and another more cumbersome one which, however, offered better forest cover and therefore minimized the risk of Allied air attack. "Ha, that saved us," a gloating Australian officer told a high-ranking Japanese official after the war. "If you had come down the Bulolo River valley in force you would have got through. At that time our strength was only one company and we had no defense positions. We had assembled the native mine-workers to look like a crowd of people, and if we had been attacked by a force with air transport it would have been all up."[16]

The continued bloodletting in New Guinea notwithstanding, the Allied forces entered into a period of relatively low activity in early 1943, following the end of the Guadalcanal campaign.[17] There was a need to reorganize and recuperate and set new strategic priorities, but at the same time, the US commanders were loath to rest on their laurels and preferred to keep the Japanese on their toes. This was the mirror image of the Japanese concerns just a year earlier, when Yamamoto and his lieutenants were bent on remaining active after the first sweeping series of conquests in the wake of Pearl Harbor.

The Japanese had been curtailed by a lack of capabilities. For the Americans in early 1943, it was rather a problem of coalition warfare. The frank, if acrimonious, debates that happened among the Allies, especially the United States and Britain, reflected a closeness of cooperation and coordination that was all but absent in the relationship between the European and Asian members of the Axis, since to all intents and purposes they were waging separate wars. This also meant, however, that sometimes Anglo-American agreement could only be obtained in the most general form. This became clear at the conference in the Moroccan city of Casablanca, held from January 14 to 24.

Meeting each other in person was in itself an experience triggering mixed emotions. Roosevelt impressed members of the British delegation with his trademark friendly and charming manner, but at the same time his physical frailty was painfully obvious.

A British delegate described the cumbersome manner in which the US president had to be taken to the garden of the villa where he stayed: "Two attendants pushed his chair to the top of the steps leading to the lawn. Then he held up his arms and they picked him up and carried him to another chair outside."[18]

The strains of fighting two major enemies at the same time necessitated some serious trade-offs and also forced the Americans especially to allocate resources carefully between the Atlantic and the Pacific. As Roosevelt had written in a letter to Churchill on November 19, 1942: "Destroyer losses and damage to destroyers in recent naval operations in the Pacific have been so serious as to necessitate an immediate return of the destroyers borrowed from the Pacific for Torch," he said, referring to the codename for the American landing in North Africa.[19]

The American interest in the Pacific somewhat paralleled the British fascination with the Mediterranean. By the same token, the Americans viewed the Mediterranean the same way that the British viewed the Pacific: as a secondary theater that could divert Allied attention away from the main objective of striking Germany in Fortress Europe. However, the Americans could hardly back down from their insistence on the importance of the Pacific. It put on display the impact of American public opinion, for whom the war against Japan had special significance after Pearl Harbor and Bataan, but it also reflected fears that the war in the Pacific could drag on indefinitely as a result of a half-hearted effort.[20]

Discussions at Casablanca on the relative importance of Europe and the Pacific went on for long days with no visible progress. "Both sides stuck to their guns, and the opposing arguments were repeated *ad nauseam*," wrote one of the British participants.[21] Among the US delegates, Admiral King emerged as a particularly strident advocate of maintaining pressure on the Japanese after the recent defeats inflicted on them, and not allowing them any breathing space. King made his argument so forcefully that his British interlocutors ended up with the impression that he placed greater emphasis on the war with Japan. "We found that the main difficulty rested in the fact that the U. S. A. Joint Planners did not agree with Germany being the primary enemy and were wishing to defeat Japan first," Alan Brooke wrote in his diary.[22]

In the talks, King cited studies he had ordered showing that only 15 percent of the total Allied resources went to the Pacific. "This is not sufficient to do more than hold; it is not enough to permit maintaining pressure on the Japanese," he told the assembled generals and admirals. "The British have definite ideas as to what the next operation should be but do not seem to have an overall plan for the conduct of the war."[23] The admiral openly expressed his doubts that Great Britain would bear its fair share of the burden of beating Japan once victory against Germany had been secured.[24] General Marshall also argued that decisive steps had to be taken in order to ensure continued Chinese participation in the war. Key to this were offensive moves in Burma, the general said, upping the ante by painting in bleak colors the consequences if this did not take place. "A situation might arise in the Pacific at any time," he warned, "that would necessitate the United States regretfully withdrawing from commitments in the European Theater."[25]

Faced with the American pressure, Churchill retorted: "If and when Hitler breaks down, all of the British resources and effort will be turned toward the defeat of Japan. Not only are British interests involved, but her honor is engaged."[26] The British promise went some way towards covering up the lingering tension, but the Casablanca Conference exposed the differences between the Americans and the British. Planners from the two sides could only agree on the broad principles of targeting Germany first and Japan second. Details about how, when, and where to strike Japan were left for the future.[27]

In light of the very general terms of the agreement with the British, American planners presented their broad strategy for 1943 in the Pacific. Japan was to be defeated with "measures which greatly resemble those which would be effective against the British Isles": blockade, bombardment and assault by sea. American planners were especially interested in bombardment, considering both the Philippines and China as bases for such an air offensive. At the end of the conference, therefore, the two sides agreed to continue the offensive through the central Pacific towards the Philippines, although it was generally assumed that an invasion of the Philippines could only take place after Germany had been defeated. US air forces in India would be expanded to prepare for an offensive in Burma.[28]

At a press conference at the end of the meetings, Roosevelt compared the close cooperation with the relationship of the Allies in World War I, when coordination had been much scarcer and much more limited in scope. "These conferences have discussed, I think for the first time in history, the whole global picture," he told the reporters. "It isn't just one front, just one ocean, or one continent—it is literally the whole world; and that is why the Prime Minister and I feel that the conference is unique in the fact that it has this global aspect."[29]

Glossing over the significant disagreement on the war against Japan, the two sides instead emphasized one result emerging from the conference: the call for the unconditional surrender of the Axis powers. The demand was suggested by Roosevelt, who was inspired by General Ulysses S. Grant's use of the term in the American Civil War.[30] He broached his idea during a private lunch for a small number of people, including Churchill. The American president's son, Elliott Roosevelt, was present and later recorded the British prime minister's reaction: "Churchill, while he slowly munched a mouthful of food, thought, frowned, thought, finally grinned, and at length announced, 'Perfect! And I can just see how Goebbels and the rest of 'em 'll squeal!'"[31] In fact, the British leader was so pleased that later the same day, he even proposed "Unconditional surrender" as the nightcap toast.[32]

★★★

In late February, Allied reconnaissance unveiled 299,000 tons of merchant shipping assembling at Rabaul, while Japanese seaplanes were searching the area around New Britain for Allied submarines. These were telltale signs that the Japanese were preparing a convoy, and signals intelligence soon confirmed that this was indeed the case.[33] George Kenney, commander of the Allied air forces in the Southwest Pacific, discussed the information with MacArthur. Everything pointed to the conclusion that the Japanese planned to land a significant number of men, perhaps an entire division, in New Guinea. Much was at stake. The four American and Australian divisions in the area were worn down by fatigue, and a Japanese land offensive would come at the worst possible time. The convoy had to be stopped before it got anywhere near its destination. It was a job for Kenney's aviators, and MacArthur ordered him to give the task top priority.[34]

The Allied commanders' analysis was fundamentally correct. The Japanese were reeling from the series of setbacks they had suffered in the Southwest Pacific towards the end of 1942, but still determined to strengthen their position in the region. New Guinea remained the first line of defense against the Allied offensive that would eventually come, and the garrison at Lae on the northeastern coast of the large island, now reduced to a mere 3,500 men, needed reinforcement. It was the destination of the convoy being prepared at Rabaul; eight transports set to carry 6,900 fresh troops to the green frontier. The men were from the 51st Infantry Division, which had so far seen service in Manchukuo and occupied China. Their transfer to the South Pacific highlighted the increasingly difficult situation there, forcing the Japanese Army, always a reluctant participant in the Navy's southern adventure, to allocate ever greater parts of its resources to that area.[35]

The Japanese prepared the convoy in every minute detail, but the Americans, too, had time to get ready. Japanese radio communication revealed that there were still a few days to go before the departure of the convoy, and the crews of low-flying American B-25 bombers spent the time practicing a new tactic not yet fully tested in battle. Instead of dropping their bombs directly onto enemy vessels, the aircraft would fly in a few yards above sea level and skip their bombs into the sides of the enemy ships, much like, a pilot explained, "a rock skips across the top of a pond when thrown on a flat angle."[36] Kenney watched as his bomber crews were drilling the maneuver on a wreck off Port Moresby and could not help but be worried that they were becoming a little too sure of themselves. "They were not taking on any high-school team this time. They were playing Notre Dame," he reminded them.[37]

For the Allies, the main question was if the Japanese convoy would travel north or south of New Britain to get to its destination. Kenney and Ennis Whitehead, the commander of Allied fighters, knew that, given the limited number of reconnaissance aircraft at their disposal, they could not cover both areas efficiently enough and had to make a choice about where to direct their attention. "Whitehead and I went over all the information at hand and tried to guess how we would run the convoy if we were Japs," Kenney said. "We decided to gamble that the Nip would take the northern route."[38] It was a risky bet but, if successful, it meant that the Allies were likely to detect the convoy early during its 260-mile voyage from Rabaul to Lae, leaving their aircraft ample time to send the Japanese vessels to the bottom of the sea.

The Allies were in luck. The convoy, reduced to a speed of seven knots by the slowest transport vessels, left Rabaul late at night on February 28, having picked the route north of New Britain, through the Bismarck Sea. The convoy was traveling under a dense cloud cover, but stayed undetected for just a few hours. In the morning of March 1, one of the reconnaissance planes sent out by Kenney came across the Japanese ships, and even though the convoy disappeared again under the clouds, Kenney's hunch about the northern route had been confirmed. The Japanese, too, knew they had been discovered. "Security and black-out orders were more rigid. All individuals arranged their belongings in order," one of the soldiers on board later remembered.[39] The measures only helped so much. The following day, the attacks began. The convoy was bombed repeatedly from high-altitude aircraft, and one of the transports was destroyed, while two others were damaged.[40]

This set the scene for the day of carnage, March 3. In Japanese folklore, it was Hinamatsuri, the traditional Doll's Festival, and the soldiers on board the convoy, many of them too young to have girlfriends, were issued candy to remind them of sisters at home and keep their focus on what they were fighting for.[41] It brought forth painful memories of more peaceful times that many of them would not live to experience again. Shortly afterwards, wave after wave of American and Australian bombers, protected by fighter escorts, appeared over the horizon and began their bloody work. One of the pilots described the action: "When within strafing range I opened fire with my forward guns. The decks were covered with troops, lined up facing the attacking plane with rifles in hand. However, my .50-calibers outranged their small arms and I saw hundreds fall and others go over the side... I then ceased fire and I made a gradual pull-up to clear the masts. My bombs skipped into the side of the ship and exploded, leaving a large hole at the waterline."[42]

The decks of the Japanese transports were crammed with Japanese soldiers, hoping to abandon ship, but making for easy targets for the aviators. Garrett Middlebrook, an American pilot, watched as a squadron of B-25 Strafers equipped with eight heavy machine guns in the nose swooped down over the Japanese vessels and chopped the dense crowds of soldiers to pieces. "Debris from the ship flew all over the water. I wondered what all the pieces of debris were and squinted harder. My God, they were human bodies!"[43] he wrote. "I realized we had not come to do battle; rather we had come to perform an execution—an execution of several thousand Japs," an American pilot said later.[44]

In a matter of just minutes that morning, all seven remaining transports as well as three destroyers were sinking or heavily damaged, but the killing did not stop there.⁴⁵ Over the next hours, the aircraft scoured the surface for survivors and machine-gunned them. There was an element of revenge in this. Early in the battle, Japanese fighters had downed an American bomber, and as the crew had bailed out and descended slowly in parachutes, the Japanese aviators had shot them up. Now it was payback time. "Every man in the squadron would have given two months' pay to be in on the strafing," an entry in the 63rd Bomb Squadron's war diary stated candidly.⁴⁶ The official historian of the US Navy in World War II, Samuel Eliot Morison, described how American patrol torpedo boats also went about the business of killing Japanese clinging to wreckage virtually within sight of the New Guinea coastline. "It was a grisly task," Morison writes, "but a military necessity since Japanese soldiers do not surrender and, within swimming distance of shore, they could not be allowed to land and join the Lae garrison."⁴⁷

At the end of the day, the convoy had ceased to exist. All eight transports had been destroyed, as had four of the destroyers. Over 3000 men had been killed.⁴⁸ For the Japanese, there was no doubt whatsoever that they had suffered a disastrous defeat. "In view of the incorrect estimate of the Allied air base strength on New Guinea, the plan to dispatch a convoy at the low speed of seven knots to Lae, where it was within effective attacking range for two days, proved ill-advised," a senior Japanese naval officer wrote in his after-action report. "This operation ended in complete failure."⁴⁹ Subsequently, the Japanese would no longer attempt to supply the Lae area with large surface ships. They had suffered a momentous, perhaps even irreversible setback in New Guinea. As MacArthur would say later, the Battle of the Bismarck Sea was "the decisive aerial engagement" of the Southwest Pacific theater.⁵⁰

In March 1943, American correspondent Theodore White and photojournalist Harrison Forman visited Henan province in central China, a sort of no-man's-land whether neither the Japanese, nor the Chinese were in complete control. Disturbing rumors had reached them about a famine of epic proportions. What they saw was a society which had been ravaged by an invisible army called starvation. It had swept through cities, towns, and villages with a force as deadly as if columns of vengeful soldiers armed to the teeth had passed through, leaving behind a barren landscape where the living envied the dead. The silence was especially frightening, and "a baby crying in a hidden room in a village sounded louder than the pounding of our horses' hooves."⁵¹

White described how corpses had been left on the side of road to either rot or be devoured by animals: "A girl no more than seventeen, slim and pretty, lay on the damp earth, her lips blue with death; her eyes were open, and the rain fell on them. People chipped at bark, pounded it by the roadside for food; vendors sold leaves at a dollar a bundle. A dog digging at a mound was exposing a human body. Ghostlike men were skimming the stagnant pools to eat the green slime of the waters."[52] No one had been spared, and the suffering of the young was particularly unbearable, the journalist wrote. "Chinese children are beautiful in health; their hair glows then with the gloss of fine natural oil, and their almond eyes sparkle. But these shrunken scarecrows had pus-filled slits where eyes should be; malnutrition had made their hair dry and brittle; hunger had bloated their bellies; weather had chapped their skins. Their voices had withered into a thin whine that called only for food."[53]

Chinese journalist Li Rui was traveling the region at the same time, recording for posterity the abject conditions he witnessed. "Famine victims are gulping down white clay into their stomachs and just wait, unmoving, for their digestive systems to decompose and eject it; we explain motherly love to our children, but in the streets there is the tragic scene of mothers selling their sons," he wrote. Equally heartbreaking, he reported about a broken woman who cursed her young son for staying alive for too long, prolonging his own suffering: "Die soon. Why haven't you died quickly?"[54] Cannibalism was rumored. Harrison Forman was told about an incident when a girl of six had starved to death. A woman had boiled the body and eaten it and was immediately arrested. She was buried alive as punishment and an example to others, a Chinese official told Forman. "If they start eating dead, they'll soon be eating live people," the official reasoned.[55]

The people of Henan were no strangers to calamities. The province had been struck by two devastating famines in the 1920s,[56] and it had also taken the brunt of the impact when Chiang Kai-shek had breached the dykes of the Yellow River in 1938 in a bid to halt the Japanese advance. In 1942, this much-tested province was once again hit by an evil fate, and its people experienced the worst drought in three generations.[57] "The famine came on very suddenly, and was really a famine blitz," the American missionary and aid worker Ernest Wampler commented.[58] This was caused mainly by a failure of the summer monsoon rains in 1941 and especially 1942.[59] The number of deaths in the Henan famine is likely to have been close to one million. It could have been far more were it not for the ancient coping mechanism of the starving masses to flee the affected areas and seek relief in neighboring provinces where the harvest had not failed to the same extent.[60]

The famines in Henan might have been caused by extreme aberrations in the summer monsoon.[61] The average rainfall in China was dramatically lower than the average, probably due to the El Niño phenomenon, characterized by high temperatures in the Pacific.[62] Giving the calamity almost Biblical overtones, locusts were an additional plague. "Half an hour after they alighted the crops had been eaten to the ground," missionary Mary Geneva Sayre reported.[63] On top of the weather and natural conditions, two additional factors combined to worsen the plight of the local farmers and push a large part of the population over the precipice. One was forced requisitioning, carried out by both Japanese and Chinese forces. The other was a rapid rise in the price of grain.

Even though it initially worsened the famine through requisitioning, the Chinese government did its level best to relocate the farmers displaced by the famine. This was not just done out of concern for the welfare of its citizens, but also reflected the need to keep up food production for the populous country. China's rulers could simply not afford to have millions of farmers remain idle, and therefore they sent many of them west to the neighboring province of Shaanxi to claim land that had been left untilled since it had been vacated in a civil war in the late 19th century. The measure doubtless saved countless lives, but it had environmental consequences as the aggressive clearance of land caused accelerated deforestation.[64]

The human flood that filled the roads of Henan in 1942 and 1943 was just one part of a massive refugee problem that affected China throughout the war years. In the period from 1937 until 1945, a staggering 95 million experienced being displaced at one point or another, corresponding to more than a quarter of the total Chinese population at the time.[65] No province was hit harder than Henan, both in absolute numbers and as a percentage of its people. During eight years of war, nearly 15 million Henan residents, or 44 percent of the total, were forced to leave their homes for an uncertain future elsewhere.[66]

At the same time, British-ruled India was experiencing its own devastating famine. "The Bengal famine of 1943 stands out as a great calamity even in an age all too familiar with human suffering and death on a tragic scale," a report prepared by the British colonial authorities stated.[67] Just as in China, famines were a horrifying collective memory from the past, which still reverberated in the minds of the people, but the subcontinent's colonial masters had grown confident that they had brought about a new society where nothing of the kind could happen again. "The old famine of history, with its dreadful death roll, is not likely to recur," a colonial administrator, who had spent more than three decades in India, had optimistically stated in 1937.[68] This was grossly over-optimistic. In fact, Bengal was teetering on the brink of famine even in normal years. The average output was the equivalent of a daily 2,000 calories per grown-up, which in itself was barely enough to survive.[69] The frightening corollary was that the availability of grain, either from domestic production or from imports from Burma, only had to drop marginally for disaster to strike. This was exactly what happened in 1942.

Hunger victims roamed the countryside, "clad in filthy rags," the surgeon-general said in a report, noting that "they were apathetic, oblivious of their surroundings or cleanliness and sometimes unconscious; the pulse was rapid and feeble, and temperature subnormal."[70] The report also pointed out that one of the features of the famine "was the mental attitude of the more advanced cases of starvation." The report continues: "The more desperate cases of hunger became childish in mind, wandering from place to place in search of food, ransacking rubbish heaps, and sometimes absconding from hospital where food and relative comfort and security were obtainable… these unfortunates seemed to be guided by an instinct compelling them to move on in fruitless and erratic attempts to find food. Irritable and unreasonable, childish and apathetic, difficult to nurse and filthy in habit, the starving sometimes cried for food even when food was before them."[71]

Had there been peace, Bengal would still have been severely affected by the harsh weather conditions that also struck in China, but the wartime conditions worsened the calamity dramatically. The Japanese invasion of Burma had deprived Bengal of a major source of rice imports. At the same time, any supplies stored in Bengal that were considered surplus were removed, lest they benefit a Japanese invasion army. Boats along the coast that could be used by the Japanese in an offensive were also withdrawn, depriving local authorities of an important means of transporting grain to areas where the famine was particularly severe. Some historians have also criticized Churchill for harboring ill will towards India, further exacerbating the situation. On September 9, 1942, the prime minister burst out in a conversation with his secretary of state for India, Leo Amery: "I hate Indians. They are a beastly people with a beastly religion." The actual extent of Churchill's culpability remains, however, disputed.[72]

News of the famine spread to Indian soldiers serving on battlefields in Europe and Asia and had a severe impact on morale. "Dear brother," read a letter sent to one such soldier serving overseas, "as regards news out here, death and death everywhere. Starvation and epidemics sweep away daily a good number. You will be astonished to see that ¼ of our neighbors have left for the better world."[73] The desperate situation caused tensions to rise. A Bengali peasant later described how he and other men from his community went to their landlord demanding grain that he stored on his property. The landlord pretended he was going to comply but instead went upstairs and shot at the peasants from a window, killing nine of them. The peasants withdrew but decided to come back, agreeing they had nothing to lose. They found the landlord defenseless: "He had no more bullets left and some of us went in and dragged him out and killed him, with eight others also from his house, to atone for the nine of us lying in his fields," the peasant said later.[74]

CHAPTER NINE

Yamamoto's Bane

April–June 1943

On April 7, a total of 67 Aichi D3A "Val" bombers and 110 Mitsubishi A6M "Zero" fighters—the largest assembly of Japanese aircraft since Pearl Harbor—were approaching Guadalcanal. "At 1400 the Russell Island radar screen became milky with traces of bogeys and Guadalcanal broadcast 'Condition Red,' followed shortly by an unprecedented 'Condition *Very* Red'," the US Navy's official historian Samuel Eliot Morison writes.[1] American intelligence had expected the attack and had scrambled 76 fighter planes from Henderson Field, ready to take on the "Zeros" when they arrived. Surface vessels anchored at Guadalcanal joined in the defense. "Everyone had a great time sawing away at the enemy planes, claiming kills and later painting Rising Suns on gun shields," according to Morison.[2]

As a result of the raid, the Japanese succeeded in sinking one destroyer, one tanker, and one corvette, in addition to downing seven American planes.[3] It was a poor trade-off, as the Japanese themselves lost 39 planes by the US count,[4] 21 by their own.[5] The Guadalcanal raid was part of a larger air offensive, Operation I-Go, which took up the first half of April and was aimed at advance Allied air bases in the Solomons and Papua. The mastermind behind the campaign, conducted with aircraft on carriers that had arrived from Truk, was Admiral Yamamoto Isoroku, who had set up his temporary headquarters at Rabaul.[6] The Japanese were initially upbeat about the result of the series of attacks. Hirohito sent a message to Yamamoto: "Please convey my satisfaction to the commander in chief, Combined Fleet, and tell him to enlarge the war result more than ever."[7]

The truth was that to the Allies it felt like pinpricks. Kenney, MacArthur's chief of aviation, even had a hard time figuring out what exactly the Japanese were trying to achieve.[8] Once the offensive was over, it was evident even to the Japanese themselves that it had hardly been worth the effort as they had been forced to sacrifice more than one quarter of all their carrier-based bombers.[9] If anything, I-Go had shown that even Yamamoto was unable to revert the dramatic shift in fortunes that had taken place in the South Pacific. This did not, however, change the fact that he was still considered a formidable foe by the Americans, viewed with a mixture of admiration and direct hatred, due to his role in planning Pearl Harbor. Halsey had put Yamamoto on a "private list of public enemies, closely trailing Hirohito and Tojo."[10]

Yamamoto was also a frequent target in American poster art, calling for revenge for the December 1941 sneak attack on the US Pacific Fleet, but propaganda aside, Yamamoto was a much more complex character than the one-dimensional image he projected among his adversaries. One of the few who was in a position to appreciate this was Henri Harold Smith-Hutton, an intelligence officer who had known Yamamoto prior to the war in Tokyo and was considered the foremost American expert on the Japanese admiral. Yamamoto was "short, heavy set, erect, and very firm, even oak-like in appearance, but gay, social and fun-loving," Smith-Hutton said. The Japanese admiral made no secret of his fondness of America, rendering him suspicious to the Japanese Army top brass who, however, forgave him because of his obvious ability.[11]

This ability was a lingering threat to the Americans, and when following I-Go they suddenly had the opportunity to "get Yamamoto," they jumped at the chance. While the Japanese carriers that had participated in the campaign withdrew to Truk, Yamamoto's next move was to visit troops in Bougainville in a bid to boost morale.

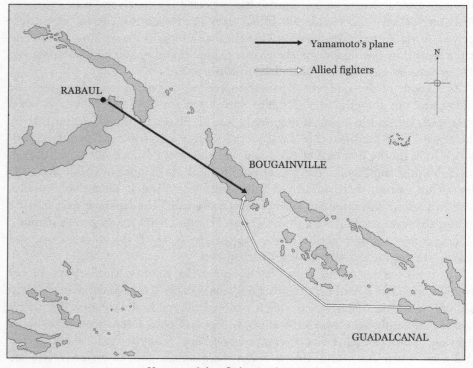

Yamamoto's last flight, April 18, 1943

American codebreakers got wind of the planned trip and set to work. "We've hit the jackpot!" an intelligence operative exclaimed when presented with the Japanese admiral's detailed itinerary. After very little debate it was decided to assassinate Yamamoto, and on the morning of April 18, when two bomber planes carrying the admiral and his staff took off from Rabaul, his death warrant had already been signed.[12]

The two bombers, along with a number of escorting fighters, reached the west side of Bougainville at 7:30 am. With an estimated 15 minutes left before the aircraft were to arrive at their destination, the ominous silhouettes of 24 Allied fighters appeared on the horizon. While the Japanese escort attempted to take up the fight with the approaching enemy, the two bomber planes dived to just above treetop level. Yamamoto was in the lead plane, and his chief of staff, Admiral Ugaki Matome, was in the second. Ugaki watched from his plane what happened as some of the Allied fighters fought their way through the Japanese escort planes and started hunting down their real target:[13]

"The first plane was staggering southward, just brushing the jungle top with reduced speed, emitting black smoke and flame. It was about four thousand meters away from us. I just said to myself, 'My God!' I could think of nothing else. I grabbed the shoulder of Air Staff Officer Muroi [Suteji], pointed to the first aircraft, and said, 'Look at the commander in chief's plane!' This became my parting with him forever. All this happened in only about twenty seconds. In the meantime, my plane turned again sharply to evade another enemy attack, and we lost sight of the commander in chief's aircraft. I waited impatiently for the plane to get back to the level while full of anxiety, though the result seemed apparent. The next glance revealed that the plane was no more to be seen, only a pall of black smoke rising to the sky from the jungle. Oh! Everything was over now!"[14]

Just hours later, a group of Japanese soldiers hacked their way through the jungle to the spot where the plane had crashed. They found most of the passengers mutilated and burned beyond recognition. One had, however, been thrown out of the fuselage, and the body was almost intact, apart from two gaping holes left by machine bullets in the lower jaw and shoulder. Even in death, he was sitting erect in his seat, his left hand clutching his ceremonial *katana* sword. It was Yamamoto.[15] "He must really have been superhuman," Ugaki wrote.[16]

The Japanese press only reported Yamamoto's death five weeks later. There was understandable concern that the growing wave of bad news from the front would affect morale at home. In the US Pacific Fleet, by contrast, the killing was a sensation. "There was so much loose talk that we in the Navy, who were responsible for security, feared that the Japanese would learn that we had broken one of the most secret codes," said Smith-Hutton.[17] The exhilaration went all the way to the top. When Halsey announced the news of Yamamoto's death at his daily conference, one of his officers whooped. "Hold on!" Halsey burst out. "What's so good about it? I'd hoped to lead that scoundrel up Pennsylvania Avenue in chains, with the rest of you kicking him where it would do the most good!"[18]

In April 1943, a new batch of guards arrived as reinforcements at Sandakan POW Camp in northern Borneo.[19] They were from the Japanese colony of Taiwan, but if the roughly 2,500 Australian and British inmates believed this would mean any improvement in their situation, they were sorely mistaken. The newcomers were just as brutal as the guards they joined, perhaps even more so, as they were at the bottom of the Japanese hierarchy and let out their frustrations on the prisoners. This coincided with a general tightening of discipline in the camp, which supplied workers for an airfield under construction nearby. A special "punishment squad" came into being, consisting of eight guards who would continuously roam the airfield equipped with clubs and immediately punish any prisoner who appeared not to be working hard enough.[20]

Sometimes these punishments were meted out collectively, and a whole group of prisoners would be lined up to pay for one man's alleged infringements. "They would give each man a couple of bashes," said an Australian prisoner. "If they whimpered or flinched they would get a bit more."[21] Getting by on a starvation diet, and exposed to a multitude of tropical diseases, the prisoners faced towering fatality rates. For those who were found guilty of disobedient or insubordinate behavior, there was "the cage," measuring six by five by four feet, barely enough to stand up or lie down.[22] Those unfortunate enough to end up this type of confinement would spend the first days without food or water. Once they were allowed to be fed, they would become a source of sinister amusement. Guards doing kitchen duty fed their dogs and the encaged prisoners at the same time, getting a kick out of watching them fight for the few scraps of meat.[23]

The Sandakan camp was just a small part of a sprawling system of forced labor which the Japanese Empire maintained in order to exploit its captured enemies. A total of 140,000 Caucasians were kept behind Japanese barbed wire, suffering abuse that rivaled that of the worst German prison camps. A Dutch internee described the dismal condition that most found themselves in after months or years in the camps: "Many developed cracked lips as a result of the heat and dust. They were unable to chew the rice and hence had to rely on eating porridge, leading to further weakening. Those whose boots had been completely worn out now had to walk on bare feet." Being without footwear could be a catastrophe for the western prisoners, who were forced to stumble along. The Dutch-Indonesian POWs who in many cases had walked barefoot since childhood "just kept trucking along."[24]

The "hell-ships," carrying prisoners from one part of the Japanese empire to another, were a particularly sinister and sad part of the story. Many became victims of the increasingly efficient submarine campaign carried out by the US Navy in the Pacific. An example was the *Lisbon Maru*, which was on the way from Hong Kong to Japan in late 1942 with 1,800 British and Canadian POWs on board. "The men on the galley could not retain their urine or their feces any longer, so we below received them with shouts of 'you dirty bastards',," said POW Bill Spooner.[25] The ship was not marked as carrying prisoners and was therefore torpedoed by American submarine USS *Grouper* off the southeastern coast of China. A mad stampede broke out among the men trapped in the hull of the ship, slipping in the urine and excrement left from days at sea. Some resigned themselves to their fate, deciding to "give the Japanese a song." Shortly afterwards, dozens of voices could be heard singing *It's a Long Way to Tipperary*. The Japanese guards opened fire on many of those prisoners who managed to escape from the hull and jump into the ocean. A total of 800 died.[26]

The humiliating treatment that the Caucasian prisoners suffered was, on the face of it, a demonstration of Japan's revenge for centuries of European colonialism. Still, the Japanese undermined their own claim to be leading Asia in a counteroffensive against the West, due to their harsh treatment of other people in the region. Asian civilians often faced Draconian punishments for the slightest act that could be interpreted as fraternizing with the Western POWs. In Hong Kong, two young Chinese who had waved to prisoners behind the barbed wire of a camp were spotted by Japanese guards. They were marched through the camp, which was located on the waterfront, and onto a jetty. "One sentry took them to the end and pointed to things in the harbor," a British eyewitness said later. "The other ran up and bayoneted them and tossed them into the harbor, then left laughing and joking."[27]

In addition to the military POWs, the Japanese also kept large numbers of civilian prisoners, typically Westerners who had been present in Asia at the time of the Japanese conquests in late 1941 and early 1942. Life in a place such as Shanghai's Zhabei Civil Assembly Prison Camp was harsh for the inmates—mainly British and American prisoners as well as a few Belgians and Dutch, with married couples taking up a large share—but the casual brutality of the POW camps was usually avoided. "There was no physical punishment," a former inmate said, "but we were warned not to try to escape. This would have been foolish because once you got into the countryside you could not lose your identity, i.e. you were not Chinese by dress and face, especially your eyes."[28]

The Western prisoners in Zhabei did benefit from a few advantages, including "the beautiful red-haired American wife of the Japanese Commandant," who allegedly threatened divorce if he treated the Western prisoners too badly. "We had another ace in the hole," a former prisoner explained. "The Japanese loved to play baseball. The young men in the camp made up a team and had quite a series going with the Japanese soldiers. When food rations were low or other problems arose our men refused to play ball. This made the Japanese very mad. Not until conditions improved did the games continue. All of us got a big laugh out of this. We were thankful for having some means of making them treat us like human beings."[29]

Allied prisoners were only taken in large numbers in the early stages of the war. Partly, this reflected the nature of the early phase of the conflict, when the Japanese made quick conquests, and often entire Allied units surrendered en masse, as in the Philippines and Singapore. Once the fighting moved to the islands of the Pacific, the Japanese had no logistical means of bringing prisoners to the camps elsewhere in the empire, and surrendering enemies were likely to be killed on the spot. Besides, rumors of the maltreatment at the hands of the Japanese caused many Allied soldiers to do everything to avoid ending up in Japanese hands, even if it meant fighting to the death.

For most Japanese, surrender was never an option. Some had exaggerated fears about the savage treatment the Allies would mete out to them, but for the majority it seems that notions about the dishonor attached to surrender formed the main motivation. During the Papuan campaign from July 1942 until January 1943, fewer than 100 Japanese were taken prisoner, most of them because they were too weakened to resist capture or kill themselves beforehand. A report from the 3rd Portable Surgical Hospital from January 1943 about 11 Japanese prisoners kept at Buna reflected the special challenges they posed. "They were a terribly malnourished and debilitated lot. As patients they were uncooperative and surly. Eight of them were placed in one tent together. The stronger ones at night would try to kick the weaker ones to death and had to be carefully watched."[30]

Half a world away, in the western United States, ethnic Japanese were experiencing a different kind of confinement. A few months into the war, in February 1942, Roosevelt had signed Executive Order 9066, which cited the risk of sabotage in authorizing the military to exclude certain American residents from important military areas. The order did not directly mention the Japanese-American community, but it was intended to form the legal basis for the internment of its members residing on the US West Coast. A total of 112,000 Japanese Americans—men, women, and children—ended up in camps which were startlingly similar in all their bleak atmosphere: "Residents were all of Japanese ancestry, of similar height and weight, with features darkened by constant exposure to the wind and sun," in the words of two modern authors. "Clothing had a uniformly drab look reflecting army surplus and leftover Sears and Roebuck; housing consisted of row after row of tar-paper barracks, and inside were identical potbelly stoves, army cots, and fine... dust."[31]

★ ★ ★

On April 26, 1943, German U-boat *U-180*, commanded by Captain Werner Musenberg, surfaced and rendezvoused with Japanese submarine *I-29* in the Indian Ocean, about 400 nautical miles east of Madagascar, in waters controlled by the

British. The German U-boat was carrying two civilian passengers who were to be transferred to the Japanese side, but the sea was too rough for this maneuver to take place right away. Instead, the submarines sailed alongside each other until early on April 28. Nearly two days had passed, and since waiting much longer could expose the surfaced submarines to considerable risk, the transfer was attempted. A hemp rope was suspended between the two submarines, and the civilian passengers were dragged on a dinghy to the waiting Japanese. On board the *I-29*, the duo were treated with the utmost respect. The Japanese commander of the submarine even offered his cabin as accommodation. Small wonder: one of the civilians was Subhas Chandra Bose, an Indian who had the potential to become Japan's most important ally in Asia.[32]

Bose, 46, was a red-blooded nationalist who was determined to rid India of the British, even if it meant cooperating with Japan and its Axis partners. Married to an Austrian woman, he had fallen out with Gandhi and arrived in Germany in the spring 1941, hoping to get Hitler's help in ending colonial rule in India. Bose had met Hitler and was disappointed to find him unwilling to retreat from anti-Indian statements that he had made in his ideological tract *Mein Kampf*.[33] Once Japan entered into the war, Bose realized they would be a more natural partner for him. However, the Japanese, too, were initially lukewarm towards harnessing him for the war effort, to the frustration of some Japanese officers who saw in the Indian politician a means to unlocking India. After all, with its 400 million people it was the second most populous nation on Earth and could theoretically by numbers alone tilt the balance in most theaters. "All the Indians whom I had come across had a great admiration for Bose, amounting almost to a religious devotion," said Lieutenant General Fujiwara Iwaichi, whose task was to stir up anti-Western feelings among Asia's populations. "I was disappointed that the Japanese government did not have on its side a great revolutionary leader who could rally his own people."[34]

Eventually Bose succeeded in arranging for his transfer to Asia. Before starting out on his U-boat voyage to Asia, he wrote a letter to his brother, who stayed on in Europe: "Today once again I am embarking on the path of danger. But this time towards home. I may not see the end of the road."[35] It was a long and arduous voyage, taking Bose along perilous routes in the Atlantic, and it was half a year until he finally reached his destination: Singapore. His sojourn in the former British colony was a success. According to British intelligence estimates, he persuaded 40,000 out of 45,000 Indian POWs to join his army. The 5,000 who stayed on the sidelines were mostly officers.[36]

Another Indian National Army had been formed from Indian POWs in Japanese camps in 1942, but those efforts had ended in failure, as the Indian commanders felt overruled by the Japanese. Even though this second attempt seemed more successful, Bose's dream of creating a free India welded together in war soon ran into problems. For one, the enormous diversity of the Indian subcontinent was an obstacle towards realizing the ideal of a unified nation. A German officer who had previously observed the recruitment of volunteers among South Asian POWs in Europe had noticed there was more that divided them than brought them together: "Muslims cannot be won over by Hindus, Gurkhas follow Gurkhas more easily and Sikhs follow Sikhs, particularly since it is usually the different languages that bind these groups."[37]

As if conditions were not difficult enough as they were, flawed decision-making on Bose's part caused him to end up with avoidable problems. In the early hours of October 24, 1943, the Provisional Government of Free India, which Bose headed, declared war on Britain and, controversially, the United States. "Why drag in America, sir?" a close collaborator asked Bose.[38] It seemed to be one of the many self-inflicted wounds that the Axis nations and their allies were prone to committing during the war years. The Roosevelt administration was openly and proudly anti-imperialist and, by refraining from targeting the United States, Bose's government could potentially have driven a wedge between Washington and London.

By the end of 1943, Bose's army was ready to enter the battlefield. Time would tell if it could make a difference. Political woes already existed. Bose was not just an Indian nationalist, but also a Pan-Asian, and he was forced to confront the awkward fact that millions of Asians were fighting *against* Japan, not *for* it. Addressing the Chongqing regime by radio, he called on Chiang Kai-shek not to send troops to India. "The Indian people really sympathize with China and the Chinese people," he said.[39] His pleas fell on deaf ears. He was appealing to the wrong Chinese. The Chinese who agreed that the future for Asia was under Japanese leadership were to be found elsewhere—in Manchuria, and in Japanese-controlled eastern China.

★ ★ ★

In Manchukuo, the three northeastern Chinese provinces welded into a Japanese-backed puppet state in the early 1930s, the official propaganda created the impression that a new society was being developed. It was allegedly a melting pot in which the best elements of Japanese, Chinese, and Manchurian culture were combined to push civilization forward. Moreover, Manchukuo was depicted as a template for the newly conquered areas further south, in China and beyond, and a litmus test for the viability of the Japanese vision of a new Asia under its leadership. "Because Pan-Asian ideals were first put into practice in Manchuria, if they are not attained here, then [it might be] assumed that they cannot be attained anywhere," wrote Kawabata Yasunari, one of Japan's most prominent authors, who would much later win the Nobel Prize for Literature.[40]

Some of Japan's most free-thinking intellectuals were sent to Manchukuo, and it showed. Until late 1943 textbooks used in schools in Manchukuo avoided extreme ideological material that was being used in other parts of the Japanese Empire and spread the notion that the Japanese were inherently superior to neighboring peoples.[41] Still, the underlying assumption remained that Japan was in a class of its own. The

Japanese authorities emphasized the need to teach the Japanese language to the young generations in Manchukuo and the colonies in Korea and Taiwan, but it was as a means of control and there was never any genuine attempt at assimilation. Rather, as modern historians have pointed out, Japan pursued a "stratification policy" intended to ensure that non-Japanese people found their proper inferior position in a hierarchical system with the Japanese at the top.[42] "By understanding the Japanese spirit," a Japanese educator told an audience of local teachers, "the Manchukuo people can learn their correct role, and carry it out faithfully."[43]

This pointed towards the dark side of Japanese rule in Manchukuo, especially after the requirements of war placed an ever more crushing burden on Japan's economy. Japan faced a growing demand for labor once it found itself embroiled in a war covering the entire Asia Pacific, and China was a major source of workers. Some were employed in China itself, some in Japan, and some in Manchukuo. Initially, Japan sought to recruit laborers on a voluntary basis, but it relied increasingly on forced conscription. For example, during a major counter-insurgency operation in 1942 aimed at Communist partisans in northern China, Japanese troops rounded up 100,000 able-bodied farmers and their families and deported them all to Manchukuo.[44] This had a curious side effect. Japan's original aim had been to distance Manchukuo from China and tie it closer to Japan economically and socially. However, the massive import of workers from China meant Manchukuo was Sinicized at a pace probably unmatched by any other period in history up to that point. It was one of the main ironies of Japan's rule in Manchukuo that it achieved the exact opposite of what it was striving to do.[45]

The most sinister expression of Japan's intentions in Manchukuo was Unit 731, established in dark brick buildings on the edge of the city of Harbin. The unit, which had conducted research into biological and chemical weaponry since the 1930s, sped up its gruesome work after the outbreak of the Pacific War, racing against time to develop new technologies that might be of use in the titanic conflict. All ethical considerations were set aside in this endeavor. Tamura Yoshio was a young uniformed employee in the Japanese Army, who took part in the vivisection of patients who had been deliberately infected with terrible diseases. He never felt sorry for his victims, he said later: "I had already gotten to where I lacked pity. After all, we were already implanted with a narrow racism."[46]

Ostensibly at the top of a rotten system, but with no real power whatsoever, was the former child emperor of China, Puyi. Perhaps due to his lack of bona fide influence, he became all the more dictatorial towards his own most immediate underlings. "I became so savage that I would have my staff beaten incessantly and even use instruments of torture on them," he wrote in his autobiography, authored late in life.[47] His arbitrary cruelty, more reminiscent of an ancient Roman ruler than of a modern head of state, made life at his court a living nightmare. "It got so that everyone was covertly watching Puyi all the time, to try and find out what mood he was in," a staff member testified later. "Puyi was completely paranoid: if you were caught eyeing him, he would bark: 'What's the matter? Why are you looking at me that way?' But if one tried to look away, he would say: 'Why are you avoiding me? What have you got to hide?'"[48]

South of Manchukuo, politicians were in a similar situation, seeing their efforts ending in results very different from what they had hoped to achieve. Wang Jingwei, Chiang Kai-shek's former collaborator who had defected to the Japanese side in the hope of saving China, was growing increasingly frustrated with the outlook for his nation. The leader of a puppet nation established in eastern China with its capital in the old city of Nanjing, he had tried his level best to avoid becoming dragged into the Pacific War. Wang succeeded for more than a year, but in January 1943, he was persuaded by his Japanese masters to declare war on the Western allies. At the same time, he studiously avoided declaring war on Chiang Kai-shek's regime, in line with his official rationale of wanting to do the best for China at a time of severe national crisis. Still, a mood of pessimism permeated the circles surrounding Wang Jingwei, and no one was more pessimistic than Wang himself, realizing that China was become more and more divided, while the Communists were growing stronger.[49]

None of the people in Wang's camp saw themselves as traitors. The attitude among many, perhaps most, of the Chinese who decided to side with the Japanese was that they were in fact doing the best they could for their nation. Described by some historians as "collaborationist nationalism,"[50] their policy nevertheless caused conditions akin to civil war. In response to continued partisan attacks, the Japanese Army decided to build massive defensive works all across the north Chinese countryside, again using forced labor. In what was nicknamed "the other Great Wall of China," due to the sheer scale of the endeavor, thousands of miles of trench lines were dug into to the hard soil, matched by thousands of miles of walls.[51] Working conditions were often wretched, and food was inadequate. Some laborers had to survive on a diet of porridge mixed with bark and leaves.[52]

Drugs became a growing problem in China in the war years, partly triggered by a Japanese need to finance the occupation of the vast nation. "The charge that the Japanese higher authorities deliberately spread the use of drugs in order to render the Chinese population more docile may be held unproven—after all they needed Chinese laborers in their factories and drug addicts do not make even moderately good workers," according to British scholar F. C. Jones, writing just a few years after the war. At the same time, he did not free the Japanese from responsibility: "They did not exercise effective control over their underlings and camp followers, whether Japanese, Korean, or Chinese, and consequently their evil record in the matter of opium, and in the even more vicious morphine and heroin traffic, both in Manchuria and in China generally, stands in glaring contrast to their glib professions of concern for the welfare and improvement of the peoples whom their armies subjugated."[53]

In an ironic twist, the Japanese even used the drugs theme as a way of rallying Chinese to their cause, pointing fingers at the British Empire for its involvement in the opium trade in earlier generations. The film *Ahen sensō* or *The Opium War* was released in early 1943, highlighting Japanese and Chinese friendship in the mid-19th century, united in defiance of sinister British opium traders. Just before the end credits, the crew of a Japanese fishing boat sail into Hong Kong harbor, singing: "We are longtime friends, we fishermen with topknots; the sound of the traditional drum encourages us; the big fish call to us: 'Come on! Come on! Bring us forth!'" With a British man-o'-war in the background, the voice-over tells the audience: "Although China was powerless, a century later, our Japan is benevolently taking up the task!"[54]

By the summer of 1943, the time had come to drive the Japanese out of the only American territory occupied by any Axis forces during the entire war—the islands of Attu and Kiska in the Aleutians. The US strategic planners were uncomfortable with the presence of Japanese troops so close to Alaska and feared they might constitute the vanguard of more ambitious operations. After all, the North Pacific formed the shortest distance between Japan and the United States, and if it had not been for the area's harsh, unpredictable weather, it would be the likeliest route of an invasion fleet in either direction. At the same time, the Aleutians could be of benefit to the Japanese in an invasion of Siberia, while by the same token, the islands would help the Americans in any joint operations with the Soviets against Japan, for example as a base for US bombers. All in all, while the Aleutians were not a top priority, there was ample rationale for offensive moves, and in November 1942, Marshall and King had set mid-May as the tentative date for attacking the Japanese in the area.[55]

The Japanese, too, recognized the importance of the Aleutians, and tried to give their garrisons the support they needed. In late March, a Japanese convoy attempted to reach the two islands, but was stopped by the US Navy in the battle of the Komandorski Islands, roughly halfway between the Aleutians and the Soviet peninsula of Kamchatka. It was an old-fashioned long-range artillery duel between two fleets over a distance of several miles, more reminiscent of World War I than the ongoing conflict, where submarines and aircraft often played decisive roles at sea.[56] US Army bombers based in the area were unable to arrive in time to assist the Navy, and the encounter was a tactical draw.[57] Strategically, however, it was a clear victory for the American side as the Japanese had to acknowledge that their garrisons in the Aleutians were now experiencing the same problems as Japanese outposts in the South Pacific. American superiority at sea and in the air meant running supplies to the isolated troops was all but impossible.

Meanwhile, the US Army was already deeply involved in preparations for the reconquest of the western Aleutians. Initially, the American planners had wanted to go straight for the more heavily fortified island of Kiska, but partly due to lack of sufficient shipping, they had opted for the less heavily garrisoned island of Attu instead. The 7th Division was picked for the task.[58] Having trained in the Mojave Desert for expected deployment in North Africa, it was now sent to subarctic conditions instead, and while the division was still aboard transport ships on its way to the Aleutians, the actual destination had been covered up in ingenious ways. The medical officers on board lectured about tropical diseases, while the winter uniforms were hidden from view.[59] Once in the staging area, at the westernmost end of the Alaskan peninsula, the soldiers and sailors realized the unforgiving nature of the freezing, deserted environment where they would have to fight. "The ships look out of place in a world that belongs so little to man," wrote a young officer on the battleship USS *Pennsylvania*.[60]

After several days of delay due to inclement weather, the 7th Infantry Division began landing on Attu began on May 11, at Massacre Bay in the south and Holtz

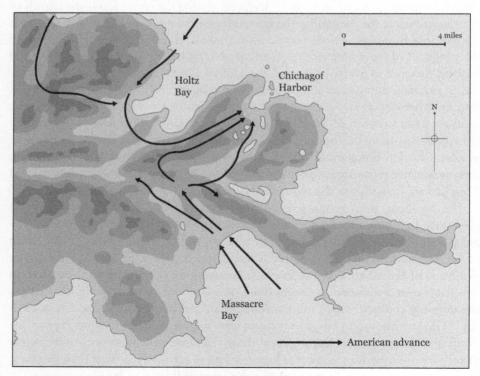

Invasion of Attu, May 11–30, 1943

Bay in the north. It was immediately clear that the weather would make up a major obstacle. Fog prevented the US Army Air Force from carrying out much of the required preparatory bombing of Japanese defenses, and it also led part of the invasion fleet to lose its way.[61] Resistance was initially surprisingly light, almost non-existent, and after brief moments of disorientation because of the dense fog, the American soldiers were relieved to be able to move inland without being shot at. "We had been in boats all day long waiting to come into the island," said Private Raymond V. Braun, of the 17th Infantry. "Then we landed in fog as thick as mashed potatoes, expecting a wild dash across the beach with bullets flying, and there weren't any."[62]

The respite was only brief. Both invasion forces soon discovered that the Japanese were nested on top of Attu's rugged hills, causing their advance to grind to a halt. Marching in the harsh landscape was an added challenge, and moving up the slopes under fire was often suicidal: "The sides were soggy where the tundra grew, and slick as grease where they were barren," a veteran of the battle said.[63] Initial reconnaissance had left the Americans with the impression that there might be as few as 500 Japanese on Attu, but in fact the number was five times as large.[64] One of the Japanese defenders was Tatsuguchi Nobuo, a medical officer who had received his education in the United States but had returned home before the outbreak of the war. His diary revealed no illusions about the American numerical superiority, but after two days of fighting he remained confident that the Japanese side could stand its ground. "Enemy strength must be a division. Our desperate defense is holding up well," he wrote on May 13.[65]

The fog was Japan's ally in the struggle for Attu. It resulted in the repeated failure of attempts by US naval artillery to hit Japanese targets in coordination with spotters onshore. "Fired on call target," the gunnery officer on board battleship USS *Nevada* wrote in his log. "Visibility nil. Cannot contact spotter on radio. May have hit him instead of target."[66] Not all was due to the weather. Some Army officers were also frustrated with the half-hearted, if not fearful support they thought the Navy was providing to the disembarked troops: "I suspected the Navy vessels emptied their magazines rapid fire into the thick fog with no targets available so they could go back… to rearm," Archibald Arnold, the second-in-command of the 7th Infantry Division, told an interviewer after the war.[67]

As the days passed without the expected gain in either invasion zone, the division's commander Albert E. Brown came under criticism from his superiors for not being aggressive enough and making excessive requests for reinforcements. "I asked him what he'd expected to build there—a stadium or a city?" said Admiral Thomas Kinkaid, in overall command of the operation to retake the Aleutians.[68] On May 16, Brown was unceremoniously pulled out of the battle and replaced with Brigadier General Eugene M. Landrum. The new commander was in luck. Just at the time he took over, the Americans in the northern sector managed a breakthrough. The northern invasion force punched through the Japanese lines, and soon were approaching the southern landing zone, threatening to trap the Japanese deployed there in a pincer movement.[69]

Little by little, American soldiers pushed inland from their two invasion beaches, forcing the Japanese into a narrow perimeter around Chichagof Harbor in the northeast of the island. Fighting was often at close quarters, and Japanese who had been overpowered were given only seconds to decide if they agreed to surrender. On May 19, soldiers of a platoon of the 17th Infantry led by Sergeant Alastair Finlayson had fought bitterly for a Japanese trench at Clevesy Pass and finally succeeded in capturing it. "The first Jap they contacted was huddled down in a hole," according to a contemporary eyewitness account. "Sergeant Finlayson hollered for him to come out but the Jap cowered lower and lower and repeated, 'No, no, no, no.' So Finlayson tossed a grenade in on him."[70]

The Japanese tactics were the same as in warmer Pacific battlefields, but the green American troops, who had for the most part never fired a weapon in anger, had to learn their lessons the hard way. Lieutenant Donald E. Dwinell from the 32nd Infantry was in a trench just yards from Japanese soldiers who did not realize how close he was. "They pulled the old trick of putting coats and helmets on rifles and moving them along their trench trying to draw our fire and thus expose our exact position," he said. "Some of the boys from farther away fired at these 'targets,' and then the Japs would dump mortar over the hillside for a while."[71] Soon no Japanese was given the benefit of doubt. A few days later, the American soldiers were involved in the grim task of clearing every little crevice of a heavily defended ridgeline with grenades and fixed bayonets. Mindful that the Japanese would often play dead, only to shoot their enemies when they turned their backs to them, the soldiers had strict order on handling Japanese bodies: "If they don't stink, stick 'em."[72]

Tatsuguchi, the medical officer, reported growing strain on the Japanese side: "Continuous flow of wounded to our field hospital caused by the fierce bombardment of enemy land and naval forces... Just lay down from fatigue in the barracks. Facial expression of the soldiers... is tense. They all went back to the firing line soon."[73] Tatsuguchi also noted that his fellow soldiers were up against a large number of African Americans. This was, however, a misunderstanding, due probably to the fact that many of the men in the 7th Division were of Mexican descent.[74] The cultural gulf between the two sides was vast, and still they tried to employ psychological warfare on each other. During lulls in the battles, English-speaking Japanese soldiers, sometimes equipped with megaphones, were shouting insults at the American lines, and fierce threats: "Damn American dogs, we massacre you!"[75]

The battles were confused and brutal. Private First Class Ira Clawson from the 32nd Infantry Regiment was surprised by Japanese machine gun fire in the open and ducked into a Japanese foxhole. He discovered a shadow huddling in panic in the corner of the hole and burst out, "Hey, how about sharing your hole, buddy?" Only then did he discover that the frightened shape belonged to a

Japanese soldier. "He made a grab for Clawson's rifle," a contemporary account said. "Clawson, like most soldiers in battle, did not wish to part with his rifle, so he grabbed it back. The Jap grabbed it again and Clawson grabbed it back. As the Jap grabbed it again Clawson felt that something should be done to break the stalemate. The Jap apparently felt the same way, and he made a grab for his knife. Clawson... having a heavy pair of wet boots on, kicked the Jap in the mouth." Two American soldiers who had watched the scene from a neighboring foxhole came over, and one of them shot the Japanese twice. At the second bullet, an explosion filled the foxhole, knocking the Americans off their feet. "Gee, I must have hit a grenade," said the GI who had fired the shots. "Those Japs sure are tricky, even the dead ones."[76]

On May 25, Tatsuguchi sensed the end was approaching, describing a devastating naval bombardment: "It felt like the... barracks blew up and things lit up tremendously. Consciousness became vague... The last line... was broken through. No hope for reinforcements."[77] A note of increasing hopelessness permeated his diary entries. Plagued by diarrhea, he tended to a continuous stream of injured coming in from the frontline. American air attacks were never-ending, and fatalistic soldiers started killing themselves. On May 28, he wrote his final diary entry, just before a suicide attack against an American artillery position was being prepared, and even the field hospital had to take part: "The last assault is to be carried out. All the patients in the hospital were made to commit suicide. Only 33 years of living and I am to die here. I have no regrets. Banzai to the Emperor."[78]

Attu had been far bloodier than expected. The victorious Americans counted 2,350 dead Japanese and took 29 prisoners.[79] In Japan, news about the debacle set off a period of more straightforward media reporting, even of defeats. The annihilation of the garrison of 2,000 on Attu was announced in full in May 1943, and in July, an editorial in the *Mainichi* newspaper warned in stern tones about hardship ahead: "At the beginning of the war, when the victories were spectacular, there was a tendency to be optimistic about the outcome... Now there is not a single Japanese who takes such an easy view. The desperate struggle on Guadalcanal, the gallant death of Admiral Yamamoto, and the heroic stand of the 2,000 soldiers at Attu have clearly shown us the grimness of the war."[80]

Altogether 549 Americans lost their lives on Attu, and 1,148 were injured. Still, the biggest cause of casualties among the Americans was not enemy fire, but exposure in the cold and wet climate. About 2,100 were evacuated due to nonbattle injuries, and among these, the most common affliction was trench foot, a painful condition caused when water seeps into the boots of a soldier, shrinking capillaries and blocking the bloodstream. In terms of the ratio of American to Japanese casualties, it was the costliest battle in the Pacific after Iwo Jima.[81] Despite the steep cost of retaking Attu, it was a strategic *cul-de-sac*, and had been even before the first American soldier set foot on its wind-swept beaches. On May 5, six days before the invasion had started, the Joint War Plans Committee, bringing together American and British chiefs of staff, had recommended that, following the seizure of the islands, no amphibious operations were to be undertaken west of the Aleutians until the Soviet Union had entered the war against Japan and combined pressure could be applied in the North Pacific.[82]

CHAPTER TEN

Jungle Neurosis

July–September 1943

Medical officers observed a strange phenomenon on the island of New Georgia in the central Solomons in the middle of July 1943. Three weeks after disembarking on the island, the US Army's 43rd Division had lost 90 soldiers killed in combat. A far larger number had become casualties due to the mental strain of fighting a faceless enemy in a radically hostile environment. In the first weeks of July, between 50 and 100 men were taken out of the line every day because of conditions categorized as "war neuroses."[1] The psychological impact on the GIs was so severe that at New Georgia, for the first time since America had been dragged into the war, entire planned operations had to be canceled because there were not enough troops available to carry them out.[2] "Their hair was matted and muddy, and beards were ½ inch in length, eyes were sunk in, dark, and had a strained expression," according to a medical officer stationed on New Georgia.[3] Another officer with the medical corps described the worst cases as "highly excited, crying, wringing their hands, mumbling incoherently, an expression of utter fright or fear, trembling all over, startled at the least sound or unusual commotion, having the appearance of trying to escape impending disaster."[4]

Frayed nerves even caused situations that came close to mass panic. After digging in for the night on July 8, men of the 43rd Division believed they heard Japanese near their bivouacs, or perhaps even among them. The frantic infantrymen began shooting and stabbing wildly. Some threw hand grenades that bounced off tree trunks and fell among their fellow soldiers. Hours later, the sun rose over a scenery of dead and injured Americans, some with deep stab wounds, but not a single Japanese among them. It had been a fight among the US soldiers themselves.[5] A war correspondent accompanying the division into battle described the conditions that could produce this kind of tragedy: "We spent every night in pitch-dark, rain-filled foxholes surrounded by snipers. In the tenseness of the long jungle nights, every sound and circumstance takes on the aspect of terror. The call of a dry-throated tree frog becomes the signaling of infiltrating Japs. Pebbles falling from the edge of a foxhole on your helmet may be thrown by Japanese trying to taunt you into showing your silhouette. After you have done this, you understand fully why men are seized by 'jungle neurosis'."[6]

The US landings on New Georgia, which had begun during the first days of July, were part of one of the most ambitious campaigns at the start of the US counteroffensive against Japan. Known as Operation Cartwheel, it was aimed at isolating the naval port of Rabaul, the main Japanese stronghold in the South Pacific. Control over New Georgia was a vital part of this drive, as the Japanese had built an airfield near an old coconut plantation at Munda Point at the southwestern tip of the island. The airfield was a convenient stop for Japanese planes attacking Guadalcanal, and attempts by Allied bombers to put it out of service had proved futile. "The Japanese ground crews, on the double, filled in the craters with crushed coral and in a matter of minutes or hours the strip was again operational," according to an official US historian.[7] Clearly, New Georgia had to be physically in American possession in order to stop its use by the Japanese.

The men of the 43rd Division constituting the main American force landing in early July on the south coast of New Georgia, five miles east of Munda, were mostly untested in battle, and the Japanese defenders took advantage of this. The history of the division's 169th Regiment, authored shortly after the battle, described the tactics applied by the Japanese after dark: "A sleepless night was spent by all under continued harassing from enemy patrols speaking English, making horror noises, firing weapons, throwing hand grenades, swinging machetes and jumping into foxholes with knives."[8] As the night reduced visibility to near zero, imagination took over. The unfamiliar smells of the jungle became poison gas in the minds of the GIs, and the land crabs covering the ground became murderous Japanese crawling towards the American positions. Soon, rumors began circulating about the Japanese methods of fighting: "Men of the 169th are reported to have told each other that Japanese nocturnal raiders wore long black robes, and that some came with hooks and ropes to drag Americans from their foxholes."[9]

Another American force had been landed in the north of the island, with the task of hindering reinforcements and supplies from being shipped in from the neighboring island of Kolombangara. Even though it had more success at maintaining cohesion among its rank and file, it initially failed in reaching its objective, as the Japanese managed to maintain a supply line to Munda in the southwest. Meanwhile, the soldiers of the 43rd Division were moving at a snail's pace towards the airfield, slowed down by the enemy, the elements, and first and foremost by "jungle neurosis."

Only after the US side fired the overall commander in charge of taking New Georgia and sent in two additional divisions, did the momentum pick up. New tactics were also introduced to cope with the Japanese pillboxes blocking the way to Munda, most of them so well camouflaged that the Americans smelled them before they saw them.[10] The flamethrower had been part of the US inventory since the start of the campaign, but it now became the central instrument in destroying Japanese positions. The official history described how this played out in an attack carried out by the 43rd Division's 103rd Regiment: "The flame throwers went forward with the infantry, which halted about twenty yards in front of the pillbox line and covered it with small arms fire. Under cover of this fire the flame thrower operators, their faces camouflaged with dirt, crawled forward. Operating in teams of two and three, they sprayed flame over three barely visible pillboxes in front of the center of the 103rd's line. Vegetation was instantly burned off. In sixty seconds the three pillboxes were knocked out and their four occupants were dead."[11]

The accumulating American pressure, combined with relentless bombing and shelling, was starting to have an impact on the defenses. Japanese rifle companies that had counted up to 170 men at the start of the battle were now down to as few as 20. Unbeknownst to the Americans, their foes, seemingly endowed with super-human stamina, were now also beginning to crack and there were cases of nervous breakdowns, even though these were never recognized as such by Japanese military medicine. Calls by the Japanese officers to "kill ten Americans for each Japanese killed," meant to make up for the quantitative imbalance between the two sides, had little effect. On the first day of August, after nearly a month of grueling jungle fighting, Munda airfield fell to the US Army.[12]

Next on the American list was the volcanic island of Kolombangara, just north of New Georgia. Admiral Halsey had planned a large-scale invasion of the island, and with an estimated 10,000 Japanese soldiers prepared to receive the disembarking Americans, it was bound to become a bloodbath. "The undue length of the Munda operation and our heavy casualties made me wary of another slugging match, but I didn't know how to avoid it. I could see no victory without Rabaul, and no Rabaul without Kolombangara," Halsey wrote with remarkable candor in his memoirs. "It was here that my staff first suggested the by-pass policy—jump over the enemy's strong points, blockade them and leave them to starve."[13] Pouring over the map, Halsey and his officers focused on the next island on the route to Rabaul. It was called Vella Lavella, and it had a garrison of just 250. "I canceled Kolombangara," Halsey said, "and wrote in Vella Lavella."[14]

It was one of the early examples of the leapfrogging or island-hopping strategy that would soon become a blood-saving element in the Allied approach to rolling back Japanese dominance of the Pacific. In this respect it was similar to the decision to invade Attu instead of Kiska in the Aleutians. The irony was that rather than being an entirely new concept emerging out of nowhere, island-hopping was in fact a rediscovery by the Americans. It had been the subject of theoretical debate in the interwar years, and it had already been envisaged in the Orange plans prepared by American strategists during the previous decade, but subsequently it had been almost forgotten.[15]

Even though Kolombangara was made redundant, it became the trigger of a naval encounter that showcased how the American superiority in the air was now matched by growing superiority at sea as well. In the battle of Vella Gulf, separating Kolombangara and Vella Lavella, the Japanese commanders attempted to reinforce their troops on Kolombangara. On the night between August 6 and 7, four destroyers—*Arashi, Hagikaze, Kawakaze*, and *Shigure*—tried to land 950 infantrymen on the island. Once again favored by their signal intelligence, the Americans knew they were coming and had a six-destroyer fleet lying in wait for them. The commander on the American side, Frederick Moosbrugger, divided his six vessels into two forces of three each.

While the Americans had the advantage of modern radar, the Japanese were disoriented by the black contour of Kolombangara obscuring the silhouettes of the Americans' enemy. In essence they were fighting blindfolded. Hara Tameichi, the captain of the *Shigure*, asked in the radio room what the other three destroyers had reported. The reply he received from a subordinate was anything but encouraging: "*Arashi* and *Kawakaze* sent brief messages saying they were hit by torpedoes. We have heard nothing from *Hagikaze*."[16] All three destroyers were sunk in the first decisive night-time US victory of the war.[17] The crew of US destroyer USS *Lang* sailed through the wreckage of the Japanese destroyers and heard a strange, otherworldly chant by the survivors floating on the surface. The moment the Americans approached in the dark, someone among the Japanese blew a whistle, and the chant immediately stopped. None was willing to be taken alive.[18]

The American victory was complete. The Japanese lost 1,210 soldiers and sailors during the brief, hectic hours of that night. A little more than 300 were able to reach the beaches of Kolombangara and were saved, for now at least.[19] By contrast, the only casualty on the US side was a gun loader whose hand was crushed in an accident.[20] It was a devastating blow to the Japanese destroyer force, and to the professional pride of its crews. At the same time, the battle was yet another example of the American command style prevailing over the more rigid procedures of their Japanese counterparts. When Moosbrugger received the order to intercept the Japanese destroyers, his superior had given him complete leeway: "You know your ships better than I do; it's up to you how to fight them."[21]

★ ★ ★

Ray Champagne, a corporal in 7th US Division, was in the first wave making a landing on Kiska on August 15, fully expecting to be shot and possibly killed. He described his amazement at finding the island completely deserted, but looking as if it had been inhabited until a few hours earlier. "The initial delight of having succeeded in making a surprise landing had turned into bewilderment. Where were they?"[22] While the landing was unopposed, it was not completely without casualties. Canadian soldiers took part in the invasion but landed on a different beach, and several firefights broke out with the Americans, causing dead and injured due to friendly fire. Marine General Holland M. Smith called it "a crushing anti-climax" caused by an American failure to carry out necessary reconnaissance. "In the Aleutians we had all the means at our disposal to determine definitely whether the Japanese had evacuated Kiska but we failed to use them. This negligence on the part of the high command was inexcusable."[23]

The Japanese had harbored no intention of staying at Kiska, and initially they had attempted to carry out a piecemeal evacuation by submarine but had been compelled to give it up as too many subs were lost in this lengthy endeavor to move the soldiers out in small groups. In the end they opted for a full-scale withdrawal taking place on July 28. The operation was put in the hands of Rear Admiral Kimura Masatomi, known throughout the Navy for an enormous moustache that would have looked more at home in the 19th century.[24] According to the Japanese military historian Chihaya Masataka, the perfect operation in battle is "as rare as the perfect game in baseball," and the Japanese forces succeeded in performing it only twice during World War II. The evacuation of Guadalcanal was one, and the withdrawal from Kiska the other.[25]

Two days after the landing at Kiska, the Allies convened for the latest in the series of conferences to coordinate the wars against Japan and Germany. This time, the setting was Quebec. It took place following not just the victory in the Aleutians, but also the continued execution of Cartwheel to isolate Rabaul, of which the drawn-out battle for New Georgia had been a recent example. Against this backdrop, it was a blow to MacArthur's plans that, according to the final report issued from the conference, "Rabaul is to be neutralized rather than captured." What this meant was that territory seized as a result of Cartwheel was to provide bases for air raids on Rabaul, but not an invasion. Rabaul was to "wither on the vine." It was the largest Japanese stronghold to do so, and the most prominent example to date of the leapfrogging strategy.[26]

Overall, the Quebec Conference focused very much on the war against Germany and plans for an invasion in northern Europe, to be carried out on the earliest possible date. Less time was allocated to the war in the Pacific, which also meant less time for British interference with American preferences. In the end, US plans for pushing towards the Japanese home islands were largely adopted. Nimitz was to be in charge of the Central Pacific drive, with invasions of Japanese-held islands in the Gilberts to begin soon. MacArthur was to proceed on his own through New Guinea, possibly moving on to the Philippines. This meant a two-pronged strategy in a situation where one offensive might have sufficed. Some might consider it wasteful, but it was deemed necessary to satisfy both the US Army and Navy.[27]

Less than a month after the Quebec Conference, on September 15, the Imperial General Headquarters met in Tokyo to make decisions of a similar long-term and far-reaching nature. It was a much-humbled Japanese top brass which now convened, settling on a new defensive line which, in the words of the official American historian, "comprised the minimum area considered essential for the attainment of Japan's war aims."[28] Delineating a somewhat modest arch from the Kuriles in the north to the Bonins, Marianas, and Carolines in the center, and onwards to New Guinea in the south and Burma in the west, it was aimed at retaining for Japan the raw materials of the East Indies. The plan called for determined fighting, but all in a defensive spirit. The tables had been turned, and to underline the gloom in Tokyo, Japan's European allies were also beginning to fall apart.

In the fall of 1943, the American and British inmates of Jiangnan prison camp near Shanghai noticed new arrivals among the POWs. They were Italians. Although the Western prisoners were kept isolated from the outside world, news was trickling in about the Allied invasion of Italy, about the fall of Benito Mussolini's Fascist government, and about the defection of the successor regime to the other side. No formal peace agreement had been signed, and therefore the unofficial leaders of the prisoners prohibited fraternization with the newcomers. Many disobeyed the order and did their level best, amid the general squalor of the camp, to make the Italians feel welcome. "Nice fellows," one of the American quipped. "Odd having Axis prisoners in with Allied prisoners."[29] Other prisoners elsewhere were less friendly towards the Italians, dismissing them as "bloody Fascists." This was highly unfair, as the vast majority of Italians ending up in Japanese prisoner camps were actually opposed to Mussolini and had decided to enter into internment exactly for that reason.[30]

The story of how Italian prisoners ended up in Japanese labor camps was a long-winded one, going back to the early part of the century. Like most other European colonial powers, Italy had wished to have a presence in China, primarily for economic reasons, and since 1901 it had been permitted to maintain a special, Italian-ruled district in the large port city of Tianjin near Beijing. After Beijing and the rest of northern China had become engulfed in the Japanese invasion in 1937, there were initially few problems for the Italians, since Tokyo and Rome were sympathetic towards each other. Following Italy's entry into the war in the summer of 1940, the Italian military presence in China was beefed up slightly in order to secure Italian vessels in Chinese ports, as it was feared they might otherwise be seized by British units.[31]

Following the armistice between Italy and the Allies in September 1943, Japan moved swiftly on any Italian military presence within its sphere of influence. A small unit of roughly 100 Italian marines were guarding a radio station in Beijing and offered resistance when the Japanese Army arrived to disarm them and place them in captivity. Even though the Italians were only equipped with small arms and hand grenades, they kept up the fight for 24 hours before raising the white flag.[32] In nearby Tianjin, a larger Italian garrison, also from the marines, received an ultimatum from a superior Japanese force and surrendered. They were then given the option of either continuing the war on the side of the Axis or becoming prisoners. The harshness of life in Japanese camps was well-known, and the majority opted for the Axis cause.[33]

At the time when news of the armistice spread, several vessels of the Italian Navy were operating in Asian waters and were facing a similar tough choice: to stay loyal to the Axis or to split, and face the dire consequences. In Shanghai, the two gunboats *Lepanto* and *Carlotto*, as well as the passenger ship *Conte Verde*, were scuttled by their crews before the Japanese managed to seize them. The same happened to the auxiliary cruiser *Calitea II* in the Japanese port of Kobe.[34] The diesel-powered sloop *Eritrea* was in waters off the west coast of Malaya and decided to make a rapid dash for the British port of Colombo in Ceylon. Even though Japanese ships and aircraft immediately took up the chase, the Italian ship succeeded in reaching its destination.[35]

Most Italian submarines on missions in the Indian Ocean stayed with the Axis but were initially met with Japanese hostility and suspicion. The submarines *Giuliani* and *Luigi Torelli* were in Singapore and their crews were interned and subjected to brutal treatment, before being released and placed under the command of the German Navy, which ran a small U-boat operation on the fringes of the Pacific out of a base in Malaya.[36] The only Italian submarine in Far Eastern waters to do otherwise was *Ammiraglio Cagni*. It was located 1,800 miles west of Singapore when news of the armistice arrived and immediately set course for the South African coast. When a few days later it arrived off the port of Durban, its captain ordered a terse message sent with its dramatic offer of surrender: "I shall arrive at Durban Harbor according to the armistice."[37]

In the autumn months of 1943, the Japanese Navy and Army commanders agreed that in order to prepare for the Allied offensive which they expected would take place in 1944, they would have to place an emphasis on the development of air power. Initially, they set an annual production target of 55,000 aircraft, but soon had to scale back their ambitions given Japan's constrained industrial capacity and its limited access to raw materials, and at a meeting on September 30, 1943, the Imperial General Headquarters decided instead on a production target of 40,000 planes for the fiscal year 1944.[38] Even this reduced level marked a drastic increase from pre-war levels, as Japan had produced a much more modest 5,088 military airplanes during all of 1941.[39] Now, less than two years on, Japan was exhausting itself, using up not just its productive capacity, but also manpower resources that could not be replaced. The same thing happened to Japanese pilots as was happening to their counterparts in the German *Luftwaffe*: they were kept in the air until they were killed. There was almost no rotation back home along the lines of the American system.[40]

It reflected how much Japan was forced to stretch its limited resources in order to stay in the war. This could not, however, change the fact that Japan could never aspire to produce more than just a fraction of what its enemies produced. Not only did the Americans have the *potential* to outproduce Japan in war materials, but they were already outproducing them long before Pearl Harbor. The US wartime shipbuilding infrastructure was close to completion when war arrived, and already by early 1943, it was running at full capacity.[41] Even at the time of its attack on Pearl Harbor in late 1941, Japan had been the underdog against America's industrial might, and this had only become more pronounced in the intervening years.

To be sure, nothing came easily to the Americans. In a situation that was a question of life and death not just for the individual, but for society itself, there was a compulsion to stretch resources to the utmost. Miracles of production that would have been considered unthinkable in peacetime now became possible. For instance, the *Casablanca*-class escort carrier was the most constructed carrier of the war, and a total of 50 left American shipyards in the period between November 1942 and July 1944. The Liberty ship program was an even more striking example of American industrial muscle. The ships were no beauties, being described by Roosevelt as "dreadful-looking objects" and receiving the popular nickname "ugly ducklings," but quantity was king.[42] "The design is the best that can be devised for an emergency product to be quickly, cheaply and simply built," a committee report from US Congress stated.[43] In an exercise meant to show how fast a Liberty ship could be built, in November 1942 workers at Permanente Metals Corporation No. 2 Shipyard in Richmond, California, succeeded in completing the SS *Robert E. Peary* in fours day, 15 hours, and 29 minutes.

Japan also introduced a "Liberty" style ship-building program to make up for the enormous losses that its merchant navy suffered due mainly to the increasingly efficient American submarine campaign, but with its scarce resources it could only do so much. About two thirds of all merchant vessels built under the expedited wartime program in force in Japan did not survive beyond the end of the war in 1945.[44] The dark fate of much of Japan's surface Navy, military and merchant, reflected the improved efficiency of the US submarine campaign. As Admiral Halsey said in his post-war memoirs, "If I had to give credit to the instruments and machines that won us the war in the Pacific, I would rank them in this order: submarines first, radar second, planes third, bulldozers fourth."[45]

By September 1943, the US Navy had finally solved the technical problems that had haunted its Mark 14 torpedo since the beginning of the war, and hit rates began rising noticeably. During the same month, the first submarines started using the Mark 18, an electric torpedo. The lengthy wait for an improved Mark 14 was not just a reflection of technical hurdles to be overcome, but also the result of bureaucratic sluggishness and even personal pride. One of the biggest problems was flaws with the magnetic influence exploder. Admiral Ralph W. Christie had played a key role in the development of the device and now, as commander of submarines in the Southwest Pacific, he refused to contemplate that they could be flawed. Only when he was directly ordered by a superior to change did he agree to upgrade his submarines.

The rising efficiency of the US submarines also reflected bolder tactics. When the war began, many of the submarine captains had been lulled by years of peace into an unimaginative, even timid leadership style. They were mercilessly weeded out and replaced by a younger breed of daring officers willing to run calculated risks. Roy Benson, one of the ace submarine captains of the war, explained one facet of how submarine missions changed within just months of war. "In some of the early patrols, submarines would go all the way from Midway to the Japanese coast running submerged all day long and only surface at night. Well, it would take forever to get there; and we never did that. Once we got into the war and learned a few things we would proceed from Pearl Harbor and Midway all the way to the Japanese coast running on the surface day and night except for the daily check dive. When we had the coast of Japan clearly in sight, then we would start submerging in the daytime and running on the surface a night to charge the batteries in addition to being able to see."[46]

The submarine campaign against Japanese shipping was instrumental in exposing one of the great ironies of the Japanese-induced Greater East Asia Co-Prosperity Sphere: it was anything but a community of growth. In fact, it was quite the opposite, dismantling many of the pre-existing patterns of free trade. The Japanese vision was for a huge common market stretching from India to the Pacific islands. What they failed to see, or at least refrained from acknowledging, was the fact that this type of common market already existed prior to the Japanese invasion as international trade was thriving, allowing areas with different natural endowments to engage in the exchange of necessary goods. Once the Japanese Empire took over the region and the US submarine offensive achieved momentum, traffic among Japan's various newly-gained possessions was greatly complicated, and self-sufficiency became the norm.[47]

Another element of the co-prosperity sphere, the expansion of existing infrastructure, was somewhat closer to becoming reality, but often at a significant cost to the people who were supposedly to benefit from the investment. Wisdom inherited from past generations had in some cases predicted what would happen. In western Java, a prophecy had circulated among locals since ancient times: the 100 miles between the two towns of Saketi and Bayah would one day be linked by an iron road, and an iron horse would travel back and forth on this road, killing thousands of people. In the early 1940s, this prophecy came true.[48] After seizing control of the Dutch East Indies in 1942, the Japanese quickly developed an interest in the coal mine of Bayah and subsequently concluded that a railroad was needed to transport the strategic resource to other parts of the island.[49]

The railroad was built through some of Java's most inhospitable terrain, but local laborers were lured into working on the project with promises of good treatment and appeals to help strengthen the nation. The moment they arrived on the scene in clean clothes and carrying suitcases, they realized they had made a mistake. The awful reality dawned on them when they saw that the workers who had got there before them were, to quote a postwar account, "men who had the task of carrying heavy loads and were as emaciated as skeletons. The causes for this lay in a shortage of food and a lack of medical care. Their bodies were no longer clothed with textiles, but with trousers and shirts made from bags."[50] They suffered from malnutrition, malaria, and tropical ulcers, where part of the patient's bone was visible, and snake bites, too, were a huge and lethal problem.[51] Beatings were common, and those who tried to flee were routinely shot. Mortality was high, and a lack of gravediggers meant that the dead were usually thrown into mass graves. "In the rainy season corpses were piled into graves half filled with water," a former laborer remembered.[52]

In theory at least, it was Japan's intention to grant independence to the colonized peoples of Asia, but not at the same time. The Philippines were to achieve self-rule even before hostilities with the Western powers were over, as it would serve as an incentive for others in the region to back the Japanese war effort. Burma could also count on independence at an early date, although the proximity to the frontline might necessitate military government for the time being. The Dutch East Indies would have to wait at least until the end of the war,[53] and a joint conference of military leaders in Tokyo in January 1943 unveiled the reason why: the Army feared that independence for the former Dutch colony might jeopardize access to the area's rich resources, which had been the rationale for the war in the first place.[54]

Despite the differences, on paper at least, Japan seemed determined to end centuries of imperialism in Asia. In practice, however, Japanese military administration turned out to be generally worse than even the most outrageous examples of Western misrule prior to the war. Right from the outset, it was emphasized that the new nations of Asia would have to accept Japanese leadership now and in the future. "The independence of various peoples of East Asia should be based on the idea of constructing East Asia as 'independent countries existing within the New Order of East Asia'," a Japanese policy paper from early 1942 stated. "This conception differs from an independence based on the idea of liberalism and national self-determination."[55]

Even if the kind of sovereignty was much less than the people of Asia had been hoping for, the new conditions under Japanese rule contributed in paradoxical ways to throwing off the shackles of imperialism. The shared experience of Japanese occupation contributed to developing a hitherto dormant national consciousness, and language often served as the glue that tied people together. "Indonesians learned to recognize a feeling which the majority of them had never known before," an official later recalled. "The more they learned to express themselves in Indonesian, the more conscious they became of the ties which linked them. The Indonesian language became the symbol of national unity."[56] The inability of the Japanese to handle the complexities of colonial government had a similar effect, as locals had to step in to make the existing bureaucracies work. "The Japanese were wholly ignorant of administrative problems and procedures in Java and as a result delegated almost all the work to Indonesians," a former occupation-era official said. "Some Japanese officials could do little more than look at and pass on reports to their superiors."[57]

In 1943, the Japanese politician Nakano Seigō was 57 years old and was regarded as a veteran conservative member of the Diet, or parliament. He was also widely known as a vocal opponent of Prime Minister Tōjō Hideki. In an opinion piece printed in the mass-circulation daily newspaper *Asahi Shimbun*, he criticized "tyranny at home," a thinly veiled attack on Tōjō, and he indirectly blamed the prime minister for not having the qualities needed in a wartime leader. Throughout 1943, Nakano's assaults on Tōjō exhibited growing boldness, but he was met with silence from the state apparatus rather than oppression, and it was only after he co-signed a public declaration in late summer accusing the prime minister of creating a medieval-style dictatorship that he was arrested along with the other signatories, all lawmakers.[58]

In a twist that would never have happened in the European dictatorships, a judge ordered Nakano and the other parliamentarians released on constitutional grounds, as their attendance was required at an extraordinary session in the Diet. Nakano participated in the meeting, but subsequently decided to take matters into his own hands. He lived with his mother, who suspected he planned to take his own life and therefore decided to hide a sharp sword he had in his possession. Instead, he took a dull knife and sharpened it on the back of his watch. "I commit suicide in the regular manner," he wrote in a note, and then performed hara-kiri.[59] He was not, as some suspected at the time, forced by the secret police to kill himself, but wanted it to be seen as his ultimate act of defiance against Tōjō.[60]

Nakano was far from the only member of the Japanese elite who allowed himself to show open defiance of Tōjō's government. Okada Keisuke, an admiral, had been prime minister in 1936 and narrowly avoided death during a coup attempt that year when his brother-in-law was mistaken for him and killed in his stead. Since this nearly miraculous escape, Okada had devoted his life to saving Japan, and in 1943, he had become convinced that national salvation necessitated Tōjō's departure, as he felt his Cabinet was leading the nation down the road of disaster. Okada sought to orchestrate a showdown between Tōjō and a group of elder statesmen, but even though he failed miserably, he faced no consequences.[61]

For Japanese outside the narrow elite circles, the risks of open opposition were, of course, infinitely larger. Kiga Sumi, a young woman recently graduated from medical college, lived in fear for her older brother's life for months on end after he had been arrested at the outbreak of the war on suspicions of Leftist sympathies. One day, she was ordered to the jail to identify his dead body. "He was lying naked on the concrete floor," she said many years later about that terrible experience. "His face was swollen. His eyes were open. I squatted down and tried to close them. I couldn't."[62] Other sad stories emerged from Japan's jails of mostly young idealists who succumbed to disease, maltreatment, or outright torture.[63]

Even so, the remarkable thing was not how many dissidents were imprisoned in Japan during the early war years, but rather how *few*. In the period from 1941 until the end of 1943, a total of 2,069 Japanese citizens were arrested for harboring "dangerous thoughts" and other violations of a law against subversion from the late 1880s, and only about one third were subsequently prosecuted. In 1943, the number of arrests under the ordinance was at an almost incredible low of 159.[64] Despite the growing authoritarianism in Japan, a level of dissent was possible that would have been unimaginable for the leaders of its Axis allies, Nazi Germany, or even Fascist Italy. The Soviet Union was also a far worse dictatorship than Japan ever became. Even at the height of the war, Japan had no system of concentration or forced labor camps for its own citizens.[65] Camps did, of course, exist both in Japan proper and in the territories it had conquered, but these were for other nationalities, either Western POWs or Asians whom Japan had allegedly liberated from oppression.

The bottom line was that the Japanese authorities often tacitly accepted lone voices of dissent. There are several possible explanations for this. Japanese society was organized in ways that severely constrained individual activism, for example through neighborhood associations, where members of small, tight-knit communities were taking on the responsibility of keeping an eye on each other. Families also exerted a great deal of control. Just as importantly, a culture of conformity meant that dissent was relatively rare and never came close to posing any threat to the regime. This was why, even at the height of war, farmers fuming over having to deliver their products at low prices could afford this kind of withering criticism: "They come and take away at a song the rice we sweated so hard to produce, to the point where it's hard for us to eat. I can't stand it. Are they telling us to work without eating? Is it good if the farmers die?"[66]

CHAPTER ELEVEN

Bloody Helen

October–December 1943

Misfortune beset the 3rd Marine Division in the pre-dawn hours of November 1, 1943, as it began landing on the large island of Bougainville in the northern Solomons.[1] The navigators taking the ships towards the invasion beach on the island's west coast had to rely on maps prepared by the German Admiralty in 1890, supplemented with more recent photos by reconnaissance planes, and surveys carried out from a submarine. The result was a significant degree of confusion as the US task force sailed across Empress Augusta Bay towards Cape Torokina where the landing was to take place. When one of the American transport vessels was still approaching the shore, the captain asked the navigating officer about his exact location at that very moment. The officer, basing his estimate on the outdated maps, answered sarcastically, "About three miles inland, sir!"[2]

Compounding an already difficult situation, a strong wind whipped up violent waves that left 86 landing craft stranded and much of their cargo destroyed. To top things off, the beach conditions were perhaps the worst encountered by the US military anywhere in the Pacific War up to then, as the narrow shoreline was framed by a steep, 12-foot embankment, and behind it, impenetrable swamp.[3] For a brief moment, the operation seemed to teeter on the verge of fiasco. However, Marines who were unloaded from ships only halfway in started walking sluggishly through chest-deep water towards the beach. Others jumped over the sides of landing craft whose ramps had been broken.[4] Japanese resistance was initially light, and one hour after the landing had started, a Marine officer sent back a reassuring message: "Old Glory flies on Torokina cape. Situation well in hand."[5]

Bougainville and its airfields were key in the revised Allied strategy of eliminating Rabaul as a threat by means of an air offensive. The Japanese fully understood the island's strategic significance, and it was occupied by a sizable garrison, including soldiers of the 6th Infantry Division, which first gained notoriety as one of the main units responsible for the massacre of civilians and unarmed POWs after the battle of Nanjing in December 1937. Now it was the underdog. The Japanese commander on

Bougainville, Hyakutake Haruyoshi, was painfully aware that he would be meeting an enemy who was superior in both numbers and the quality of materiel, and in desperation, perhaps, he had to rely on the notion that superior morale alone would be enough to carry the day. "The battle plan," he announced to his subordinates before the American assault, "is to resist the enemy's material strength with perseverance, while at the same time displaying our spiritual strength and conducting raids and furious attacks against the enemy flanks and rear. On this basis we will secure the key to victory within the dead spaces produced in enemy strength, and, losing no opportunities, we will exploit successes and annihilate the enemy."[6]

Like the Guadalcanal campaign, the battle of Bougainville was fought as much at sea as on land. The initial American landing on Guadalcanal had seen an early setback in the Battle of Savo Island, when a Japanese task force had surprised the American surface fleet and sent it fleeing. The Japanese attempted a repeat of this feat at Empress Augusta Bay in the night between November 1 and 2, when they attacked the American fleet covering the landing. The attempt ended in failure, as the Japanese lost one light cruiser and one destroyer, while on the American side, several ships were damaged, but none sunk. After daybreak, 65 bombers from Rabaul had a second go at the American ships, and 17 were shot down.[7] "The scene was of an organized hell in which it was impossible to speak, hear or even think," Admiral Aaron Merrill, the commander of the US fleet at Bougainville, said in his after-action report. "The air seemed completely filled with bursting shrapnel and, to our great glee, enemy planes in a severe state of disrepair."[8]

On November 4, American scouts reported a Japanese task force consisting of eight heavy cruisers, two light cruisers and eight destroyers heading from Truk to Rabaul, but presumably under orders to move on from there to Bougainville. Halsey had only one option, to send two carrier groups, *Princeton* and *Saratoga*, against the Japanese armada at Rabaul. This had the potential to go horribly wrong and both carriers risked being sunk or severely damaged. "Every one of us knew what was going through the Admiral's mind," said Vice Admiral Robert B. Carney, on Halsey's staff. "It showed in his face, which suddenly looked 150 years old."[9] Halsey pondered briefly if the carrier task force should be put on the line, and then simply said, "Let 'er go."[10] It was a gamble but it paid off. Aircraft from the two US carriers succeeded in breaking through to Rabaul destroying 25 Japanese fighters and damaging six cruisers and two destroyers. After this debacle, the Japanese fleet was forced to return to Truk.[11]

Meanwhile, the Marines were fighting their own battles in Bougainville's green hell, where even basic orientation was close to impossible. Edward A. Craig, commander of the 9th Marines on the island, was barely able to chart his own troop dispositions on a map since he only had a hazy notion of where the various units were located. He found an ingenious solution to the problem, ordering each company in the frontline to put up small weather balloons above the treetops and then having a plane photograph the area: "The small white dots made by the balloons gave a true picture finally of just how my defensive lines ran in a particularly thick part of the jungle," he said in a post-war testimony. "It was the only time during the early part of the campaign that I got a really good idea as to exactly how my lines ran."[12]

According to the official Marine history of the campaign, this type of can-do attitude soon become characteristic of all American soldiers fighting in the hostile environment, as there was no other way to defeat the elements, let alone prevail over the Japanese: "This fight for survival against enemy and hardship in the midst of a sodden, almost impenetrable jungle had molded a battlewise and resourceful soldier, one who faced the threat of death with the same fortitude with which he regarded the endless swamps and forest and the continual rain. Danger was constant, and there were few comforts even in reserve bivouac positions."[13]

In this way, day after day, the Marines and soldiers on Bougainville gradually pushed the Japanese back. It was a long-drawn-out slugfest, which did not really end until 1945. Similar lengthy campaigns were being waged in New Guinea, where Americans and Australians fought alongside each other. However, the fact was that by the end of 1943 the Solomons and New Guinea were running the risk of becoming sideshows. Rabaul was no longer the all-consuming center of attention after the supreme Allied commanders had agreed it could be bypassed. New Guinea held the promise of moving on to the Dutch East Indies and the Philippines, but it was not the most direct way to Tokyo. The Central Pacific was where the Americans planned to strike the next blow. Once again, the Marines were leading the way.

Most men of the 2nd Marine Division thought they were going on another amphibious exercise when they shipped out of Wellington aboard 16 transports in late October. In fact, they were leaving for the real thing. They were slated to carry out the invasion of the heavily fortified atoll of Tarawa, but their commanders could not tell them yet. Most of the Marines had local girlfriends, and it could not be known that the division was taking off permanently. "The word would have passed all the way to Tokyo. But it didn't pass, we were just out on another amphibious exercise—and zip—we're on our way," said Carl W. Hoffman, then a Marine captain.[14] The deception was so elaborate that a rumor was spread deliberately that the Marines would be back in Wellington for a scheduled dance. "Maybe we didn't leave many broken hearts in New Zealand," said Julian Smith, the division commander, "but we certainly left a lot of broken dates."[15]

The invasion of Tarawa, part of the Gilbert Islands, was a key step in the Central Pacific strategy. Approaching the bloated Japanese empire in this area meant hitting it in its eastern flank, where it was most vulnerable, and where America's relative strength was growing steadily and inexorably because of the massive US shipbuilding

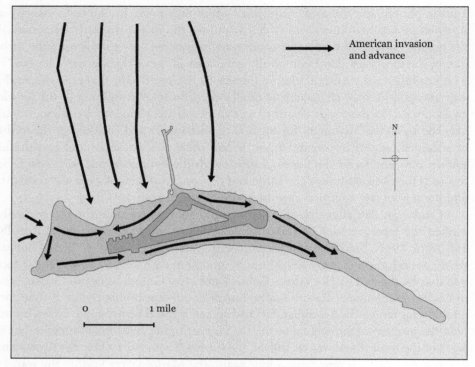

Invasion of Tarawa, November 20–23, 1943

program.[16] The US side knew that the Central Pacific had to be conquered in piece-meal fashion. Achieving control of the Gilberts was a necessary precondition for an attack on the Marshalls, cutting in half the flight time of American bombers to those islands. At the same time, once the Stars and Stripes were flying over Tarawa, it placed Samoa outside Japanese reach, opening up a more direct route for the vital shipping links between the United States and Australia.[17]

Tarawa was an atoll consisting of several islands, and the invasion force would concentrate its effort on Betio, the most heavily fortified of these. Betio, codenamed "Helen," did not seem like much. The island was three miles long and 600 yards across at its widest point. It was almost entirely flat, and no natural feature was more than 10 feet above sea level.[18] How many Japanese were on the island? Extensive reconnaissance work went before the attack, and intelligence officers equipped with the most recent aerial photographs of the island attempted to estimate the size of the Japanese garrison based on the number of shoreline latrines.[19] They ended up with the conclusion that there were between 2,500 and 3,100 Japanese troops, in addition to a couple of thousand laborers, both Japanese and Koreans.[20] The estimate was remarkably accurate. In fact, the Japanese garrison consisted of 2,619 soldiers, and they were ready to fight. Alerted to US amphibious capabilities by the Guadalcanal debacle, they had built up defenses on Tarawa and other islands in the area in an expedited program over the summer of 1943.[21] Now, according to Rear Admiral Shibazaki Keiji, commander of the Japanese garrison, "a million men cannot take Tarawa in a hundred years."[22]

The Japanese rear admiral's claim was about to be put to the test. The invasion fleet arrived off Tarawa in the night between November 19 and 20. At 5:07 am the naval artillery commenced fire on the Japanese positions, only interrupted when the job was taken over by aircraft.[23] Rear Admiral Harry W. Hill, in command of the naval forces that would land the Marines, had promised a heavy bombardment with the navy's 16-inch guns supplemented by 2,000-pound bombs dropped from the air. "We're not only going to annihilate, we're going to obliterate the island," he told the Marine officers in a pre-invasion briefing. Marine Lieutenant Colonel Raymond L. Murray, who was among Hill's audience, thought to himself, "My God, there is not going to be anybody left to fight when we get on that island. We're just going to be able to walk over it."[24]

Murray, who was set to arrive in a late attack wave with the 6th Marine Regiment, joked with Major Henry Pierson "Jim" Crowe, "Please leave enough Japs so that when the 6th Marines get ashore, we'll have a few to shoot."[25] Murray later said, "We were disappointed that we were not in the assault initially. I think that everybody always wants to be in the main assault..."[26] It was the type of self-assured attitude that was only to be expected from an elite force that had trained for its mission for months, but General Julian Smith, the commander of the 2nd Marine Division, was not convinced it would be a smooth landing. "OK," he said, "you can bomb these people all you want to but there'll be just enough left that can give us trouble, and when those Marines go ashore there won't be anything protecting them but their khaki shirts or their dungarees."[27]

Smith's word of caution proved on the mark. The men in the landing force were soon disabused of any notion that the Japanese had all been wiped out. War correspondent Robert Sherrod, observing the operation from an American warship, watched a shell hit the water 50 yards from the stern of his vessel, assuming it was friendly fire. "My God, what wide shooting!" he exclaimed. "Those boys need some practice." A Marine major looked at the journalist: "You don't think that's our own guns doing that shooting, do you?" Sherrod realized his error, and for the first time awoke to the fact that Japanese enemies had survived the fierce bombardment and were prepared to fight back. All he could say, feeling like a man who had swallowed a piece of steak without chewing it, was: "Oh."[28]

The fact was that key Japanese positions had been left intact and untouched by what looked like an impressive pre-invasion bombardment. Many naval commanders were aware that if the shells of their artillery landed in the water in front of the island, their lack of precision would be there for anyone to see. They wanted to be sure that their shells hit inland, and as a result major positions and pillboxes located near the water line often escaped destruction. "Therefore inland Tarawa really got pounded but the shoreline not so much," a Marine said later.[29]

Another problem was a reef which stretched parallel to the beach 800 to 1,000 yards out. Landing vehicles known as amphibious tractors or "amtraks" got stuck and had to unload the soldiers there, exposing them to fierce enemy fire, and a long way to wade in.[30] "We never thought it'd be as bad as it was," said Marine Major Wood B. Kyle. "We thought we could cross the reef, and we couldn't—we just couldn't get in at the time we landed. At high tide possibly we could have."[31] The Marines caught in the open in this manner also were targeted by murderous mortar and artillery fire. "It was almost uncanny from time to time to watch a ramp go down and a bunch of guys make a surge to come out and a shell explode right in their face," said Marine Norman T. Hatch. "Like the guy had dead aim and was looking right down into that boat and fired right into it, and it didn't happen once. It happened a dozen times that I saw, you know, and the boat blown completely out of the water and smashed and bodies all over the place."[32]

A pier stretching several hundred yards out into the ocean offered some protection for the shocked Marines, who crouched next to its wooden structure, unwilling to move further. Major "Jim" Crowe was the only one who was standing upright. Without a helmet, holding a gun in his hand, and clenching a cigar in his teeth, he trudged back and forth among the scattered groups of men, kicking their butts and yelling, "Look, the son of a bitches can't hit me. Why do you think they can hit you? Get moving. Go." Through example combined with robust coercion, he managed to get the men to leave the protection of the pier.[33]

Intense Japanese machine-gun fire forced the Marines to keep a low profile as they moved towards the beach. "They were all down on their hands and knees in the water and all that was sticking out were the helmets. Nobody was standing up and walking," said Marine Norman T. Hatch.[34] Movement towards the beach took place at a snail's pace, since the men were weighed down by equipment made even heavier from being soaked in water. After what seemed an eternity, Hatch crawled onto the island and sought cover. The first thing he saw was a Marine with his buttock shot off. "He was just lying there with all the flesh exposed and bleeding, and my face was like about two and a half feet away from it, and I thought, Jesus… That could be me. It could be anybody I know."[35]

Many of the troops that reached the beach had been injured on the way in and were now waiting for help. Even those left unscathed from enemy fire were only able to offer sporadic resistance. Some were completely demoralized and apathetic, while others wanted to shoot back but had lost their weapons. Communications were "terrible," according to Smith. "We had the best equipment that the United States had at that time, but so much of it got wet," he remarked years later.[36] As the unarmed Marines picked up rifles from the dead and wounded, they joined those actively engaged in combat. The American fire became more steady, but it remained disorganized. "It was just a melee," Smith said. "Of course, there was progress being made in that we were killing more of them than they were killing of us. But there was no advance over the land."[37]

Little by little, however, the Marines were able to advance, squirming from one obstacle to the next, until they were able to identify the Japanese positions which their trouble was coming from. Once they knew where the enemy was located, they were able to call in precise naval gun fire, obliterating dugouts a mere 40 or 50 feet away. This lifted morale considerably, and the Marines started moving out. Carl W. Hoffman, the Marine captain, reached the edge of the airfield and dropped into a shell hole, ending up on his back next to another Marine. Then he looked up in a battered palm tree right above him and saw a Japanese staring down. "I literally thought my heart was going to stop. I whispered to the guy next to me, 'There's a Japanese up above us.' He gasped, 'What are we going to do?' I replied, 'I don't know. If I make any move or you make any move he's going to shoot us. Why he hasn't already, I don't know.' We remained frozen for what seemed an eternity and finally figured out this Jap wasn't ever going to move because he was dead."[38]

Once they had established a foothold, the Marines set about reorganizing, forming ad hoc outfits from scattered men that had been separated from their units. One company commander ended up with soldiers from up to 14 different units, including sailors from boats that had somehow ended up on the island.[39] As the Marines prepared for the first night, the beach was becoming crowded with Americans, including large numbers of injured waiting for a chance to be transported to ships offshore. Once it was dark, there was a considerable risk that they would begin shooting among themselves, believing each other to be Japanese, and Crowe walked from position to position admonishing his men: "I don't want anybody firing on the beach tonight. I don't care what it is. I don't care who comes in there over the sea wall. Nobody fires a weapon unless I give the word."[40]

At the same time as Marines set foot on Tarawa, further to the north the Americans were returning to Makin, the atoll which had been the target of a brief diversionary raid the year before in a mission involving President Roosevelt's son. The Soldiers approaching the beach in their landing craft, from the 27th Infantry Division, were in high spirits, talking about souvenirs they planned to take home. "The hell with an ear," one of them joked. "I'm sending home a whole Jap. Preserve it in alcohol and keep it in the living room."[41] The first few minutes of the landing only added to the enthusiasm. "I jumped down from my boat," one of the soldiers later said, "and stood straight up for two or three minutes, waiting for somebody to shoot me. Nobody shot! I saw many other soldiers doing the same thing."[42]

The mood quickly subsided. Landing craft carrying 15 tanks in the second attack wave were stuck on a reef 150 to 200 yards out and had to let down their ramps, leaving it to the vehicles to reach the beach through shallow water by themselves. Only two of the tanks actually made it that far, and once there, both ended up in shell holes. One of the tank commanders later described his predicament: "We went forward about 25 yards and hit a shell hole. We got out of that and went about 15 yards more and hit another. The water was about 7 feet deep and our tank drowned out. The tank immediately filled with smoke after hitting the second shell hole. My driver said the tank was on fire. The crew dismounted right there with great speed... I remained inside the tank. As soon as the crew got out of the tank they were machine gunned from the shore and with more speed they came back inside the tank."[43]

As they proceeded to clear out the atoll, the GIs were targeted by Japanese snipers tied with ropes to the treetops, "Even after they were dead, they didn't fall out, but just hung there, ludicrously and foolishly," a war correspondent remarked.[44] More unnerving to the Americans, most of whom saw battle for the first time, the Japanese resorted to psychological tactics reminiscent of New Georgia. "The Japanese periodically set up a tom-tom-like beating all over the front of the perimeter. Periodically, also, they would yell or sing, apparently under the influence of sake," the official history of the invasion states.[45] The tactics worked, and some of the inexperienced American soldiers began seeing enemies where there was none. In one instance, a panicking soldier ran along the beach yelling, "There's a hundred and fifty Japs in the trees!" setting off a wave of aimless shooting. The shooting was only stopped, with great difficulty, after the soldier admitted he had not actually seen any Japanese.[46]

The battle for Makin lasted for three days, and in the end, the Japanese themselves were driven to desperation. An unnamed Japanese soldier was part of a group that had dispersed into the jungle and was now evading the Americans. "The whereabouts of each platoon leader is unknown. We are surrounded by tanks but will stick it out to the finish," the soldier wrote in his diary. "We did not care about the fire from the machine guns and the guns on the tanks... The tanks could not come close because of the swamp... We know that we are to die... and plan to fight to the beautiful finish."[47]

Offshore, Michael Bak, a young sailor on board the destroyer USS *Franks*, was following the fighting on Makin. He was as green as many of the soldiers on the island, and initially never thought he could actually be hurt in the war. "I always knew I'd be back sooner or later—just a matter of time," he said in a post-war interview. "In six months we'd wipe the Japs off the face of the earth and we'd be back home. I mean, it was a we-couldn't-lose situation. And most of the friends I was with aboard ship had the same feeling. It was just a good, happy feeling. It was like a picnic, going to war, you know, raising the flag."[48]

That changed when on the third day of the Makin operation, he watched the carrier USS *Liscome Bay* be sunk by a Japanese submarine, with the loss of 644 American lives. "It was dark out there, and I remember it was just like putting a candle out. The ball of fire was snuffed out as the ship sank... as soon as the carrier exploded, we went to general quarters. We watched the whole thing. We were just dumbfounded that the ship was blown up."[49] It was the first time he experienced the horrors of war, Bak later explained. "It sort of scared everybody. They just sort of felt, 'My gosh, this is for real.' Everybody wanted to get out to the war zone as quick as possible, myself included. 'Let's get out there and, boy, we'll show them what we can do and how we're going to beat the Japs in a short time.' We found out it wasn't so easy."[50]

On Tarawa, the battle continued, bloody and grueling. The task facing the invasion force was complicated by the fact that part of the island's garrison consisted of Korean laborers with no desire to sacrifice themselves for the Japanese Empire, and they gave themselves up as quickly as they could. On the first evening a group of Koreans, who had surrendered, were taken to the beach. Escaping the attention of the Americans, a Japanese soldier had mixed into the crowd, and after sunset he started crawling around, stabbing wounded soldiers in their sleep. One of the injured men woke up and sounded the alarm. The Japanese soldier was overpowered and killed with knives. No shot was fired, as ordered by Crowe.[51]

The first morning, the Marines were shot at from the sea. It turned out a group of Japanese had swum to the wrecks of the amtracks and boats from the day before and were shooting from inside the hulls. Several rounds of mortar fire were needed to silence them.[52] The entire incident might have left many of the Marines with the impression that the situation was precarious and could go either way, but in reality, victory was within their grasp. Only a few hours on, in heavy fighting around midday on November 21, the battle was decided. Shortly before noon, Colonel David M. Shoup, a regimental commander who had led his men on the island since the day before, reported "Situation ashore uncertain." At 1:45 pm he followed up with a terse "Doing our best." At 5:06 pm he radioed: "Casualties many. Percentage dead not known. Combat efficiency—we are winning."[53]

A day of ugly struggle lay ahead. The second morning, sniper fire killed two Marines on the beach within just seconds of each other. The rifle bullets were traced to a tank turret dug into the sand. The sniper had either been hiding since the invasion or had snuck in during the night. The Marines unleashed a hail of fire against the turret, but to no effect. Then an engineer dropped a satchel charge onto the turret, and a soldier with a flamethrower fired a shot of flame. "The door opens on the side, and the guy comes running out, and he runs right straight towards us, towards the sea wall," a Marine recalled later. "He's all on fire and he falls down in front of us, and his ammunition pouch starts to go off, and there were pieces of metal flying in all directions... Then, of course, they pump him full of bullets."[54]

After Tarawa had been taken, some Marines went souvenir-hunting among the dead Japanese. This was a dangerous activity. One Marine went into a dugout full of Japanese who had killed themselves. He let out a yell and came crawling out again. "What's the matter?" one of his friends asked. He answered, "There's somebody still alive in there." Among the pile of dead bodies there was a wounded Japanese who had played dead, but when the Marine crawled over him, he had let out a noise. The Marines quickly dragged him out and killed him.[55]

Nimitz visited Tarawa only days later, at a time when surviving Japanese soldiers might still emerge from hiding trying to kill unsuspecting Americans. "I have never seen such a desolate spot as Tarawa," he wrote to his wife, comparing it to the moonscapes of the Western Front of the previous war, where battles had been raging for weeks, not just days, as was the case here. The stench from the unburied dead was so penetrating that he was relieved when he could move to another island in the atoll. "Even there," he confided in his letter, "we could still get occasional whiffs when the wind shifted."[56]

Tarawa had been paid for dearly, and a sense of fatigue and weariness descended over many of the participants. Only little by little did it become clear that an important turning point was being reached. Victory was finally within reach, not as something that would happen at some point in the distant future, but as an event that would likely take place within a foreseeable number of years. Smith-Hutton, the Navy intelligence officer, described the situation at the end of 1943 as one that was generally brighter than generally acknowledged. "In the Pacific Theater," he said, "our situation had greatly improved, but I must say we didn't fully realize it at the time."[57] Meanwhile, relations with one of America's most important allies were being transformed, and opinions were changing, not always for the better. At the very moment when Tarawa and Makin were being conquered, attention was focusing in on China.

Two years into the war, the ordinary American could be in little doubt of the importance of the China-Burma-India theater. Known by the abbreviation CBI, it had initially been designed as one of the main staging areas for offensive operations against Japan, and US propaganda gave due emphasis to the Americans serving in the area. Towards the end of 1943, news reporting from that theater continued unabated, even though senior US military leaders had gradually come to the conclusion that the Central Pacific provided the most direct route to Japanese surrender.

Even so, the United States carried on its effort to keep China in the war, not only through the "Hump" supply route, but also by preparing large numbers of Chinese soldiers in India for eventual deployment in Burma and southwest China. The interaction of Chinese and Americans in these camps was a study in cultural differences. Zhou Wenxing, a private Chinese soldier training in India, commented on how radically different leadership philosophies clashed: "Americans were strongly opposed to physical punishment, which was quite commonplace in the Chinese army among veteran squad and platoon leaders, and they would wave their hands saying, 'No good! No good!' However, our officers didn't pay attention to their advice; instead they believed in our ancient doctrine that 'sticks and clubs bring out good men!'"[58]

A cultural divide at quite another level was in evidence when Chiang Kai-shek met with his American and British counterparts, Roosevelt and Churchill, at the Cairo Conference in late November 1943. It was the only time during the war that Chiang sat down with the two leaders, and he did not make a good impression, especially on his British interlocutors. Field Marshal Alan Brooke found him "shrewd and foxy" and thought he had "no grasp of the larger aspects of war, but was determined to get the best of all bargains."[59] The suspicion went both ways. The Chinese, concerned about British intentions after more than a century of imperialist pressure, went so far as to deny British access to aerial photos of Chinese territory, taken by US reconnaissance planes. "It's not hard to appreciate their point of view," Roosevelt said in a private conversation. "They're aware that the British want a look at them for commercial reasons... commercial, postwar reasons."[60]

The US intelligence officer Henri Smith-Hutton was in Cairo, and got an impression of an opportunistic Chinese leader, bent on squeezing as much out of his Allies as possible, at the lowest possible cost. "Chiang Kai-shek seemed to live in a dream world. In considering the problems of using Chinese troops against the Japanese in China and in Burma, the first thing President Chiang Kai-shek did was to demand that the amounts of equipment supplied by us be practically doubled. He wanted the Burma airlifts to be increased even more. For instance, he talked about a ten thousand ton monthly figure for the Burma airlift, which was, of course, fantastic. His emphasis was not on using Chinese troops, but on how much equipment they would need."[61]

To Smith-Hutton, Chiang seemed to spend little time on the practical matters of waging war, a feature he shared with most of his senior officers. "It seemed that he was uninterested in any details, that he didn't have any real knowledge of what had been supplied already and how it had been used. He did promise to consider a counter proposal which President Roosevelt made in regard to the supplies, and then shortly after the conference was finished, he telephoned that no, he couldn't agree to it. At the same time the Chinese staff officers also showed that they had no real grasp of modern military problems. They had little concept of what they would have to do to clear important areas of their country of the Japanese invaders."[62]

Unlike previous conferences, the Cairo meetings focused mainly on the Pacific, and several decisions made at the time had a bearing on how early the Allies could expect to end the war against Japan. The participants discussed an offensive in Burma combined with an amphibious landing on the Andaman Islands in the Bay of Bengal. The United States wanted the offensive partly to secure bases for a long-range bombing campaign against Japan and to secure more active Chinese participation in the war. Churchill was lukewarm, thinking the relief of China would not pay off. He was also concerned that resources spent in northern Burma could be put to better use in the Mediterranean or to retake Singapore and Hong Kong. Chiang, by contrast, agreed to commit forces in southwest China towards Burma.[63]

A draft of the so-called Cairo Declaration stated that "all the territories Japan has stolen from the Chinese, including particularly Manchuria and Formosa, shall be restored to the Republic of China." Churchill hastily added to this draft that the Pescadores, an archipelago in the straits between Formosa and the mainland, should also be added to these territories to be returned by Japan.[64] In separate talks with Soviet leader, Josef Stalin, held later at Tehran without Chiang's attendance, Roosevelt and Churchill also secured a promise that the Soviet Union would enter into the war against Japan following victory over Germany.

One of the consequences of the Soviet pledge to assist in the war against Japan was a lessening in the urgency to build up China as a base of operations against Japan. Therefore, the invasion in Andaman Islands was called off. Roosevelt told Stilwell, his top man in China, that he had been fighting "as stubborn as a mule for four days. But the British just won't do it."[65] To compensate for this, the Hump flights were to be boosted.[66] The Cairo Conference marked the turning point in Allied views of China. The China and Burma front became secondary to the Central Pacific as the theater where the war against Japan was to be decided.[67] Afterwards, even Roosevelt saw China as a less significant ally.

In a speech to parliament at the end of 1943, Premier Tōjō Hideki, who was now concurrently minister of war, admitted that the Japanese Empire was on the defensive: "The counter-offensive of the enemy is becoming more full-fledged, and everywhere severe and violent battles are occurring. With regard to local battles, there are some ups and downs in them, but with the close co-operation of the Navy the general strategic position which has already been gained by us is secure and is not challenged. Our officers and men on the first line, with great ardor and energy, are meeting the counter-offensive… with a single mind they are forging ahead toward the complete achievement of the objects of the war."[68]

In one area only did the Japanese maintain the capacity to seize the initiative and take the war deep into enemy territory: China. In November 1943, the Japanese Army in that theater of war, now a battleground for more than six years, carried out one of its most ambitious offensive operations in several months. It put the

11th Japanese Army, which had fought in Central China since the late 1930s, in charge of driving deep into Hunan province, targeting the major city of Changde. Even though the attack was to take place in the heart of China, its objective was to weaken Allied war efforts in faraway Burma. In other words, the Americans were not alone in viewing China, Burma, and India as an integrated theater of war.

The chief of Japan's China Expeditionary Army outlined the general thrust of the operation: "The 11th Army will advance to the Changde area, attack vigorously and weaken the enemy's will to continue the war. At the same time, the Army will suppress the enemy's diversion of strength to the Burma area and will coordinate with the operation of the Southern Army."[69] A more detailed operations plan drawn up subsequently made clear that possession of Changde was not an objective in itself. The forces advancing towards Changde were instructed to "destroy the enemy everywhere en route." Once Changde had been taken, "the enemy assembling in and counterattacking from the Changde area will be sought out and destroyed." Upon achieving these objectives, the Japanese forces were to withdraw."[70]

After lengthy preparation, on November 23, the China Expeditionary Army ordered the 116th Japanese Division, supported by elements of two other divisions, to capture Changde. The attack began two days later, but the Chinese Army's 57th

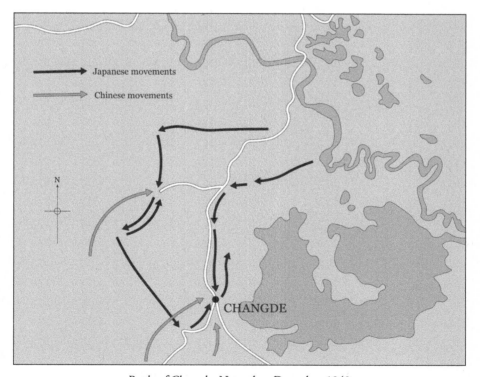

Battle of Changde, November–December, 1943

Division, which occupied the city, put up vigorous resistance, and proved hard to drive out. Other Chinese units fared less well: reinforcements arriving to relieve the division inside Changde were caught in a pincer movement carried out by the two supporting Japanese divisions and suffered severe losses. By early December, Changde was under Japanese control.[71]

At this point, the Imperial Headquarters sent a message to the forces in Changde, inquiring if the city could be held until the following year. A major offensive was being prepared in deep secrecy. Its name was Ichi-Go, and it would become one of the largest Japanese operations of the entire war. The China Expeditionary Army refused, and instead it ordered a general withdrawal from the city on December 9. In their haste to get out, the Japanese piled their dead, along with some severely wounded, into several houses, and burned them down.[72] The pullout was completed four days later. The operation had ended in what looked like defeat. But there was little doubt that this was only temporary. Preparations for the coming offensive went ahead. Japan would be back one last time the following year. The scene was set for a bloody 1944.

Endnotes

Chapter One

1   Arthur J. Marder, *Old Friends, New Enemies: The Royal Navy and the Imperial Japanese Navy. Strategic Illusions, 1936–1941* (Oxford: Clarendon Press, 1981), 369–370.

2   "Prince of Wales and Repulse Were Sunk By Aerial Torpedoes, Survivors Declare," *New York Times*, December 12, 1941:14.

3   John W. Dower, *War Without Mercy: Race and Power in the Pacific War* (New York NY: Pantheon Books, 1986), 101, quoting Cecil Brown, *Suez to Singapore: Cecil Brown's Story* (New York NY: Halcyon House, 1943).

4   Fletcher Pratt, *Sea Power and Today's War* (New York NY: Harrison-Hilton Books, 1939), 178.

5   Adrian Stewart, *The Underrated Enemy: Britain's War with Japan, December 1941–May 1942* (London: William Kimber, 1987), 38.

6   James Leasor, *Singapore: The Battle that Changed the World* (Kelly Bray: House of Stratus, 2001), 102, n15.

7   S. W. Roskill, *The War At Sea 1939–1945, Volume 1: The Defensive* (London: Her Majesty's Stationery Office, 1954), 564.

8   Samuel Eliot Morison, *The Rising Sun in the Pacific 1931–April 1942* [*History of the United States Naval Operations in World War II*, vol. 3] (Boston MA: Little, Brown and Co., 1948), 189.

9   Roskill, *The War At Sea*, 564–565.

10 The air group was named after the city in Korea where it had been formed in 1940, Genzan, today Wonsan.

11 Arthur Nicholson, *Hostages of Fortune: Winston Churchill and the Loss of the Prince of Wales and Repulse* (Stroud: Sutton Publishing, 2005), 131.

12 Ibid., 126.

13 Marder, *Old Friends*, 467.

14 Nicholson, *Hostages of Fortune*, 126–127.

15 Marder, *Old Friends*, 468.

16 "Diary of Battle Observer," *New York Times*, December 12, 1941: 14.

17 Marder, *Old Friends*, 471.

18 "Diary of Battle Observer," *New York Times*, December 12, 1941: 14.

19 Marder, *Old Friends*, 473.

20 Roskill, *The War At Sea*, 566.

21 David Hein, "Vulnerable: HMS Prince of Wales in 1941," *Journal of Military History*, vol. 77 (July 2013): 982–983.

22 John Toland, *The Rising Sun: The Decline and Fall of the Japanese Empire 1936–1945* (New York NY: Random House, 1970), 242.

23 Marder, *Old Friends*, 476–477.

24 Roskill, *The War At Sea*, 567.

25 "Extract from Report of Flight-Lieutenant T. A. Vigors to C.-in-C., Far Eastern Fleet, Dated 11th December, 1941, from R.A.A.F. Station, Sembawang," in BR 1736 (8), 1955, Naval Staff History, Second World War: Battle Summary No. 14, p. 39.

26 Marder, *Old Friends*, 390–391.

27 Winston S. Churchill, *The Second World War, Vol. III: The Grand Alliance* (New York NY: Houghton Mifflin, 1950), 551.

28 Harold Macmillan, *The Blast of War 1939–1945* (London: Macmillan, 1967), 140–141.

29 John Kennedy, *The Business of War: The war narrative of Major-General Sir John Kennedy* (London: Hutchinson & Co., 1957), 184.

30 Ernst Wickert, *Mut und Übermut: Geschichten aus meinem Leben* (Stuttgart: Deutsche Verlags-Anstalt, 1992), 355.

31 Robert Guillain, *Orient Extrême: Une vie en Asie* (Paris: Seuil, 1986), 83.

32 Wickert, *Mut*, 360.

33 Toland, *Rising Sun*, 228.

34 Frank Gibney (ed.), *Sensō: The Japanese Remember the Pacific War* (Armonk NY: M.E. Sharpe, 1995), 125.

35 Samuel Hideo Yamashita, *Daily Life in Wartime Japan* (Lawrence KS: University Press of Kansas, 2015), 17.

36 Haruko Taya Cook and Theodore F. Cook, *Japan at War: An Oral History* (New York NY: The New Press, 1992), 77.

37 Stephen Large, *Emperor Hirohito and Showa Japan: A Political Biography* (London and New York NY: Routledge, 1992), 115.

38 Joseph C. Grew, *Ten Years in Japan* (London: Hammond, Hammond & Co., 1945), 432.

39 Otto D. Tolischus, *Tokyo Record* (New York NY: Reynal and Hitchcock, 1943), 328.

40 Ibid., 333.

41 Testimony by Kido Kōichi, The International Military Tribunal for the Far East (IMTFE), *Transcript of Proceedings*, 31,051–31,053.

42 Jonathan Parshall and Anthony Tully, *Shattered Sword: The Untold Story of the Battle of Midway* (Herndon VA: Potomac Books, 2005), 29.

43 Testimony by Kido Kōichi, IMTFE, *Transcript of Proceedings*, 31,051–31,053.

44 Galeazzo Ciano, *The Ciano Diaries 1939–1943*, edited by Hugh Gibson (Garden City NY: Doubleday and Company, 1946), 416.

45 Gobbels diary entry for December 8, 1941, in Joseph Goebbels, *Die Tagebücher von Joseph Goebbels*, Teil II: Diktate 1941–1945, Band 2: Oktober–Dezember 1941, ed. Elke Fröhlich (Munich: K. G. Saur, 1996) (online edition).

46 Wilhelm Koppen, "Der erschlichene Krieg," *Völkischer Beobachter*, December 9, 1941: 1–2.

47 Gobbels diary entry for December 10, 1941, in Goebbels, *Tagebücher* (online edition).

48 Ian Kershaw, *Fateful Choices: Ten Decisions That Changed the World, 1940–1941* (New York NY: The Penguin Press, 2007), 416–430.

49 Gobbels diary entry for December 13, 1941, in Goebbels, *Tagebücher* (online edition).

50 Gobbels diary entry for December 8, 1941, in Goebbels, *Tagebücher* (online edition).

51 Ugaki, *Fading Victory*, 52.

52 Henry Frei, *Guns of February: Ordinary Japanese Soldiers' View of the Malayan Campaign and the Fall of Singapore, 1941–42* (Singapore: NUS Press, 2004), 42–4.

53 Dower, *War Without Mercy*, 101–102, quoting Brown, *Suez to Singapore*.

54 K. D. Bhargava and K. N. V. Sastri, *Campaigns in South-East Asia 1941–42 [Official History of the Indian Armed Forces in the Second World War 1939–45]* (New Delhi: Ministry of Defence, 1960), 85.

55 Petra Groen, "The Invasion of the Dutch East Indies: An Impressive Japanese Source," *International Journal of Military History and Historiography*, 36 (2016): 53.

56 *Reports of General MacArthur: Japanese Operations in the Southwest Pacific Area*, vol. 2, pt. 1, 33 n14, quoting *Konoye Ayamaro Ko Shuki [Memoirs of Prince Ayamaro Konoe]*, 3.

57 The War History Office of the National Defense College of Japan, *The Invasion of the Dutch East Indies*, ed. and transl. by Willem Remmelink (Leiden: Leiden University Press, 2015), 25–26.

58 Groen, "The Invasion of the Dutch East Indies"

59 H. P. Willmott, *The Barrier and the Javelin: Japanese and Allied Pacific Strategies, February to June 1942* (Annapolis MD: Naval Institute Press, 1983), 14–15.

60 John Donovan, letter to family, accession number 1992.479.004, December 8, 1941, John Donovan Papers, Box 1, National Naval Aviation Museum.

61 Frank O. Hough et al., *Pearl Harbor to Guadalcanal [History of U.S. Marine Corps Operations in World War II, Volume 1]* (Washington DC: United States Marine Corps, 1958), 75–78.

62 George J. McMillin, "Surrender of Guam to the Japanese," *Guam Recorder* (April–September 1972): 11.

63 Paul S. Dull, *A Battle History of the Imperial Japanese Navy (1941–1945)* (Annapolis MD: Naval Institute Press, 1978), 23–24.

64 R. D. Heinl, *The Defense of Wake* (Washington DC: Historical Section, Division of Public Information, U.S. Marine Corps, 1947), 23.

65 Ibid., 25. This is contradicted by Japanese accounts, which state that the *Yubari* did not receive any hits, see Dull, *Navy*, 24.

66 Heinl, *Wake*, 25; Dull, *Navy*, 24.

67 United States Strategic Bombing Survey (Pacific), Naval Analysis Division, *Interrogations of Japanese Officials*, vol. 1 (Washington DC: Government Printing Office, 1946), 55.

68 Dull, *Navy*, 26.

69 Heinl, *Wake*, 43.

70 John Gotte, *Japan Fights for Asia* (New York NY: Harcourt, Brace and Company 1943), 94.

71 Ibid., 94.

72 Heinl, *Wake*, 56.

73 Ibid., 49; Hough, *Pearl Harbor to Guadalcanal*, 98.

74 Heinl, *Wake*, 52.

75 James P. S. Devereux, *The Story of Wake Island* (Philadelphia PA: J. P. Lippincott, 1947), 174.

76 Heinl, *Wake*, 52; Devereux, *Wake Island*, 179.

77 Louis Morton, *Strategy and Command: The First Two Years [U.S. Army in World War II: The War in the Pacific]* (Washington DC: Office of the Chief of Military History, Department of the Army, 1962), 133–134; Heinl, *Wake*, 39; John B. Lundstrom, *Black Shoe Carrier Admiral: Frank Jack Fletcher at Coral Sea, Midway, and Guadalcanal* (Annapolis MD: Naval Institute Press, 2006), 41.

78 Heinl, *Wake*, 39; Lundstrom, *Black Shoe Carrier Admiral*, 42–47.

Chapter Two

1 Shimada Kōichi, "The Opening Air Offensive Against the Philippines," in *The Japanese Navy in World War Two*, ed. David C. Evans (Annapolis MD: Naval Institute Press, 1986), 99.

2 Louis Morton, *Fall of the Philippines [United States Army in World War II: The War in the Pacific]* (Washington DC: Office of the Chief of Military History, Department of the Army, 1953), 14.

3 Richard Fuller, *Shōkan: Hirohito's Samurai* (London: Arms and Armor, 1992), 103.

4 Morton, *Fall of the Philippines*, 103–105.

5   Ibid., 108.
6   Shimada, "The Opening Air Offensive Against the Philippines," 95.
7   Jonathan M. Wainwright, *General Wainwright's Story: The Account of Four Years of Humiliating Defeat, Surrender, and Captivity* (Garden City NY: Doubleday, 1946), 27.
8   Morton, *Fall of the Philippines*, 107.
9   Wainwright, *General Wainwright's Story*, 27.
10 Morton, *Fall of the Philippines*, 110.
11 Ibid., 123–132.
12 Thomas Dooley, "The First U.S. Tank Action in WWII," *Armor* (July–August 1983): 12; Morton, *Fall of the Philippines*, 134.
13 Benjamin R. Morin, "My Story." http://heurisko.org/uncle.html
14 Morton, *Fall of the Philippines*, 207–208.
15 Interview with William H. Gentry, July 31, 1985 Nunn Center for Oral History, University of Kentucky.
16 Ibid.
17 Morton, *Fall of the Philippines*, 129–144.
18 D. Clayton James, *Years of MacArthur* (Boston MA: Houghton Mifflin Company, 1970–1985), vol. 2, 26–27.
19 Cecil S. King, Oral History, US Naval Institute Oral History Program, 179–180.
20 Robert W. Levering, *Horror Trek: A True Story of Bataan, the Death March and Three and One-Half Years in Japanese Prison Camps* (Dayton OH: Hortsman Printing Co., 1948), 40.
21 King, Oral History, 188.
22 F. Spencer Chapman, *The Jungle is Neutral* (London: Chatto and Windus, 1950), 29.
23 Stanley Woodburn Kirby, *The Loss of Singapore [History of the Second World War. United Kingdom Military Series. The War against Japan, vol. 1]* (London: HMSO, 1957), 164.
24 Tsuji Masanobu, *Singapore: 1941–1942: The Japanese Version of the Malayan Campaign of World War II* (Singapore: Oxford University Press, 1988), 129.
25 Fuller, *Shōkan*, 236–238.
26 Ron Magarry, *The Battalion Story: 2/26th Infantry Battalion, 8th Division, AIF* (Jindalee, Queensland: Magarry, 1995), 56.
27 Leslie Gordon Gaffney interviewed by Caroline Gaden about his service with 8th Division Headquarters in Malaya and Singapore, and his experiences as a prisoner of war of the Japanese, 1941–45, oral history, Australian War Memorial, accession number S01738.
28 Kaushik Roy, *Sepoys against the Rising Sun: The Indian Army in Far East and South-East Asia, 1941–45* (Leiden: Brill, 2016), 84.
29 Ibid., 69.
30 Tsuji, *Singapore*, 5.
31 Ibid., 6.
32 Lionel Wigmore, *The Japanese Thrust [Australia in the War of 1939–1945, Series 1 (Army), vol. 4]* (Canberra: Australian War Memorial, 1957), 167.
33 Arthur Percival, "Operations of Malaya Command, From 8th December, 1941 to 15th February, 1942," *Second Supplement to the London Gazette*, January 27, 1948: 12
34 Cecil Brown, "Malay Jungle War," *Life*, January 12, 1942; reprinted in *Reporting World War II, Part One: American Journalism 1938–1944* (New York NY: Library of America, 1995), 280.
35 "H. P. Willmott, *Empires in the Balance: Japanese and Allied Pacific Strategies to April 1942* (Annapolis MD: Naval Institute Press, 1989), 172.
36 Kirby, *Singapore*, 230; Wigmore, *Thrust*, 161.
37 Jonathan Moffatt and Audrey Holmes McCormick, *Moon over Malaya: A Tale of Argylls and Marines* (Cheltenham: The History Press, 2003), 95.

38 Christopher Shores and Brian Cull with Izawa Yasuho, *Bloody Shambles* (London: Grub Street, 1992), 130 and 132.

39 Peter Elphick, "Cover-ups and the Singapore Traitor Affair," Fall of Singapore 60th Anniversary Conference, November 2001. Published online by Four Corners, Australian Broadcasting Corporation, 2002.

40 Wong Chi Man and Tsoi Yiu Lun, *Eastern Fortress: A Military History of Hong Kong, 1840–1970* (Hong Kong: Hong Kong University Press, 2014), 73.

41 Ibid., 83–84 and 94.

42 Ibid., 122–123.

43 Robert Brooke-Popham, "Operations in the Far East, From 17th October, 1940 to 27th December, 1941," *Supplement to the London Gazette*, January 22, 1948: 541.

44 C. P. Stacey, *Six Years of War: The Army in Canada, Britain and the Pacific [Official History of the Canadian Army in the Second World War, vol. 1]* (Ottawa: Queen's Printer, 1955), 465.

45 Ibid., 470.

46 Tim Carew, *The Fall of Hong Kong* (London: Blond, 1961), 16.

47 Roy, *Sepoys*, 54-55.

48 C. M. Maltby, "Operations in Hong Kong from 8th to 25th December, 1941," *Supplement to the London Gazette*, January 27, 1948: 700.

49 Mary Monro, *Stranger In My Heart* (London: Unbound, 2018), 24–25.

50 Maltby, "Operations," 701.

51 Charles G. Roland, "Massacre and Rape in Hong Kong: Two Case Studies Involving Medical Personnel and Patients," *Journal of Contemporary History*, vol. 32, no. 1 (January 1997): 47.

52 Roy, *Sepoys*, 62.

53 Stacey, *Six Years*, 473.

54 Maltby, "Operations," 715.

55 Stacey, *Six Years*, 482.

56 Basil Collier, *War in the Far East 1941–1945: A Military History* (London: Heinemann, 1969), 154.

57 Kirby, *Singapore*, 147.

58 Ibid., 146.

59 Maltby, "Operations," 719.

60 Wenzell Brown, *Hong Kong Aftermath* (New York NY: Smith & Durrell, 1943), 11–12.

61 Ibid., 12.

62 Churchill, *Grand Alliance*, 634.

63 Maltby, "Operations," 724.

64 Ibid., 714.

65 Stacey, *Six Years*, 481.

66 Roland, "Massacre," 53.

67 Ibid., 54.

68 Roland, "Massacre," 48.

Chapter Three

1 Harrison Foreman, untitled report, *New York Times*, January 15, 1942, 5.

2 Theodore H. White and Annalee Jacoby, *Thunder out of China* (New York NY: William Sloane Associates, 1946), 181.

3 Lin Yutang, *The Vigil of a Nation* (New York NY: The John Day, 1945), 63.

4 Guo Rugui, *Zhongguo Kangri Zhanzheng zhengmian zhanchang zuozhanji [China's War of Resistance against Japan: An Account of Frontline Battles]* (Nanjing: Jiangsu Renmin Chubanshe, 2006), vol. 2, 1099.

5   *Army Operations in China December 1941–December 1943* [Japanese Monograph no. 71] (Tokyo: Headquarters USAFFE, 1956), 54.
6   Hsu Long-hsuen and Chang Ming-kai, *History of the Sino-Japanese War (1937–1945)* (Taipei: Chung Wu Publishing, 1971), 374.
7   Guo, *Zhongguo*, 1106–1107.
8   Edward L. Dreyer, *China at War 1901–1949* (London and New York NY: Longman, 1995), 277; Hsu and Chang, *Sino-Japanese War* 362–375.
9   Dreyer, China at War, 243–244, 277.
10 *Army Operations in China December 1941–December 1943*, 71.
11 Hsu and Chang, *Sino-Japanese War*, 374.
12 Guo, *Zhongguo*, vol. 2, 1107.
13 Foreman, *New York Times*, January 15, 1942, 5.
14 Yang Zhenghua, "Changsha baoweizhan shimo" ["The Defense of Changsha from Beginning to End"] in *Hunan Sida Huizhan: Yuan Guomindang jiangling Kangri Zhanzheng qinliji [The Four Big Battles of Hunan: Personal Recollections from the War of Resistance against Japan by Former Nationalist Commanders]* (Beijing: Zhongguo Wenshi Chubanshe, 1995), 236.
15 Guo, *Zhongguo*, 1098.
16 *Army Operations in China December 1941–December 1943*, 53.
17 David Tucker, "Labor Policy and the Construction Industry in Manchukuo: Systems of Recruitment, Management, and Control," in *Asian Labor in the Wartime Japanese Empire: Unknown Histories,* ed. Paul H. Kratoska (Armonk NY: Sharpe, 2005), 34.
18 Brown, *Hong Kong Aftermath*, 11.
19 Iriye Akira, *Power and Culture: The Japanese-American War 1941–1945* (Cambridge MA: Harvard University Press, 1981), 52.
20 Owen Lattimore, *China Memoirs: Chiang Kai-shek and the War Against Japan* (Tokyo: University of Tokyo Press, 1990), 164.
21 Winston S. Churchill, *The Second World War, Vol. IV: The Hinge of Fate* (New York NY: Houghton Mifflin, 1950), 134.
22 Churchill, *Hinge*, 133.
23 Grace Person Hayes, *The History of the Joint Chiefs of Staff in World War II: The War Against Japan* (Annapolis MD: Naval Institute Press, 1982), 74.
24 Claire Lee Chennault, *Way of a Fighter* (New York NY: G.P. Putnam's Sons, 1949), 127–128.
25 Chennault cited later rumors that in fact only one Japanese bomber had returned from the mission. Chennault, *Way of a Fighter*, 130.
26 Interview with Brig Gen David Lee "Tex" Hill, September 20, 2003. Admiral Nimitz Historic Site, National Museum of the Pacific War, 7.
27 Bill Yenne, *When Tigers Ruled the Sky: The Flying Tigers American Outlaw Pilots over China in World War II* (New York NY: Berkley Caliber, 2016), 174.
28 Forrest C. Pogue, *George C. Marshall: Ordeal and Hope 1939–1942* (New York NY: Viking, 1966), 355–357.
29 Joseph W. Stilwell, *The Stilwell Papers* (New York NY: William Sloane Associates, 1948), 25–26. This conversation predates a more frequently cited conversation on January 23 with George C. Marshall in which Stilwell made the same reply upon learning that he was going to China. See Clayton R. Newell, *Burma, 1942* (Washington DC: United States Army Center of Military History, 1995), 10–11; and Charles F. Romanus and Riley Sunderland, *Stilwell's Mission to China [United States Army in World War II: China-Burma-India Theater]* (Washington DC: United States Army Center of Military History, 1953), 72–73.
30 Hayes, *The History of the Joint Chiefs of Staff in World War II*, 34–35.
31 Ibid., 35; Pogue, *Ordeal and Hope*, 244.

32 Hayes, *The History of the Joint Chiefs of Staff in World War II*, 35.

33 Margaret Utinsky, *"Miss U"* (San Antonio TX: The Naylor Company, 1948), 1.

34 Morton, *Fall of the Philippines*, 236.

35 Wainwright, *Wainwright's Story*, 46.

36 Morton, *Fall of the Philippines*, 261–262.

37 Edwin Price Ramsey and Stephen J. Rivele, *Lieutenant Ramsey's War: From Horse Soldier to Guerrilla Commander* (New York NY: Knightsbridge, 1990), 66.

38 Geoffry Perret, *Old Soldiers Never Die* (Avon MA: Adams Media, 1996), 271.

39 Carol Morris Petillo, *Douglas MacArthur: The Philippine Years* (Bloomington IN: Indiana University Press, 1981), 205; see also Carol Morris Petillo, "Douglas MacArthur and Manuel Quezon: A Note on an Imperial Bond," *Pacific Historical Review*, vol. 48, no. 1 (February 1979): 107–117.

40 Perret, *Old Soldiers Never Die*, 271.

41 Kennedy, *Business*, 185.

42 Hayes, *The History of the Joint Chiefs of Staff in World War II*, 46.

43 John Connell, *Wavell: Supreme Commander 1941–1943* (London: Collins, 1969), 69.

44 Churchill, *Alliance*, 607.

45 Maurice Matloff and Edwin M. Snell, *Strategic Planning for Coalition Warfare 1941–1942 [United States Army in World War II: The War Department]* (Washington DC: Office of the Chief of Military History, Department of the Army, 1953), 123.

46 Ibid., 122.

47 Ibid., 45.

48 Connell, *Wavell*, 71.

49 Ibid., 84.

50 Ibid., 85.

51 Percival, "Operations of Malaya Command," 1276.

52 *Japanese Night Combat* (Tokyo: Eighth United States Army, Military History Section, 1955), 123.

53 From the oral history interview of Winston Arthur Reginald Mathews (accession no. 002685/ reel no. 5), Oral History Centre, National Archives of Singapore.

54 Ibid.

55 F. Tillman Durdin, "Australian Army Shows Democracy," *The New York Times*, January 20, 1942: 3.

56 F. Spencer Chapman, *The Jungle is Neutral* (London: Chatto and Windus, 1950), 27–28.

57 War History Office of the National Defense College of Japan, *Invasion of the Dutch East Indies*, 6.

58 Ibid., 177.

59 Ibid.

60 Peter Williams, *The Kokoda Campaign 1942: Myth and Reality* (Cambridge: Cambridge University Press, 2012), 17.

61 Wigmore, *Thrust*, 403.

62 Ibid., 403–410.

63 War History Office of the National Defense College of Japan, *Invasion of the Dutch East Indies*, 132–133.

64 Ibid., 151–152.

65 Clay Blair Jr. *Silent Victory: The U.S. Submarine War against Japan.* (Philadelphia PA and New York NY: J. B. Lippincott, 1975), pp. 117–119. Mike Ostlund. *Find 'Em, Chase 'Em, Sink 'Em: The Mysterious Loss of the WWII Submarine USS Gudgeon.* (Guilford CT: Lyons Press, 2012).

66 Joel Ira Holwitt, "'Execute Against Japan': Freedom-of-the-Seas, the U.S. Navy, Fleet Submarines, and the U.S. Decision to Conduct Unrestricted Warfare, 1919–1941" (PhD diss., Ohio State University, 2005), 215–220.

67 Mark P. Parillo, *The Japanese Merchant Marine in World War II*. (Annapolis MD: Naval Institute Press, 1993), p. 97.

68 David C. Evans and Mark R. Peattie. *Kaigun: Strategy, Tactics and Technology of the Imperial Japanese Navy 1887–1941* (Annapolis MD: Naval Institute Press, 1997), p. 434.

69 Theodore Roscoe, *United States Submarine Operations in World War II*. (Annapolis MD: Naval Institute Press, 1949), p. 12.

70 Evans and Peattie, *Kaigun*, 437–438.

71 Blair, *Silent Victory*, 92.

Chapter Four

1 Louis Allen, *Burma: The Longest War 1941–45* (London: Orion Publishing, 2000), 32.

2 Connell, *Wavell: Supreme Commander*, 133.

3 William Slim, *Defeat into Victory* (London: Cassell & Co., 1956), 13

4 Interview with Neville Hogan, Imperial War Museum (IWM SR 12342).

5 Slim, *Defeat into Victory*, 13

6 Churchill, *Hinge*, 146–148.

7 Ibid.

8 Allen, *Burma*, 57.

9 Slim, *Defeat into Victory*, 29.

10 Tony Mains, *Retreat from Burma* (London: W. Foulsham & Co., 1973), 63.

11 Slim, *Defeat into Victory*, 30.

12 Guido Samarani, "Shaping the Future of Asia: Chiang Kai-shek, Nehru and China-India Relations During the Second World War Period," *Working papers in contemporary Asian studies*, No. 11, Centre for East and South-East Asian Studies, Lund University (2005), 13.

13 Message from Churchill to Chiang, February 12, 1942. CHAR 20/70 1 bound file (136 folios) Official: Prime Minister: Personal telegrams, The Churchill Archive.

14 "Discussions with Chiang Kai-shek and Wife," in *The Collected Works of Mahatma Gandhi* (Ahmedabad: Ministry of Information and Broadcasting, 1979), vol. 75, 333–334; Xiao Ruping, "Kangzhan shiqi Jiang Jieshi fangwen Yindu de zai kaocha" ["A Reassessment of Chiang Kai-shek's visit to India during the War of Resistance"], *Zhejiang Daxue Xuebao*, vol. 48, no. 5 (September 2018): 89.

15 "Letter to Walabhbhai Patel," February 25, 1942, in *The Collected Works of Mahatma Gandhi*, vol, 75, 359.

16 S. P. Shukla, "Chiang Kai Shek in India: An episode in the Sino-Indian relationship," *Proceedings of the Indian History Congress*, vol. 36 (1975): 449.

17 "Chinese Spokesman Comments," *New York Times*, February 23, 1942: 2.

18 Stilwell, *Papers*, 48.

19 Hayes, *History of the Joint Chiefs of Staff*, 81.

20 Pogue, *Ordeal and Hope*, 256.

21 Stilwell, *Papers*, 77.

22 Ibid., 68.

23 Ibid., 66.

24 Hans van de Ven, *War and Nationalism in China 1925–1945* (London: RoutledgeCurzon, 2003), 33.

25 Mains, *Retreat*, 65.

26 Ibid., 64–65.

27 Ernest B. Miller, *Bataan Uncensored* (Long Prairie MN: Hart Publications, 1949), 174–175.

28 Ibid., 72.
29 Petillo, *Philippine Years*, 206.
30 Forrest C. Pogue, *George C. Marshall: Ordeal and Hope 1939–1942* (New York NY: Viking Press, 1966), 246.
31 Robert H. Ferrell (ed.), *The Eisenhower Diaries* (New York NY: W. W. Norton, 1981), 49.
32 Morton, *Fall of the Philippines*, 545.
33 Ibid., 542–545.
34 Ibid., 542.
35 Ferrell (ed.), *Eisenhower Diaries*, 49.
36 Pogue, *Ordeal and Hope*, 248–251.
37 Alistair Urquhart, *The Forgotten Highlander* (London: Abacus, 2010), 90.
38 Arthur Bryant, *The Turn of the Tide 1939–1943: A Study based on the Diaries and Autobiographical Notes of Field Marshal The Viscount Alanbrooke* (London: Collins, 1957), 295.
39 Bryant, *Turn*, 304.
40 Tsuji, *Singapore*, 212–213.
41 Ibid., 216.
42 Urquhart, *Highlander*, 94.
43 "Bullwinkel obituary," *Daily Telegraph*, July 17, 2000.
44 *Canberra Times*, September 18, 1945.
45 Elizabeth Yu, Oral History, Singapore National Archives, Accession no. 000597, reel no. 1.
46 Kevin Blackburn, "The Collective Memory of the Sook Ching Massacre and the Creation of the Civilian War Memorial of Singapore," *Journal of the Malaysian Branch of the Royal Asiatic Society*, vol. 73, no. 2 (2000): 74.
47 Ibid., 74–75.
48 Kennedy, *Business*, 198.
49 Hayes, *Joint Chiefs*, 45.
50 War History Office of the National Defense College of Japan, *Invasion of the Dutch East Indies*, 269.
51 Ibid., 22–23.
52 Ibid., 183–184.
53 Shores, Cull and Izawa, *Bloody Shambles*, vol. 2, 94.
54 Ibid., 102.
55 Ibid., 104.
56 Ibid., 105–106.
57 Morison, *Rising Sun*, 292.
58 G. Hermon Gill, *The Royal Australian Navy 1939–1942 [Australia in the War of 1939–1945, Series 2 (Navy), vol. 1]* (Canberra: Australian War Memorial, 1957), 593.
59 Steven Bullard, "Japanese Strategy and Intentions Toward Australia," in *Australia 1942: In the Shadow of War*, ed. Peter J. Dean (Port Melbourne: Cambridge University Press, 2013), 133–137.
60 United States Strategic Bombing Survey (Pacific), Naval Analysis Division, *Interrogations of Japanese Officials*, vol. 1 (Washington DC: Government Printing Office, 1946), 70.
61 Richard J. Samuels, *Special Duty: A History of the Japanese Intelligence Community* (Ithaca NY: Cornell University Press, 2019), 67.
62 Elliott R. Thorpe, *East Wind, Rain* (Boston MA: Gambit, 1969), 109.
63 Donald M. Kehn, *In the Highest Degree Tragic: The Sacrifice of the U.S. Asiatic Fleet in the East Indies during World War II* (Lincoln NE: Potomac Books, 2017), 295.
64 Hara Tameichi, *Japanese Destroyer Captain* (Annapolis MD: Naval Institute Press, 2011), 72–73.
65 T. J. Cain and A. V. Sellwood, *H. M. S. Electra* (London: Frederick Muller, 1959), 234.

66 Cook and Cook, *Japan at War*, 89.

67 L. de Jong, *Het Koninkrijk der Nederlanden in de Tweede Wereldoorlog [The Kingdom Of The Netherlands In The Second World War]* (The Hague: Staatsuitgeverij), vol. 11a, 2nd vol., p. 947.

68 Johannes Vandenbroek, "A Teacher Turned Soldier and Imprisoned," in *The Defining Years of the Dutch East Indies, 1942–1949: Survivors' Accounts of Japanese Invasion and Enslavement of Europeans and the Revolution That Created Free Indonesia*, ed. Jan A. Krancher (Jefferson NC and London: MacFarland & Co., 1996), 67.

69 Barend A. van Nooten, "The Mouse-Deer and the Tiger," in *The Defining Years of the Dutch East Indies, 1942–1949: Survivors' Accounts of Japanese Invasion and Enslavement of Europeans and the Revolution That Created Free Indonesia*, ed. Jan A. Krancher (Jefferson NC and London: MacFarland & Co., 1996), 107–109.

70 Walter D. Edmonds, *They Fought With What They Had* (Boston MA: Little, Brown and Company, 1951), 437.

71 L. de Jong, *Het Koninkrijk der Nederlanden in de Tweede Wereldoorlog. Nederlands-Indië I (2e band)* (Leiden: Martinus Nijhof, 1984), 965.

72 Ohmae Toshikazu, "Japanese Operations in the Indian Ocean," in *The Japanese Navy in World War Two*, ed. David C. Evans (Annapolis MD: Naval Institute Press, 1986), 108.

73 Stanley Woodburn Kirby, *India's Most Dangerous Hour [History of the Second World War. United Kingdom Military Series. The War against Japan, vol. 2]* (London: Her Majesty's Stationery Office, 1958), 119–120.

74 Abe Zenji, *The Emperor's Sea Eagle* (Honolulu HI: Arizona Memorial Museum Association, 2006), 88–91.

75 Willmott, *Empires*, 438.

76 Edwin P. Hoyt, *Hirohito: The Emperor and the Man* (Westport CT: Praeger Publishers, 1992), 131–132; Stephen S. Large, *Hirohito*, 115.

77 *IMTFE*, 31,052-31,057.

78 Kawamura Noriko, *Emperor Hirohito and the Pacific War* (Seattle WA: University of Washington Press, 2015), 112.

79 Large, *Hirohito*, 117.

80 Edward J. Drea, *In the Service of the Emperor: Essays on the Imperial Japanese Army* (Lincoln NE: University of Nebraska Press, 1998), 33–35.

Chapter Five

1   Jacob Eierman, "I Helped Bomb Japan," in *Popular Science* (July 1943): 66.

2   Craig L. Symonds, *The Battle of Midway* (Oxford: Oxford University Press, 2011), 117.

3   James H. "Jimmy" Doolittle with Carroll V. Glines, *I Could Never Be So Lucky Again* (New York NY: Bantam Books, 1991), 1–2.

4   Kramer J. Rohfleisch, "Drawing the Battle Line in the Pacific," in Wesley Frank Craven and James Lea Cate (eds.), *Plans and Early Operations, January 1939 to August 1942 [The Army Air Forces in World War II]* (Chicago IL: University of Chicago Press, 1948), 439.

5   H. P. Willmott, *Barrier and the Javelin*, 174.

6   Joe Dwinell, "Heroes of a Generation: Lynnfield Vet Recalls Daring Doolittle Raid," *Boston Herald*, June 29, 2019.

7   Ted W. Lawson, *Thirty Seconds Over Tokyo* (New York NY: Random House, 1943), 66.

8   Lawson, *Thirty Seconds*, 66.

9   Eierman, "I Helped," 67–68.

10 Robert A. Fearey, "My Year with Ambassador Joseph C. Grew, 1941–1942: A Personal Account," *The Journal of American-East Asian Relations*, vol. 1, no. 1 (spring 1992): 115.

11 Grew, *Ten Years*, 453.

12 Hayes, *History of the Joint Chiefs of Staff*, 127.

13 Rohfleisch, "Drawing the Battle Line," 444.

14 "A Blow at Japan's Heart," *New York Times*, April 20, 1942: 20.

15 Fearey, "My Year," 115.

16 Ugaki, *Fading Victory*, 113.

17 Abe, *Sea Eagle*, 94.

18 Hayes, *History of the Joint Chiefs of Staff*, 127.

19 James M. Scott, *Target Tokyo: Jimmy Doolittle and the Raid that Avenged Pearl Harbor* (New York NY: W. W. Norton 2015), 382.

20 Ibid.

21 Ibid.

22 Slim, *Defeat into Victory*, 65.

23 Ibid.

24 White (ed.), *Stilwell Papers*, 115–116.

25 Gordon S. Seagrave, *Burma Surgeon* (London: Victor Gollancz, 1944), 107.

26 Shi Linxian, "Personal Experience," in Deng Xian (ed.), *Under the Same Army Flag* (Beijing: China Intercontinental Press, 2005), 151–152.

27 Mains, *Retreat*, 92.

28 Ibid., 87.

29 Interview with Pearl "Prue" Brewis, Imperial War Museum (IWM SR 22741).

30 Hugh Tinker, "A Forgotten Long March: The Indian Exodus from Burma, 1942," *Journal of Southeast Asian Studies*, vol. 6, no. 1 (March 1975): 6.

31 Ibid., 13–14.

32 Slim, *Defeat into Victory*, 105.

33 Kirby, *India's Most Dangerous Hour*, 210.

34 Headquarters, American Army Forces, China, Burma and India, "The Campaign in Burma," Stilwell Papers, quoted in M. S. Venkataramani and B. K. Shrivastava, *Quit India: The American Response to the 1942 Struggle* (New Delhi: Vikas Publishing House, 1979), 178–179.

35 *The Years of MacArthur*, vol. 2, 36–37.

36 Melvin H. McCoy and S. M. Mellnik, with Welbourn Kelly, *Ten Escape from Tojo* (New York NY: Farrar & Rinehart, 1944), 41–42.

37 Miller, *Bataan Uncensored*, 225.

38 Ibid.

39 James, *Years of MacArthur*, vol. 2, 150.

40 Morton, *Fall of the Philippines*, 538.

41 Clark Lee, *They Call It Pacific: An Eyewitness Story of Our War Against Japan from Bataan to the Solomons* (New York NY: The Viking Press, 1943), 169.

42 Uno Kazumaro, *Corregidor: Island of Delusion* (Shanghai: Mercury Press, 1942).

43 Wainwright, *General Wainwright's Story*, 122.

44 John Prados, *Combined Fleet Decoded: The Secret History of American Intelligence and the Japanese Navy in World War II* (New York NY: Random House, 1995), 301.

45 Prados, *Combined Fleet*, 301.

46 Shindo Hiroyuki, "The Japanese Army's 'Unplanned' South Pacific Campaign," in *Australia 1942: In the Shadow of War*, ed. Peter J. Dean (Port Melbourne: Cambridge University Press, 2013), 112–113

47 Hayes, *History of the Joint Chiefs of Staff*, 129.

48 Edwin T. Layton, Oral History, US Naval Institute Oral History Program, 88.

49 E. B. Potter, *Nimitz* (Annapolis MD: Naval Institute Press,1976), 67.

50 Lundstrom, *Black Shoe Carrier Admiral*, 132.

51 Dull, *Imperial Japanese Navy*, 121.

52 Ibid., 121–122.

53 CSM R. J. Dickens, USN, "Personal observations of Sims #409 disaster," May 13, 1942, included in USS Neosho (AO-23) War Diary, 1 April 1942–7 May 1942, Record Group 38, National Archives and Records Administration, College Park, MD.

54 Stuart D. Ludlum, *They Turned the War Around at Coral Sea and Midway: Going to War with Yorktown's Air Group Five* (Bennington VT: Merriam Press, 2006), 119.

55 Symonds, *Midway*, 176.

56 Paul D. Stroop, Oral History, US Naval Institute Oral History Program, 93–94.

57 Dull, *Imperial Japanese Navy*, 125.

58 Ugaki, *Fading Victory*, 353–354.

59 Paul D. Stroop, Oral History, Naval Institute, 93.

60 United States Strategic Bombing Survey, *Interrogations of Japanese Officials*, vol. 1 (Washington DC: US Government Printing Office, 1946), 54.

61 Stroop, Oral History, 94.

62 Ibid., 97.

63 Ludlum, *They Turned the War Around*, 127.

64 Ibid., 131.

65 Office of Naval Intelligence, *Combat Report Coral Sea* (Washington DC: Navy Department, 1943), 22.

66 United States Strategic Bombing Survey, *Interrogations of Japanese Officials*, vol. 1 (Washington DC: US Government Printing Office, 1946), 54.

67 Stroop, Oral History, 101.

68 Okumiya Masatake and Horikoshi Jiro with Martin Caidin, *Zero! The Story of Japan's Air War in the Pacific 1941-45* (New York NY: Ballantine Books, 1957), 104–105.

69 Stroop, Oral History, 103.

70 Noel A. M. Gayler, Oral History, Naval Institute Oral History Program, 109.

71 Stroop, Oral History, 105.

72 Ibid., 107.

73 Ibid., 108.

74 Gayler, Oral History, 110.

75 Hayes, *History of the Joint Chiefs of Staff in World War II*, 128–129.

76 Prados, *Combined Fleet*, 319.

77 Ibid., 318–319.

78 Layton, *Oral History*, 79.

79 Ibid., 123.

80 Potter, *Nimitz*, 83.

81 United States Strategic Bombing Survey, *Interrogations of Japanese Officials*, vol. 1 (Washington DC: US Government Printing Office, 1946), 250.

82 Parshall and Tully, *Shattered Sword*, 36–37.

83 Lundstrom, *Black Shoe Carrier Admiral*, 238.

84 Recollections of Lieutenant George Gay, USNR, Naval History and Heritage Command.

85 Ibid.

86 James S. Gray, "Decision at Midway," accessed at The Battle of Midway Roundtable, http://www.midway42.org.

87 United States Strategic Bombing Survey, *Interrogations of Japanese Officials*, vol. 1 (Washington DC: US Government Printing Office, 1946), 6.

88 Ibid., 142.

89 E. T. Wooldridge (ed.), *Carrier Warfare in the Pacific: An Oral History Collection* (Washington DC: Smithsonian Institution Press, 1993), 57.
90 Ludlum, *They Turned the War Around*, 131.
91 Gayler, Oral History, 108.
92 Since the battle itself there has been a widely repeated myth that the American dive bombers hit at the exact moment when the Japanese planes were on the decks of all four Japanese carriers, refueling and all but ready to take off. This adds an extra dramatic element to the story, as well as a note of tragedy, if viewed from the Japanese angle. According to this version, if only the Japanese planes had been given five more minutes to take off, disaster could have been prevented. However, a careful analysis of the available sources has led the foremost historians of the battle to the conclusion that the decks of the carriers were almost empty at the time of the attack. This does not diminish the importance of the victory at Midway, but it undermines the idea that the result was in the balance, and the US win came at the tiniest of margins. Parshall and Tully, *Shattered Sword*, 229–231. The concept of the "fateful five minutes" can be traced partly to a flawed account given by the former Japanese aviator Fuchida Mitsuo in the postwar work he co-authored with Okumiya Masatake, *Midway: The Battle that Doomed Japan* (Annapolis MD: Naval Institute Press, 1955) 155–156.
93 Gibney (ed.), *Sensō*, 130.
94 John Muse Worthington, Oral History, Naval Institute Oral History Program, 179.
95 Recollections of the Battle of Midway by LT Joseph P. Pollard, MC, USN, Naval History and Heritage Command.
96 Parshall and Tully, *Shattered Sword*, 352.
97 Thomas B. Buell, *The Quiet Warrior: A Biography of Admiral Raymond A. Spruance* (Annapolis MD: Naval Institute Press, 1987), 163.
98 Large, *Hirohito*, 117.
99 Kawamura, *Hirohito*, 116.
100 Ibid., 112.
101 United States Strategic Bombing Survey, *Interrogations of Japanese Officials, vol. 1* (Washington DC: US Government Printing Office, 1946), 25.
102 Ibid., 269.

Chapter Six

1   Jon T. Hoffmann, *From Makin to Bougainville: Marine Raiders in the Pacific War* (Washington DC: United States Marine Corps, 1995), 6–9.
2   H. P. Willmott, *The Second World War in the Far East* (London: Cassell, 1999), 84.
3   Hayes, *The History of the Joint Chiefs of Staff in World War II*, 146.
4   Ferrell, *Eisenhower Diaries*, 50.
5   Ronald H. Spector. *Eagle Against the Sun: The American War with Japan* (New York NY: Vintage Books, 1985), 185.
6   Hayes, *The History of the Joint Chiefs of Staff in World War II*, 148.
7   Henry W. Buse, Oral History, USMC, 39.
8   Edwin Pollock, Oral History, USMC, 118.
9   John Miller Jr. *Guadalcanal: The First Offensive [United States Army in World War II: The War in the Pacific]* (Washington DC: Center of Military History, 1995), 59–60.
10 Stanley Coleman Jersey, *Hell's Islands: The Untold Story of Guadalcanal* (College Station TX: Texas A&M University Press, 2008), 114.

11 Ohmae Toshikazu, "The Battle of Savo Island," in David C. Evans (ed.), *The Japanese Navy in World War Two: In the Words of Former Japanese Naval Officers* (Annapolis MD: Naval Institute Press), 223.

12 Jersey, *Hell's Islands*, 114.

13 Robert Leckie, *Helmet for My Pillow* (New York NY: Bantam, 2010), 59.

14 Justice M. Chambers, Oral History, USMC, 321.

15 Lewis J. Fields, Oral History, USMC, 75.

16 Ibid., 77.

17 Chambers, Oral History, 305.

18 Ibid., 312–313.

19 Theodore R. Cummings Collection (AFC/2001/001/78232), Veterans History Project, American Folklife Center, Library of Congress.

20 Miller, *First Offensive*, 65.

21 Cummings Collection.

22 Ohmae, "Savo Island," 236.

23 Bruce M. Petty, *Voices from the Pacific War: Bluejackets Remember* (Annapolis MD: Naval Institute Press, 2004), 77.

24 James D. Hornfischer, *Neptune's Inferno: The U.S. Navy at Guadalcanal.* (New York NY: Bantam, 2012), 44; Robert L. Eichelberger with Milton MacKaye, *Our Jungle Road to Tokyo* (New York NY: The Viking Press, 1950), 18.

25 Eichelberger with MacKaye, *Jungle Road*, 18.

26 Dudley McCarthy, *South-West Pacific Area First Year: Kokoda to Wau [Australia in the War of 1939–1945, Series 1 (Army), vol. 5]* (Canberra: Australian War Memorial, 1959), 133–134.

27 McCarthy, *South-West*, 135.

28 Ibid.

29 Ibid., 136.

30 Ibid.

31 Williams, *Kokoda*, 10.

32 *Japanese Army Operations in the South Pacific Area: New Britain and Papua Campaigns, 1942–43*, translated by Steven Bullard (Canberra: Australian War Memorial, 2007), 130.

33 Raymond Paull, *Retreat from Kokoda: The Australian Campaign in New Guinea 1942* (London: Secker & Warburg, 1983), 34.

34 Williams, *Kokoda*, 66–67.

35 Allan S. Walker, *The Island Campaigns [Australia in the War of 1939–1945, Series 5 (Medical), vol. 3]* (Canberra: Australian War Memorial, 1957), 21.

36 McCarthy, *South-West*, 176.

37 Ibid., 142.

38 Miller, *First Offensive*, 91.

39 Jim McEnery, *Hell in the Pacific: A Marine Rifleman's Journey from Guadalcanal to Peleliu.* (New York NY: Simon and Schuster, 2012), 66.

40 Miller, *First Offensive*, 95.

41 The Ilu River was erroneously confused with the Tenaru River nearby, and the action on August 21 was often by mistake referred to as the Battle of the Tenaru in contemporary records, see Gordon L. Rottman, *World War II Pacific Island Guide: A Geo-Military Study* (Westport CT: Grenwood Press, 2002), 107.

42 Pollock, Oral History, 133.

43 Fields, Oral History, 82.

44 John P. Leonard, Oral History, USMC, 48.

45 Pollock, Oral History, 140–141.
46 Leonard, Oral History, 48.
47 Michael S. Smith. *Bloody Ridge: The Battle That Saved Guadalcanal.* (New York NY: Presidio Press, 2000), 92.
48 Pollock, Oral History, 147–148.
49 *New York Times*, September 29, 1942, 10.
50 "Four Years of My Life, January 2, 1942 thru February 1, 1946," Library of Congress.
51 Miller, *First Offensive*,109.
52 Davis, Oral History, 122–123.
53 Roy H. Elrod, *We Were Going to Win, or Die There: With the Marines at Guadalcanal, Tarawa, and Saipan* (Denton TX: University of North Texas Press, 2017), 114–115.
54 Buse, Oral History, 54.
55 Recollections of Pharmacist's Mate First Class Louis Ortega, Naval History and Heritage Command.

Chapter Seven

1   William, *Kokoda Campaign*, 209.
2   *Japanese Army Operations in the South Pacific Area*, 172.
3   McCarthy, *South-West Pacific Area*, 271.
4   *Japanese Army Operations in the South Pacific Area*, 174.
5   Robert Odell, "Personal Notes on the Papuan Campaign," December 1942, 9, in Records of the office of the Surgeon General-Army (RG 112) E 145, Box 104 NADC; quoted from Josephine Callisen Bresnahan, "Dangers in Paradise: The Battle Against Combat Fatigue in the Pacific War" (PhD diss., Harvard University, 1999), 107–108.
6   Eichelberger with MacKaye, *Jungle Road*, 21.
7   Ibid., 17.
8   Williams, *Kokoda*, 13.
9   Mark R. Peattie, *Sunburst: The Rise of Japanese Naval Air Power, 1909–1941* (Annapolis MD: Naval Institute Press, 2001), 172, 174.
10 Eric M. Bergerud, *Fire in the Sky: The Air War in the South Pacific* (New York NY: Basic Books, 2001), 247.
11 Ibid., 203.
12 Hough et al., *Pearl Harbor to Guadalcanal*, 292.
13 Bergerud, *Fire in the Sky*, 264.
14 Douglas Napier Gillison, *Royal Australian Air Force 1939–1942 [Australia in the War of 1939–1945, Series 3 (Air), vol. 1]* (Canberra: Australian War Memorial, 1962), 676.
15 Miller, *First Offensive*, 65.
16 Marlin Groft and Larry Alexander. *Bloody Ridge and Beyond: A World War II Marine's Memoir of Edson's Raiders in the Pacific.* (New York NY: Berkley, 2014), 54.
17 Charles H. Walker, *Combat Officer: A Memoir of War in the South Pacific* (New York NY: Ballantine Books, 2004), 24.
18 John L. Zimmermann, *The Guadalcanal Campaign* (Washington DC: Historical Division United States Marine Corps, 1949), 62.
19 John Hersey, *Into the Valley: A Skirmish of the Marines* (Lincoln NE: University of Nebraska Press, 2002) 10–11.
20 Walker, *Combat Officer*, 21–22.

21 Joseph H. Alexander, *Edson's Raiders: The 1st Marine Raider Battalion in World War II* (Annapolis MD: Naval Institute Press, 2010), 153–154.

22 Ulrich A. Straus. *The Anguish of Surrender: Japanese POWs of World War II.* (Seattle WA: University of Washington Press, 2005), 116–117.

23 Leckie, *Helmet*, 84.

24 Eric M. Bergerud, *Touched With Fire: The Land War in the South Pacific* (New York NY: Penguin Books, 1997), 412.

25 Elrod, *We Were Going to Win*, 118.

26 George MacDonald Fraser, *Quartered Safe Out Here* (New York NY: Skyhorse Publishing, 2007), 3.

27 Walker, *Combat Officer*, 31–32.

28 Murray, Oral History, 137.

29 Richard Tregaskis, *Guadalcanal Diary.* (New York NY: Modern Library, 2000), 152.

30 Zimmermann, *Guadalcanal Campaign*, 67–68.

31 Ibid., 144.

32 John Paton Davies Jr., *China Hand: An Autobiography* (Philadelphia PA: University of Pennsylvania Press, 2012), 47.

33 Romanus and Sunderland, *Stilwell's Mission to China*, 8.

34 John Donovan, letter to family, accession number 1992.479.004, undated, John Donovan Papers, Box 1, National Naval Aviation Museum.

35 John D. Plating, *The Hump: America's Strategy for Keeping China in World War II* (College Station TX: Texas A&M Press, 2011), 98.

36 Plating, *Hump*, 118.

37 Wooldridge, *Carrier Warfare*, 70.

38 Ibid.

39 William F. Halsey, *Admiral Halsey's Story* (New York NY: Whittlesey House, 1947), 120.

40 Buse, Oral History, 51.

41 Halsey, *Admiral Halsey's Story*, 123.

42 Ibid., 121.

43 Wooldridge, *Carrier Warfare*, 82.

44 Ibid., 83.

45 Ibid., 72.

46 Dull, *Japanese Navy*, 230.

47 Wooldridge, *Carrier Warfare*, 84.

48 Ibid., 75.

49 John B. Lundstrom, *The First Team and the Guadalcanal Campaign: Naval Fighter Combat from August to November 1942* (Annapolis MD: Naval Institute Press, 1994), 446.

50 Tanaka Raizō, "The Struggle for Guadalcanal", in *The Japanese Navy in World War Two*, ed. David C. Evans (Annapolis MD: Naval Institute Press, 1986) 185.

51 Halsey, *Admiral Halsey's Story*, 122.

52 United States Strategic Bombing Survey [Pacific]. Naval Analysis Division, *Interrogations of Japanese Officials* Volume 2, 461.

53 Drea, *Service*, 189.

54 Kawamura, *Hirohito*, 117.

55 Matsudaira Yasumasa, "Appendix: The Japanese Emperor and the War," *Reports of General MacArthur: Japanese Operations in the Southwest Pacific Area*, vol. 2, pt. 2, 763. It is perhaps easy to suspect a certain degree of hindsight in Hirohito's assertion. However, a modern historian has advocated the idea that the defeat on the Kokoda Trail was indeed a decisive point in changing the emperor's mind about the war, Drea, *Service*, 256.

56   Bix, *Hirohito*, 458.
57   Ibid., 461.
58   Kawamura, *Hirohito*, 112–113.

Chapter Eight

1   *Papuan Campaign: the Buna-Sanananda Operation* (Washington DC: Historical Division, War Department, 1945), 9.
2   Very few Japanese survived to tell the story of conditions inside Buna Mission Station, and details about the situation are based mainly on the testimony of local inhabitants who had worked as servants for the Japanese and managed to escape at the last moment, see F. Tillman Durdin, "Buna Area Wind-Up An American Saga," *New York Times*, January 8, 1943: 4.
3   Durdin, "Buna Area," 4.
4   Samuel Milner, *Victory in Papua [United States Army in World War II: The War in the Pacific]* (Washington DC: Office of the Chief of Military History, Department of the Army, 1957), 317.
5   Eichelberger, *Jungle Road*, 49.
6   Drea, *Service*, 103.
7   *Japanese Army Operations in the South Pacific Area*, v, 174.
8   Drea, *Service*, 189.
9   Large, *Hirohito*, 116.
10   Gibney (ed.), *Sensō*, 132.
11   Mary H. Williams, *Chronology [United States Army in World War II: Special Studies]* (Washington DC: Office of the Chief of Military History, Department of the Army, 1960), 91. Americal Division is a contraction of "American, New Caledonian Division."
12   Shindo Hiroyuki, "The Japanese Army's Search for a New South Pacific Strategy, 1943," in *Australia 1943: The Liberation of New Guinea*, ed. Peter J. Dean (Port Melbourne: Cambridge University Press, 2014), 69–70.
13   Yoshihara Tsutomu, Chief of Staff, 18th Army, Imperial Japanese Army, translation by Doris Heath of manuscript titled 'Southern Cross', AWM MSS0725.
14   Diary of Tamura Yoshikazu, Australian War Memorial.
15   Phillip Bradley, *The Battle for Wau: New Guinea's Frontline 1942–1943* (Melbourne: Cambridge University Press, 2008), 225.
16   Yoshihara Tsutomu, Chief of Staff, 18th Army, Imperial Japanese Army, translation by Doris Heath of manuscript titled 'Southern Cross', AWM MSS0725.
17   Thomas E. Griess, *Second World War: Asia and the Pacific* (West Point NY: United States Military Academy, 1977), 141.
18   Kennedy, *Business*, 286.
19   Francis L. Loewenheim, Harold D. Langley, and Manfred Jonas (eds.), *Roosevelt and Churchill: Their Secret Wartime Correspondence* (New York NY: Saturday Review Press, 1975), 282.
20   Morton, *Strategy and Command*, 381–382.
21   Kennedy, *Business*, 281.
22   Bryant, *Tide*, 549.
23   *Casablanca Conference, January 1943. Joint Chiefs of Staff. Minutes of Meetings* (Washington DC: Office of the Combined Chiefs of Staff, 1943), 59.
24   *Casablanca Conference, January 1943. Papers and Minutes of Meetings* (Washington DC: Office of the Combined Chiefs of Staff, 1943), 192; Kennedy, *Business*, 281.
25   *Casablanca Conference, January 1943. Papers and Minutes of Meetings* (Washington DC: Office of the Combined Chiefs of Staff, 1943), 227–228.

26 Ibid., 144.
27 Morton, *Strategy and Command*, 384–385.
28 Ibid., 385.
29 Loewenheim et al. (eds.), *Roosevelt and Churchill*, 309.
30 Robert E. Sherwood, *Roosevelt and Hopkins: An Intimate History* (New York NY: Harper, 1948), 696.
31 Elliott Roosevelt, *As He Saw It* (New York NY: Duell, Sloan and Pearce, 1945), 117.
32 Roosevelt, *As He Saw It*, 119. In his wartime memoirs, Churchill provides an alternative account, suggesting that the term may have appeared in his conversations with Roosevelt earlier during their private talks at Casablanca; however, he agrees that it was not a spontaneous, off-the-cuff remark made by Roosevelt at the final press conference. Churchill, *Hinge*, 613–614.
33 Gregory P. Gilbert, *The Battle of the Bismarck Sea March 1943* (Canberra: Air Power Development Centre, 2013), 33; Prados, *Combined Fleet*, 450.
34 George C. Kenney, *General Kenney Reports: A Personal History of the Pacific War* (New York NY: Duell, Sloan, and Pearce, 1949), 198.
35 Dull, *Japanese Navy*, 268–269.
36 Garrett Middlebrook, *Air Combat at 20 Feet* (Bloomington IN: AuthorHouse 2004), 152.
37 Kenney, *Reports*, 201.
38 Ibid., 199; on the gamble, see also O. G. Haywood Jr., "Military Decision and Game Theory," *Journal of the Operations Research Society of America*, vol. 2, no. 4 (November 1954): 365–385.
39 Gilbert, *Bismarck Sea*, 34.
40 Ibid., 33–39
41 Ibid., 44.
42 Samuel Eliot Morison, *Breaking the Bismarcks Barrier 22 July 1942–1 May 1944* [*History of the United States Naval Operations in World War II*, vol. 6] (Boston MA: Little, Brown and Co., 1950), 60.
43 Middlebrook, *Air Combat*, 159.
44 Ibid., 160.
45 Gilbert, *Bismarck Sea*, 55.
46 Bruce Gamble, *Fortress Rabaul: The Battle for the Southwest Pacific, January 1942–April 1943* (Minneapolis MN: Zenith Press, 2010), 313.
47 Morison, *Bismarcks Barrier*, 62.
48 Gilbert, *Bismarck Sea*, 69.
49 Prados, *Combined Fleet*, 451.
50 Richard L. Watson, "Battle of the Bismarck Sea," in Wesley Frank Craven and James Lea Cate (eds.), *The Pacific: Guadalcanal to Saipan, August 1942 to July 1944* [*The Army Air Forces in World War II*] (Chicago IL: University of Chicago Press, 1951), 146.
51 Theodore H. White and Annalee Jacoby, *Thunder Out of China* (London: Victor Gollancz, 1947), 162.
52 Ibid.
53 Ibid.
54 Li Rui, *Qianfengbao*, April 14, 1943, quoted from Mark Baker, "The Slow, the Quick and the Dead: Environment, Politics and Temporality in the Henan Famine, 1942–43," *International Review of Environmental History*, vol. 4, no. 2 (2018): 104.
55 Harrison Forman, *Diary*, 38. Forman's diary from the visit to Henan in 1943, kept at University of Wisconsin-Milwaukee. https://collections.lib.uwm.edu/digital/collection/forman/id/50.
56 Baker, "The Slow, the Quick and the Dead," 94.
57 Anthony Garnaut, "A Quantitative Description of the Henan Famine," *Modern Asian Studies*, vol. 47, no. 6 (2013): 2018.

58 Ernest Wampler, *China Suffers: Or, My Six Years of Work During the Incident* (Elgin IL: Brethren Publishing, 1945), 229.

59 Garnaut, "Famine," 2043.

60 The recent estimate of less than one million starvation deaths in the Henan famine is from Garnaut, "Famine," and is based primarily on analyses of available demographic statistics. It contrasts with earlier numbers of more than three million deaths, which according to Garnaut are based on exaggerated contemporary claims by journalists and cannot be substantiated by more careful research. A toll of three million is mentioned in several texts, including Song Zhixin, *1942: Henan dajihuang [1942: The Great Henan Famine]* (Wuhan, Hubei renmin chubanshe, 2012), 2–3.

61 Garnaut, "Famine," 2011.

62 S. Brönnimann et al., "Extreme climate of the global troposphere and stratosphere in 1940–42 related to El Niño," *Nature*, vol. 431, no. 7011 (October 2004): 971–974.

63 Mary Geneva Sayre, *Missionary Triumphs in Occupied China* (Winona Lake IN: The Women's Missionary Society of the Free Methodist Church, 1945), 93.

64 Micah S. Muscolino, "Violence Against People and the Land: The Environment and Refugee Migration From China's Henan Province, 1938–1945," *Environment and History*, vol. 17, no. 2 (May 2011): 291–311.

65 Hsi-sheng Ch'i, "The Military Dimension, 1942–1945," in *China's Bitter Victory*, eds. James C. Hsiung and Steven I. Levine (Armonk NY: M. E. Sharpe, 1992), 180.

66 Ibid.

67 Famine Inquiry Commission, *Report on Bengal* (New Delhi: Government of India, 1945), 1.

68 Edward Blunt, *I.C.S.: The Indian Civil Service* (London: Faber and Faber, 1937), 184.

69 Cormac Ó Gráda, "'Sufficiency and Sufficiency and Sufficiency': Revisiting the Bengal Famine of 1943–44," UCD Centre for Economic Research, *Working Paper Series* (2010), 12.

70 Quoted in Janam Mukherjee, *Hungry Bengal: War, Famine and the End of Empire* (Oxford: Oxford University Press, 2015), 129.

71 Mukherjee, *Hungry Bengal*, 129–130.

72 John Barnes and David Nicholson (eds.), *The Empire at Bay: The Leo Amery Diaries* (London: Hutchinson, 1988), 832. Much has been made in recent writing of Churchill's alleged dislike of Indians, but some of it seems based on hyperbole and a distortion of historical sources. See, for example, "The dark side of Winston Churchill's legacy no one should forget," *The Washington Post*, February 3, 2015: "Amery vented in his private diaries, writing 'on the subject of India, Winston is not quite sane' and that he didn't 'see much difference between [Churchill's] outlook and Hitler's'." A more complete excerpt from Amery's diary of August 4, 1944 shows that Amery did not make the comparison with the German dictator in "private," but to Churchill's face in a state of great emotion while the two were involved in a heated argument, and therefore should probably not be taken at face value. The context is a remark by Amery on the Indian caste system: "This let loose Winston in a state of great exultation describing how after the war he was going to go back on all the shameful story of the last twenty years of surrender, how once we had won the war there was no obligation to honour promises made at a time of difficulty, and not taken up by the Indians, and carry out a great regeneration of India based on extinguishing landlords and oppressive industrialists and uplift the peasant and untouchable, probably by collectivisation on Russian lines. It might be necessary to get rid of wretched sentimentalists like Wavell and most of the present English officials in India, who were more Indian than the Indians, and send out new men. What was all my professed patriotism worth if I did not stand up for my own countrymen against Indian money-lenders? Naturally I lost patience and couldn't help telling him that I didn't see much difference between his outlook and Hitler's which annoyed him no little. I am by no means sure whether on this subject of India he is really quite sane." Ibid., 992–993.

73 Srinath Raghavan, *India's War: The Making of Modern South Asia 1939–1945* (London: Allen Lane, 2016), 353.

74 Paul R. Greenough, *Prosperity and Misery in Modern Bengal: The Famine of 1943–1944* (Oxford: Oxford University Press, 1982), 160.

Chapter Nine

1   Morison, *Bismarcks Barrier*, 120.

2   Ibid., 124.

3   Ibid.

4   Kramer J. Rohfleisch, "The Central Solomons," in Wesley Frank Craven and James Lea Cate (eds.), *The Pacific: Guadalcanal to Saipan, August 1942 to July 1944 [The Army Air Forces in World War II]* (Chicago IL: University of Chicago Press, 1948), 213.

5   Ugaki, *Fading Victory*, 329.

6   Ibid., 319.

7   Ibid., 328.

8   Kenney, *General Kenney Reports*, 225.

9   Ugaki, *Fading Victory*, 330.

10 Halsey, *Admiral Halsey's Story*, 155.

11 Smith-Hutton, Oral History, US Naval Institute Oral History Program, 595.

12 Prados, *Combined Fleet*, 459–460.

13 Donald M. Goldstein and Katherine V. Dillon (eds.), *Fading Victory: The Diary of Admiral Matome Ugaki 1941–1945* (Annapolis MD: Naval Institute Press, 1991), 353–354.

14 Ibid.

15 Adonis C. Arvanitakis, *Killing a Peacock: A Case Study of the Targeted Killing of Admiral Isoroku Yamamoto* (Fort Leavenworth KS: School of Advanced Military Studies, United States Army Command and General Staff College, 2015), 1–3.

16 Goldstein and Dillon (eds.), *Fading Victory*, 359.

17 Smith-Hutton, Oral History, 597.

18 Halsey, *Admiral Halsey's Story*, 157.

19 Richard Reid, *Laden, Fevered, Starved: The POWs of Sandakan, North Borneo, 1945* (Canberra: Commonwealth Department of Veterans' Affairs, 1999), 19.

20 Tanaka Yukiko, *Hidden Horrors Japanese War Crimes In World War II* (Boulder CO: Westview Press, 1996), 35.

21 Reid, *Laden, Fevered, Starved*, 19.

22 Tanaka, *Hidden Horrors*, 35.

23 Reid, *Laden, Fevered, Starved*, 21.

24 Frans J. Nicholaas Ponder, "A Soldier in the Royal Netherlands-Indies Army," in *The Defining Years of the Dutch East Indies, 1942–1949: Survivors' Accounts of Japanese Invasion and Enslavement of Europeans and the Revolution That Created Free Indonesia*, ed. Jan A. Krancher (Jefferson NC and London: MacFarland & Co., 1996), 29.

25 Tony Banham, *The Sinking of the Lisbon Maru: Britain's Forgotten Wartime Tragedy* (Hong Kong: Hong Kong University Press, 2011), 77.

26 Banham, *Lisbon Maru*, 81.

27 Ibid., 36.

28 Chester Fritz and Dan Rylance, *Ever Westward to the Far East: The Story of Chester Fritz* (Grand Forks ND: University of North Dakota, 1982), 151–152.

29 Barbara Bernard McGee and Ruth Dorval Jones, *Barney: Journals of Harry Virden Bernard* (Smithfield NC: McGee Press, 1982), 239.

30 Quarterly Report, Headquarters, 3d Portable Surgical Hospital, USASOS, 1 Jan.–31 Mar. 1943, dated 1 July 1943, quoted in Robert S. Anderson (ed.), *Medical Department, United States Army: Preventive Medicine in World War II, vol. 9: Special Fields* (Washington DC: Department of the Army, 1969), 403.

31 Harry H. L. Kitano and Roger Daniels, "Introduction," in *Japanese Americans: From Relocation to Redress*, eds. Roger Daniels, Sandra C. Taylor and Harry H. L. Kitano (Seattle WA: University of Washington Press, 1991), 22.

32 Sugata Bose, *His Majesty's Opponent: Subhas Chandra Bose and India's Struggle against Empire* (Cambridge MA: The Belknap Press of Harvard University Press, 2011), 235.

33 Bose, *His Majesty's Opponent*, 219; Horst Geerken, *Hitlers Griff nach Asien*, vol. 2 (Bonn: BukitCinta, 2015), 65.

34 Fujiwara Iwaichi, *F. Kikan: Japanese Army Intelligence Operations in Southeast Asia during World War Two* (Hong Kong: Heinemann Asia, 1983), 89.

35 Bose, *His Majesty's Opponent*, 231.

36 Ibid., 242.

37 Rudolf Hartog, *The Sign of the Tiger* (New Delhi: Rupa, 2001), 61.

38 Bose, *His Majesty's Opponent*, 258.

39 Ibid., 262.

40 Annika A. Culver, "Manchukuo and the Creation of a New Multi-Ethnic Literature: Kawabata Yasunari's Promotion of 'Manchurian' Culture, 1941–1942," in *Sino-Japanese Transculturation: Late Nineteenth Century to the End of the Pacific War*, eds. Richard King, Cody Poulton and Endo Katsuhiko (Lanham MD: Lexington Books, 2011, 170.

41 Andrew Hall, "The Word Is Mightier than the Throne: Bucking Colonial Education Trends in Manchukuo," *The Journal of Asian Studies*, vol. 68, no. 3 (August 2009): 909–910.

42 Hall, "Word," 904.

43 Ibid., 906.

44 Ju Zhifen, "Northern Chinese Laborers and Manchukuo," in *Asian Labor in the Wartime Japanese Empire: Unknown Histories*, ed. Paul H. Kratoska (Armonk NY: Sharpe, 2005), 69.

45 David Tucker, "Labor Policy and the Construction Industry in Manchukuo: Systems of Recruitment, Management, and Control," in *Asian Labor in the Wartime Japanese Empire: Unknown Histories*, ed. Paul H. Kratoska (Armonk NY: Sharpe, 2005), 54.

46 Cook and Cook, *Japan at War*, 164.

47 Aisin-Gioro Pu Yi, *From Emperor to Citizen* (Beijing: Foreign Languages Press, 1979), vol. 2, 304.

48 Edward Behr, *The Last Emperor* (Toronto: Futura, 1987), 245.

49 Gerald E. Bunker, *The Peace Conspiracy: Wang Ching-wei and the China War, 1937–1941* (Cambridge MA: Harvard University Press, 1972), 271–280.

50 Timothy Brook, "Collaborationist Nationalism in Occupied Wartime China," in *Nation Work: Asian Elites and National Identities*, eds. Timothy Brook and Andre Schmid (Ann Arbor MI: University of Michigan Press, 2000), 159–190.

51 Ju, "Northern," 74.

52 Ibid.

53 F. C. Jones, *Manchuria since 1931* (London: Royal Institute of International Affairs, 1949), 134.

54 Miriam Kingsberg, *Moral Nation: Modern Japan and Narcotics in Global History* (Berkeley CA: University of California Press, 2013), 90.

55 Hayes, *Joint Chiefs*, 272–273.

56 Samuel Eliot Morison, *Aleutians, Gilbert and Marshalls June 1942–April 1944* [*History of the United States Naval Operations in World War II*, vol. 7] (Boston MA: Little, Brown and Co., 1951), 22–36.

57 Stetson Conn, Rose C. Engelman and Byron Fairchild, *Guarding the United States and Its Outpost* [*United States Army in World War II: The Western Hemisphere*] (Washington DC: Office of the Chief of Military History, Department of the Army, 1961), 278–279.

58 Conn et al., *Guarding*, 279.

59 Morison, *Aleutians, Gilbert and Marshalls*, 38.

60 Ibid., 38–39.

61 Conn et al., *Guarding*, 285.

62 Sewell T. Tyng, Nelson L. Drummond and Robert J. Mitchell, *The Capture of Attu As Told by the Men Who Fought There* (Washington DC: War Department, 1944), 31.

63 Tyng et al., *Capture of Attu*, 36.

64 John Haile Cloe, *Attu: The Forgotten Battle* (Anchorage AK: National Park Service, 2017), 40.

65 Cloe, *Attu*, 79.

66 Brian Garfield, *The Thousand-Mile War: World War II in Alaska and the Aleutians* (Fairbanks AK: University of Alaska Press, 1995), 290–291.

67 Ibid., 296.

68 Ibid., 307.

69 Spector, *Eagle*, 181.

70 Tyng et al., *Capture of Attu*, 41.

71 Ibid., 50.

72 Garfield, *Thousand-Mile War*, 322.

73 Cloe, *Attu*, 88.

74 Ibid.

75 Garfield, *Thousand-Mile War*, 292 and 297.

76 Tyng et al., *Capture of Attu*, 42–43.

77 Cloe, *Attu*, 104.

78 Ibid., 107.

79 Conn et al., *Guarding*, 295.

80 Ben-Ami Shillony, *Politics and Culture in Wartime Japan* (Oxford: Clarendon Press, 1981), 96.

81 Conn et al., *Guarding*, 295.

82 Hayes, *Joint Chiefs*, 371.

Chapter Ten

1 John Miller, *Cartwheel: The Reduction of Rabaul* [*United States Army in World War II: The War in the Pacific*] (Washington DC: Office of the Chief of Military History, Department of the Army, 1959), 120.

2 Josephine Callisen Bresnahan, "Dangers in Paradise: The Battle Against Combat Fatigue in the Pacific War" (PhD diss., Harvard University, 1999), 184.

3 Miller, *Cartwheel*, 121.

4 Ibid.

5 Ibid., 112–113

6 Charles Edmundson, "Battle of the Pacific," *Time*, August 9, 1943, 40.

7 Morison, *Bismarcks Barrier*, 90–91.

8 *169th Infantry History*, p. 4, quoted in Miller, *Cartwheel*, 109.

9 Miller, *Cartwheel*, 108–109.

10 Ibid., 133.

11 Ibid., 148.

12 Ibid., 159.

13 Halsey, *Admiral Halsey's Story*, 170–171.

14 Ibid., 171.

15 Edward S. Miller, *War Plan Orange: The U.S. Strategy to Defeat Japan, 1897–1945* (Annapolis MD: Naval Institute Press, 1991), 351.

16 Hara, *Destroyer Captain*, 179.

17 Potter, *Nimitz*, 245–246.

18 Morison, *Bismarcks Barrier*, 220.

19 Dull, *Imperial Japanese Navy*, 278–279.

20 Morison, *Bismarcks Barrier*, 220.

21 Ibid., 213.

22 Chihaya, "Withdrawal," 276–277.

23 Holland M. Smith and Percy Finch, *Coral and Brass* (New York NY: Charles Scribner's Sons, 1949), 106.

24 Chihaya Masataka, "The Withdrawal from Kiska," in *The Japanese Navy in World War Two*, ed. David C. Evans (Annapolis MD: Naval Institute Press, 1986), 255

25 Chihaya, "Withdrawal," 246.

26 Morton, *Strategy and Command*, 652.

27 Ibid., 520.

28 Ibid., 546.

29 Gregory J. W. Urwin, *Victory in Defeat: The Wake Island Defenders in Captivity* (Annapolis MD: Naval Institute Press, 2011), 252–252.

30 Guido Samarani, "An Historical Turning Point: Italy's Relations with China before and after 8 September 1943," *Journal of Modern Italian Studies*, vol. 15, no. 4 (2010): 598.

31 Samarani, "Turning Point," 597.

32 Sandro Bassetti, *Colonia Italiana in Cina* (Milano: Lampa di Stampa, 2014), 340.

33 Ibid., 340–341.

34 Ibid., 339.

35 Ibid., 338.

36 Ibid., 338–339.

37 Bassetti, *Colonia Italiana*, 339; "Italian Submarine Safe," *New York Times*, September 21, 1943, 4.

38 *Reports of General MacArthur: Japanese Operations in the Southwest Pacific Area*, vol. 2, pt. 1, 251.

39 Alvin D. Coox, "The Rise and Fall of the Imperial Japanese Air Forces," in Alfred F. Hurley and Robert C. Ehrhart (eds.), *Air Power and Warfare* (Washington DC: US Government Printing Office, 1979), 91.

40 A. Sutherland Brown William Rodney, "Burma Banzai: The Air War in Burma through Japanese Eyes," *Canadian Military History*, vol. 11, no. 2 (2012): 52.

41 Morton, *Strategy and Command*, 449.

42 L. A. Sawyer and W. H. Mitchell, *The Liberty Ships: The History of the 'Emergency' Cargo Ships Constructed in the United States during World War II* (Newton Abbot: David & Charles, 1970), 13.

43 Sawyer and Mitchell, *Liberty Ships*, 14.

44 S. C. Heal, *Ugly Ducklings: Japan's WWII Liberty Type Standards Ships* (Annapolis MD: Naval Institute Press, 2003).

45 Halsey, *Admiral Halsey's Story*, 69.

46 Roy Benson, *Oral History*, 188–189.

47 Shigeru Sato: "'Economic soldiers' in Java: Indonesian Laborers Mobilized for Agricultural Projects," in *Asian Labor in the Wartime Japanese Empire: Unknown Histories*, ed. Paul H. Kratoska (Armonk NY: Sharpe, 2005), 130–131.

48 Harry A. Poeze, "The Road to Hell: The Construction of a Railway Line in West Java during the Japanese Occupation," in *Asian Labor in the Wartime Japanese Empire: Unknown Histories*, ed. Paul H. Kratoska (Armonk NY: Sharpe, 2005), 164.

49 Ibid., 158–162.

50 Ibid., 163.

51 Ibid., 162.

52 Ibid., 165.

53 "Establishment of East Asia: Maneuvers for the First Period of Total War," *IMFTE*, Exhibit no. 1335, 17–19.

54 "Course of Events Leading up to Decisions on Political Control and Reversion of the East Indies in the Second World War," *IMFTE*, Exhibit no. 1344, 1. The decision was publicly announced by the end of the same month, see "Tojo Message Greeted with Joy," *Nippon Times Evening*, January 29, 1943, 1.

55 "Draft of Basic Plan for Establishment of Greater East Asian Co-Prosperity Sphere," *IMFTE*, Exhibit no. 1336, 10.

56 George S. Kanahele, "The Japanese occupation of Indonesia, prelude to independence," (unpublished Ph.D. dissert.), 69.

57 R. Pandji Seoroso, interviewed in Jakarta, August 27, 1964. Kanahele, "Japanese occupation," 61.

58 Ben-Ami Shillony, "Wartime Japan: A Military Dictatorship," in *Military and State in Modern Asia* ed. Harold Z. Schiffrin (Jerusalem: Academic Press, 1976), 75–76.

59 Katō Masuo, *The Lost War: A Japanese Reporter's Inside Story* (New York NY: Alfred A. Knopf, 1946), 105.

60 Shillony, "Wartime," 76; Najita Tetsuo, "Nakano Seigō and the Spirit of the Meiji Restoration in Twentieth-Century Japan," in *Dilemmas of Growth in Prewar Japan*, ed. James W. Morley (Princeton NJ: Princeton University Press, 1971), 415–416.

61 Shillony, *Politics and Culture in Wartime Japan* (Oxford: Clarendon Press, 1991), 52–53.

62 Cook and Cook, *Japan at War*, 230.

63 Frank Gibney (ed.), *Sensō: The Japanese Remember the Pacific War* (Armonk NY: M. E. Sharpe, 1995), 178–179.

64 Elise Tipton, *The Japanese Police State: The Tokkō in Interwar Japan* (Honolulu HI: University of Hawaii Press, 1990), 157.

65 Ibid., 149.

66 Thomas R. H. Havens, *Valley of Darkness: The Japanese People and World War Two* (New York NY: W. W. Norton, 1978), 99.

Chapter Eleven

1 Williams, *Chronology*, 143.

2 Morison, *Breaking the Bismarcks Barrier*, 298–299.

3 Halsey, *Admiral Halsey's Story*, 181.

4 Shaw and Kane, *Isolation of Rabaul*, 210.

5 Ibid., 214.

6 Miller, *Cartwheel*, 239.

7 Halsey, *Admiral Halsey's Story*, 180.

8 Morison, *Breaking the Bismarcks Barrier*, 319.

9 Halsey, *Admiral Halsey's Story*, 181.

10 Ibid.

11   Ibid.
12   Shaw and Kane, *Isolation of Rabaul*, 226.
13   Ibid., 253.
14   Hoffman, Oral History, 16.
15   Henry I. Shaw Jr., Bernard C. Nalty and Edwin J. Turnbladh, *History of U.S. Marine Corps Operations in World War II, vol. 3: Central Pacific Drive* (Washington DC: U.S. Government Printing Office, 1966), 51.
16   Morton, *Strategy and Command*, 448–449.
17   Shaw, Nalty and Turnbladh, *Central Pacific Drive*, 23–25, 28.
18   Ibid., 30.
19   Ibid., 29.
20   Ibid., 30.
21   Morton, *Strategy and Command*, 446–447.
22   John Wukovits, *One Square Mile of Hell: The Battle for Tarawa* (New York NY: NAL Caliber, 2007), 74.
23   Shaw, Nalty and Turnbladh, *Central Pacific Drive*, 53–54.
24   Murray, Oral History, 141.
25   Ibid., 141–142.
26   Ibid., 146.
27   Carl W. Hoffman, Oral History, 16–17.
28   Robert Sherrod, *Tarawa: The Story of a Battle* (New York NY: Duell, Sloan and Pearce, 1944), 62–63.
29   Carl W. Hoffman, Oral History, 17–18.
30   Ibid., 18–19.
31   Wood B. Kyle, Oral History, 55.
32   Norman T. Hatch, Oral History, 98.
33   Hatch, Oral History, 97–98.
34   Ibid., 94.
35   Ibid., 95–96.
36   Ibid., 292.
37   Ibid., 293.
38   Carl W. Hoffman, Oral History 20–21.
39   Wood B. Kyle, Oral History, 55.
40   Hatch, Oral History, 100.
41   Merle Miller, "The Battle for Makin," *Yank* (December 3, 1943): 5; quoted in Josephine Callisen Bresnahan, "Dangers in Paradise: The Battle Against Combat Fatigue in the Pacific War" (PhD diss., Harvard University, 1999), 82.
42   Philip A. Crowl and Edmund G. Love, *Seizure of the Gilberts and Marshalls [United States Army in World War II: The War in the Pacific]* (Washington DC: Office of the Chief of Military History, Department of the Army, 1953), 85.
43   Crowl and Love, *Gilberts and Marshalls*, 85.
44   Miller, "Makin," 83.
45   Crowl and Love, *Gilberts and Marshalls*, 123.
46   Ibid., 108.
47   Jennifer N. Johnson, "'We're still alive today': A Captured Japanese Diary from the Pacific Theater," *Prologue: The Journal of the National Archives*, vol. 45, no. 2 (Summer 2013): 57.
48   Oral History, Naval Institute, 58.
49   Ibid., 91.

50 Ibid., 91–92.
51 Hatch, Oral History, 101.
52 Ibid., 102.
53 Shaw, Nalty and Turnbladh, *Central Pacific Drive*, 79.
54 Hatch, Oral History, 103–104.
55 Ibid., 113.
56 Potter, *Nimitz*, 261–262.
57 Smith-Hutton, Oral History, 438.
58 Zhou Wenxing, "Wenxing (Literary Star), Wuxing (Military Star), and a Patriotic Heart," in Deng Xian (ed.), *Under the Same Army Flag* (Beijing: China Intercontinental Press, 2005), 93.
59 Keith Sainsbury, *The Turning Point: Roosevelt, Stalin, Churchill and Chiang-Kai-Shek, 1943: The Moscow, Cairo, and Teheran Conferences* (Oxford: Oxford University Press, 1985), 184–185.
60 Roosevelt, *As He Saw It*, 163.
61 Smith-Hutton, Oral History, 418–419.
62 Ibid., 419.
63 *Roosevelt and Churchill: Their Secret Wartime Correspondence*, 274–275.
64 United States Department of State, *Foreign relations of the United States diplomatic papers: The Conferences at Cairo and Tehran* (Washington DC: US Government Printing Office, 1943), 404.
65 Sainsbury, *Turning Point*, 287.
66 *Roosevelt and Churchill: Their Secret Wartime Correspondence*, 276.
67 Sainsbury, *Turning Point*, 307.
68 "Tojo Reports Developments of War to Diet," *Nippon Times*, December 28, 1943, 1.
69 *Army Operations in China December 1941–December 1943*, 161.
70 Ibid.
71 Ibid., 169.
72 Brooks Atkinson, "Changteh Blasted Off Map by War; City May Rise Again on a New Site," *New York Times*, December 30, 1943: 1.

Bibliography

Literature

Abe Zenji. *The Emperor's Sea Eagle*. Honolulu HI: Arizona Memorial Museum Association, 2006.

Alexander, Joseph H. *Edson's Raiders: The 1st Marine Raider Battalion in World War II*. Annapolis MD: Naval Institute Press, 2010.

Allen, Louis. *Burma: The Longest War 1941–45*. London: Orion Publishing, 2000.

Amery, Leo. *The Empire at Bay: The Leo Amery Diaries*, edited by John Barnes and David Nicholson. London: Hutchinson, 1988.

Anderson, Robert S., ed. *Medical Department, United States Army: Preventive Medicine in World War II, vol. 9: Special Fields*. Washington DC: Department of the Army, 1969.

Army Operations in China December 1941–December 1943 [Japanese Monograph no. 71]. Tokyo: Headquarters USAFFE, 1956.

Arvanitakis, Adonis C. *Killing a Peacock: A Case Study of the Targeted Killing of Admiral Isoroku Yamamoto*. Fort Leavenworth KS: School of Advanced Military Studies, United States Army Command and General Staff College, 2015.

Baker, Mark. "The Slow, the Quick and the Dead: Environment, Politics and Temporality in the Henan Famine, 1942–43." *International Review of Environmental History*, vol. 4, no. 2 (2018).

Banham, Tony. *The Sinking of the Lisbon Maru: Britain's Forgotten Wartime Tragedy*. Hong Kong: Hong Kong University Press, 2011.

Bassetti, Sandro. *Colonia Italiana in Cina*. Milano: Lampa di Stampa, 2014.

Behr, Edward. *The Last Emperor*. Toronto: Futura, 1987.

Bergerud, Eric M. *Fire in the Sky: The Air War in the South Pacific*. New York NY: Basic Books, 2001.

—. *Touched With Fire: The Land War in the South Pacific*. New York NY: Penguin Books, 1997.

Bhargava, K. D. and K. N. V. Sastri. *Campaigns in South-East Asia 1941–42 [Official History of the Indian Armed Forces in the Second World War 1939–45]*. New Delhi: Ministry of Defence, 1960.

Blackburn, Kevin. "The Collective Memory of the Sook Ching Massacre and the Creation of the Civilian War Memorial of Singapore." *Journal of the Malaysian Branch of the Royal Asiatic Society*, vol. 73, no. 2 (2000).

Blair, Clay. *Silent Victory: The U.S. Submarine War against Japan*. Philadelphia PA and New York NY: J. B. Lippincott, 1975.

Blunt, Edward. *I.C.S.: The Indian Civil Service*. London: Faber and Faber, 1937.

Bose, Sugata. *His Majesty's Opponent: Subhas Chandra Bose and India's Struggle against Empire*. Cambridge MA: The Belknap Press of Harvard University Press, 2011.

Bradley, Phillip. *The Battle for Wau: New Guinea's Frontline 1942–1943*. Melbourne: Cambridge University Press, 2008.

Bresnahan, Josephine Callisen. "Dangers in Paradise: The Battle Against Combat Fatigue in the Pacific War." PhD diss., Harvard University, 1999.

Brönnimann, S. et al., "Extreme climate of the global troposphere and stratosphere in 1940–42 related to El Niño." *Nature*, vol. 431, no. 7011 (October 2004).

Brook, Timothy. "Collaborationist Nationalism in Occupied Wartime China." In *Nation Work: Asian Elites and National Identities*, edited by Timothy Brook and Andre Schmid. Ann Arbor MI: University of Michigan Press, 2000.

Brooke-Popham, Robert. "Operations in the Far East, From 17th October, 1940 to 27th December, 1941." *Supplement to the London Gazette*, January 22, 1948.

Brown, Cecil. *Suez to Singapore: Cecil Brown's Story*. New York NY: Halcyon House, 1943.

Brown, A. Sutherland and William Rodney. "Burma Banzai: The Air War in Burma through Japanese Eyes." *Canadian Military History*, vol. 11, no. 2 (2012).

Brown, Wenzell. *Hong Kong Aftermath*. New York NY: Smith & Durrell, 1943.

Buell, Thomas B. *The Quiet Warrior: A Biography of Admiral Raymond A. Spruance*. Annapolis MD: Naval Institute Press, 1987.

Bullard, Steven. "Japanese Strategy and Intentions Toward Australia." In *Australia 1942: In the Shadow of War*, edited by Peter J. Dean. Port Melbourne: Cambridge University Press, 2013.

Bunker, Gerald E. *The Peace Conspiracy: Wang Ching-wei and the China War, 1937–1941*. Cambridge MA: Harvard University Press, 1972.

Bryant, Arthur. *The Turn of the Tide 1939–1943: A Study based on the Diaries and Autobiographical Notes of Field Marshal The Viscount Alanbrooke*. London: Collins, 1957.

Cain, T. J. and A. V. Sellwood. *H. M. S. Electra*. London: Frederick Muller, 1959.

Carew, Tim. *The Fall of Hong Kong*. London: Blond, 1961.

Casablanca Conference, January 1943. Joint Chiefs of Staff. Minutes of Meetings. Washington DC: Office of the Combined Chiefs of Staff, 1943.

Chapman, F. Spencer. *The Jungle is Neutral*. London: Chatto and Windus, 1950.

Chennault, Claire Lee. *Way of a Fighter*. New York NY: G.P. Putnam's Sons, 1949.

Ch'i Hsi-sheng. "The Military Dimension, 1942–1945." In *China's Bitter Victory*, edited by James C. Hsiung and Steven I. Levine. Armonk NY: M. E. Sharpe, 1992.

Chihaya Masataka. "The Withdrawal from Kiska." In *The Japanese Navy in World War Two*, edited by David C. Evans. Annapolis MD: Naval Institute Press, 1986.

Chloe, John Haile. *Attu: The Forgotten Battle*. Anchorage AK: National Park Service, 2017.

Churchill, Winston S. *The Second World War, Vol. III: The Grand Alliance*. New York NY: Houghton Mifflin, 1950.

Ciano, Galeazzo. *The Ciano Diaries 1939–1943*, edited by Hugh Gibson. Garden City NY: Doubleday and Company, 1946.

Collier, Basil. *War in the Far East 1941–1945: A Military History*. London: Heinemann, 1969.

Conn, Stetson, Rose C. Engelman and Byron Fairchild. *Guarding the United States and Its Outpost [United States Army in World War II: The Western Hemisphere]*. Washington DC: Office of the Chief of Military History, Department of the Army, 1961.

Connell, John. *Wavell: Supreme Commander 1941–1943*. London: Collins, 1969.

Cook, Haruko Taya and Theodore F. Cook. *Japan At War: An Oral History*. New York NY: The New Press, 1992.

Coox, Alvin D. "The Rise and Fall of the Imperial Japanese Air Forces." In *Air Power and Warfare*, edited by Alfred F. Hurley and Robert C. Ehrhart. Washington DC: US Government Printing Office, 1979.

Crowl, Philip A. and Edmund G. Love. *Seizure of the Gilberts and Marshalls [United States Army in World War II: The War in the Pacific]*. Washington DC: Office of the Chief of Military History, Department of the Army, 1953.

Culver, Annika A. "Manchukuo and the Creation of a New Multi-Ethnic Literature: Kawabata Yasunari's Promotion of 'Manchurian' Culture, 1941–1942." In *Sino-Japanese Transculturation: Late Nineteenth Century to the End of the Pacific War,* edited by Richard King, Cody Poulton and Endo Katsuhiko. Lanham MD: Lexington Books, 2011.

Davies Jr., John Paton. *China Hand: An Autobiography.* Philadelphia PA: University of Pennsylvania Press, 2012.

Devereux, James P. S. *The Story of Wake Island.* Philadelphia PA: J. P. Lippincott, 1947.

Dooley, Thomas. "The First U.S. Tank Action in WWII." *Armor* (July–August 1983).

Doolittle, James H. "Jimmy" with Carroll V. Glines. *I Could Never Be So Lucky Again.* New York NY: Bantam Books, 1991.

Dower, John W. *War Without Mercy: Race and Power in the Pacific War.* New York NY: Pantheon Books, 1986.

Drea, Edward J. *In the Service of the Emperor: Essays on the Imperial Japanese Army.* Lincoln NE: University of Nebraska Press, 1998.

Dreyer, Edward L. *China at War 1901–1949.* London and New York NY: Longman, 1995.

Dull, Paul S. *A Battle History of the Imperial Japanese Navy (1941–1945).* Annapolis MD: Naval Institute Press, 1978.

Edmonds, Walter D. *They Fought with What They Had.* Boston MA: Little, Brown and Company, 1951.

Eichelberger, Robert L. with Milton MacKaye. *Our Jungle Road to Tokyo.* New York NY: The Viking Press, 1950.

Eierman, Jacob. "I Helped Bomb Japan." *Popular Science* (July 1943).

Eisenhower, Dwight D. *The Eisenhower Diaries,* edited by Robert H. Ferrell. New York NY: W. W. Norton, 1981.

Elphick, Peter. "Cover-ups and the Singapore Traitor Affair." Fall of Singapore 60th Anniversary Conference, November 2001. Published online by Four Corners, Australian Broadcasting Corporation, 2002.

Elrod, Roy H. *We Were Going to Win, or Die There: With the Marines at Guadalcanal, Tarawa, and Saipan.* Denton TX: University of North Texas Press, 2017.

Evans, David C. and Mark R. Peattie. *Kaigun: Strategy, Tactics and Technology of the Imperial Japanese Navy 1887–1941.* Annapolis MD: Naval Institute Press, 1997.

Famine Inquiry Commission. *Report on Bengal.* New Delhi: Government of India, 1945.

Fearey, Robert A. "My Year with Ambassador Joseph C. Grew, 1941–1942: A Personal Account." *The Journal of American-East Asian Relations,* vol. 1, no. 1 (spring 1992).

Fraser, George MacDonald. *Quartered Safe Out Here.* New York NY: Skyhorse Publishing, 2007.

Frei, Henry. *Guns of February: Ordinary Japanese Soldiers' View of the Malayan Campaign and the Fall of Singapore, 1941–42.* Singapore: NUS Press, 2004.

Fritz, Chester and Dan Rylance. *Ever Westward to the Far East: The Story of Chester Fritz.* Grand Forks ND: University of North Dakota, 1982.

Fuchida Mitsuo and Okumiya Masatake. *Midway: The Battle that Doomed Japan.* Annapolis MD: Naval Institute Press, 1955.

Fujiwara Iwaichi, F. *Kikan: Japanese Army Intelligence Operations in Southeast Asia during World War Two.* Hong Kong: Heinemann Asia, 1983.

Fuller, Richard. *Shōkan: Hirohito's Samurai.* London: Arms and Armor, 1992.

Gamble, Bruce. *Fortress Rabaul: The Battle for the Southwest Pacific, January 1942–April 1943.* Minneapolis MN: Zenith Press, 2010.

Gandhi, Mahatma. *The Collected Works of Mahatma Gandhi.* Ahmedabad: Ministry of Information and Broadcasting, 1979.

Garfield, Brian. *The Thousand-Mile War: World War II in Alaska and the Aleutians*. Fairbanks AK: University of Alaska Press, 1995.

Garnaut, Anthony. "A Quantitative Description of the Henan Famine." *Modern Asian Studies*, vol. 47, no. 6 (2013).

Geerken, Horst. *Hitlers Griff nach Asien*, vol. 2. Bonn: BukitCinta, 2015.

Gibney, Frank, ed. *Sensō: The Japanese Remember the Pacific War*. Armonk NY: M.E. Sharpe, 1995.

Gilbert, Gregory P. *The Battle of the Bismarck Sea, March 1943*. Canberra: Air Power Development Centre, 2013.

Gill, G. Hermon. *The Royal Australian Navy 1939–1942 [Australia in the War of 1939–1945, Series 2 (Navy), vol. 1]*. Canberra: Australian War Memorial, 1957.

Gillison, Douglas Napier. *Royal Australian Air Force 1939–1942 [Australia in the War of 1939–1945, Series 3 (Air), vol. 1]*. Canberra: Australian War Memorial, 1962.

Goebbels, Joseph. *Die Tagebücher von Joseph Goebbels*. Edited by Elke Fröhlich. Munich: K. G. Saur, 1996.

Gotte, John. *Japan Fights for Asia*. New York NY: Harcourt, Brace and Company, 1943.

Greenough, Paul R. *Prosperity and Misery in Modern Bengal: The Famine of 1943–1944*. Oxford: Oxford University Press, 1982.

Grew, Joseph C. *Ten Years in Japan*. London: Hammond, Hammond & Co., 1945.

Griess, Thomas E. *Second World War: Asia and the Pacific*. West Point NY: United States Military Academy, 1977.

Groen, Petra. "The Invasion of the Dutch East Indies: An Impressive Japanese Source." *International Journal of Military History and Historiography*, 36 (2016).

Groft, Marlin and Larry Alexander. *Bloody Ridge and Beyond: A World War II Marine's Memoir of Edson's Raiders in the Pacific*. New York NY: Berkley, 2014.

Guillain, Robert. *Orient Extrême: Une vie en Asie*. Paris: Seuil, 1986.

Guo Rugui. *Zhongguo Kangri Zhanzheng zhengmian zhanchang zuozhanji [China's War of Resistance against Japan: An Account of Frontline Battles]*. Nanjing: Jiangsu Renmin Chubanshe, 2006.

Hall, Andrew. "The Word Is Mightier than the Throne: Bucking Colonial Education Trends in Manchukuo." *The Journal of Asian Studies*, vol. 68, no. 3 (August 2009).

Halsey, William F. *Admiral Halsey's Story*. New York NY: Whittlesey House, 1947.

Hara Tameichi. *Japanese Destroyer Captain*. Annapolis MD: Naval Institute Press, 2011.

Hartog, Rudolf. *The Sign of the Tiger*. New Delhi: Rupa, 2001.

Havens, Thomas R. H. *Valley of Darkness: The Japanese People and World War Two*. New York NY: W. W. Norton, 1978.

Hayes, Grace Person. *The History of the Joint Chiefs of Staff in World War II: The War Against Japan*. Annapolis MD: Naval Institute Press, 1982.

Haywood Jr., O. G. "Military Decision and Game Theory." *Journal of the Operations Research Society of America*, vol. 2, no. 4 (November 1954).

Heal, S. C. *Ugly Ducklings: Japan's WWII Liberty Type Standards Ships*. Annapolis MD: Naval Institute Press, 2003.

Hein, David. "Vulnerable: HMS Prince of Wales in 1941." *Journal of Military History*, vol. 77 (July 2013).

Heinl, R. D. *The Defense of Wake*. Washington DC: Historical Section, Division of Public Information, U.S. Marine Corps, 1947.

Hersey, John. *Into the Valley: A Skirmish of the Marines*. Lincoln NE: University of Nebraska Press, 2002.

Hoffmann, Jon T. *From Makin to Bougainville: Marine Raiders in the Pacific War*. Washington DC: United States Marine Corps, 1995.

Holwitt, Joel Ira. "'Execute Against Japan': Freedom-of-the-Seas, the U.S. Navy, Fleet Submarines, and the U.S. Decision to Conduct Unrestricted Warfare, 1919–1941." PhD diss., Ohio State University, 2005.

Hornfischer, James D. *Neptune's Inferno: The U.S. Navy at Guadalcanal.* New York NY: Bantam, 2012.

Hough, Frank O. et al. *Pearl Harbor to Guadalcanal [History of U.S. Marine Corps Operations in World War II, Volume 1].* Washington DC: United States Marine Corps, 1958.

Hoyt, Edwin P. *Hirohito: The Emperor and the Man.* Westport CT: Praeger Publishers, 1992.

Hsu Long-hsuen and Chang Ming-kai. *History of the Sino-Japanese War (1937–1945).* Taipei: Chung Wu Publishing, 1971.

International Military Tribunal for the Far East. *Transcript of Proceedings.*

Iriye Akira. *Power and Culture: The Japanese-American War 1941–1945.* Cambridge MA: Harvard University Press, 1981.

James, D. Clayton. *Years of MacArthur.* Boston MA: Houghton Mifflin Company, 1970–1985.

Japanese Army Operations in the South Pacific Area: New Britain and Papua Campaigns, 1942–43. Translated by Steven Bullard. Canberra: Australian War Memorial, 2007.

Japanese Night Combat. Tokyo: Eighth United States Army, Military History Section, 1955.

Jersey, Stanley Coleman. *Hell's Islands: The Untold Story of Guadalcanal.* College Station TX: Texas A&M University Press, 2008.

Johnson, Jennifer N. "'We're still alive today': A Captured Japanese Diary from the Pacific Theater." *Prologue: The Journal of the National Archives,* vol. 45, no. 2 (Summer 2013).

Jones, F. C. *Manchuria since 1931.* London: Royal Institute of International Affairs, 1949.

de Jong, L. *Het Koninkrijk der Nederlanden in de Tweede Wereldoorlog [The Kingdom Of The Netherlands In The Second World War].* The Hague: Staatsuitgeverij, 1969–1994.

Ju Zhifen. "Northern Chinese Laborers and Manchukuo." In *Asian Labor in the Wartime Japanese Empire: Unknown Histories,* edited by Paul H. Kratoska. Armonk NY: Sharpe, 2005.

Kanahele, George S. "The Japanese occupation of Indonesia, prelude to independence." Ph.D. diss. Cornell University, 1967.

Katō Masuo. *The Lost War: A Japanese Reporter's Inside Story.* New York NY: Alfred A. Knopf, 1946.

Kawamura Noriko. *Emperor Hirohito and the Pacific War.* Seattle WA: University of Washington Press, 2015.

Kehn, Donald M. *In the Highest Degree Tragic: The Sacrifice of the U.S. Asiatic Fleet in the East Indies during World War II.* Lincoln NE: Potomac Books, 2017.

Kennedy, John. *The Business of War: The war narrative of Major-General Sir John Kennedy.* London: Hutchinson & Co., 1957.

Kenney, George C. *General Kenney Reports: A Personal History of the Pacific War.* New York NY: Duell, Sloan, and Pearce, 1949.

Kershaw, Ian. *Fateful Choices: Ten Decisions That Changed the World, 1940–1941.* New York NY: The Penguin Press, 2007.

Kingsberg, Miriam. *Moral Nation: Modern Japan and Narcotics in Global History.* Berkeley CA: University of California Press, 2013.

Kirby, Stanley Woodburn. *India's Most Dangerous Hour [History of the Second World War. United Kingdom Military Series. The War against Japan, vol. 2].* London: Her Majesty's Stationery Office, 1958.

—, *The Loss of Singapore [History of the Second World War. United Kingdom Military Series. The War against Japan, vol. 1].* London: Her Majesty's Stationery Office, 1957.

Kitano, Harry H. L. and Roger Daniels. "Introduction." In *Japanese Americans: From Relocation to Redress,* edited by Roger Daniels, Sandra C. Taylor and Harry H. L. Kitano. Seattle WA: University of Washington Press, 1991.

Large, Stephen. *Emperor Hirohito and Showa Japan: A Political Biography.* London and New York NY: Routledge, 1992.

Lattimore, Owen. *China Memoirs: Chiang Kai-shek and the War Against Japan.* Tokyo: University of Tokyo Press, 1990.

Lawson, Ted W. *Thirty Seconds Over Tokyo*. New York NY: Random House, 1943.

Leasor, James. *Singapore: The Battle that Changed the World*. Kelly Bray: House of Stratus, 2001.

Leckie, Robert. *Helmet for My Pillow*. New York NY: Bantam, 2010.

Lee, Clark. *They Call It Pacific: An Eyewitness Story of Our War Against Japan from Bataan to the Solomons.* New York NY: The Viking Press, 1943.

Levering, Robert W. *Horror Trek: A True Story of Bataan, the Death March and Three and One-Half Years in Japanese Prison Camps*. Dayton OH: Hortsman Printing Co., 1948.

Lin Yutang. *The Vigil of a Nation*. New York NY: The John Day, 1945.

Loewenheim, Francis L., Harold D. Langley and Manfred Jonas, eds. *Roosevelt and Churchill: Their Secret Wartime Correspondence*. New York NY: Saturday Review Press, 1975.

Ludlum, Stuart D. *They Turned the War Around at Coral Sea and Midway: Going to War with Yorktown's Air Group Five*. Bennington VT: Merriam Press, 2006.

Lundstrom, John B. *Black Shoe Carrier Admiral: Frank Jack Fletcher at Coral Sea, Midway, and Guadalcanal*. Annapolis MD: Naval Institute Press, 2006.

—, *The First Team and the Guadalcanal Campaign: Naval Fighter Combat from August to November 1942*. Annapolis MD: Naval Institute Press, 1994.

MacMillan, Harold. *The Blast of War 1939–1945*. London: Macmillan, 1967.

Magarry, Ron. *The Battalion Story: 2/26th Infantry Battalion, 8th Division, AIF*. Jindalee, Queensland: Magarry, 1995.

Mains, Tony. *Retreat from Burma*. London: W. Foulsham & Co., 1973.

Maltby, C. M. "Operations in Hong Kong from 8th to 25th December, 1941." *Supplement to the London Gazette*, January 27, 1948.

Man, Kwong Chi and Tsoi Yiu Lun. *Eastern Fortress: A Military History of Hong Kong, 1840–1970*. Hong Kong: Hong Kong University Press, 2014.

Marder, Arthur J. *Old Friends, New Enemies: The Royal Navy and the Imperial Japanese Navy. Strategic Illusions, 1936–1941*. Oxford: Clarendon Press, 1981.

Matloff, Maurice and Edwin M. Snell. *Strategic Planning for Coalition Warfare 1941–1942 [United States Army in World War II: The War Department]*. Washington DC: Office of the Chief of Military History, Department of the Army, 1953.

McCarthy, Dudley. *South-West Pacific Area First Year: Kokoda to Wau [Australia in the War of 1939–1945, Series 1 (Army), vol. 5]*. Canberra: Australian War Memorial, 1959.

McCoy, Melvin H. and S. M. Mellnik, with Welbourn Kelly. *Ten Escape from Tojo*. New York NY: Farrar & Rinehart, 1944.

McEnery, Jim. *Hell in the Pacific: A Marine Rifleman's Journey from Guadalcanal to Peleliu*. New York NY: Simon and Schuster, 2012.

McGee, Barbara Bernard and Ruth Dorval Jones. *Barney: Journals of Harry Virden Bernard*. Smithfield NC: McGee Press, 1982.

McMillin, George J. "Surrender of Guam to the Japanese." *Guam Recorder*. April–September 1972.

Middlebrook, Garrett. *Air Combat at 20 Feet*. Bloomington IN: AuthorHouse 2004.

Miller, Edward S. *War Plan Orange: The U.S. Strategy to Defeat Japan, 1897–1945*. Annapolis MD: Naval Institute Press, 1991.

Miller, Ernest B. *Bataan Uncensored*. Long Prairie MN: Hart Publications, 1949.

Miller, John. *Cartwheel: The Reduction of Rabaul [United States Army in World War II: The War in the Pacific]*. Washington DC: Office of the Chief of Military History, Department of the Army, 1959.

—. *Guadalcanal: The First Offensive [United States Army in World War II: The War in the Pacific]*. Washington DC: Center of Military History, 1995.

Milner, Samuel. *Victory in Papua [United States Army in World War II: The War in the Pacific]*. Washington DC: Office of the Chief of Military History, Department of the Army, 1957.

Moffatt, Jonathan and Audrey Holmes McCormick. *Moon over Malaya: A Tale of Argylls and Marines.* Cheltenham: The History Press, 2003.

Monro, Mary. *Stranger In My Heart.* London: Unbound, 2018.

Morison, Samuel Eliot. *Aleutians, Gilbert and Marshalls June 1942–April 1944 [History of the United States Naval Operations in World War II, vol. 7].* Boston MA: Little, Brown and Co., 1951.

—, *Breaking the Bismarcks Barrier 22 July 1942–1 May 1944 [History of the United States Naval Operations in World War II, vol. 6].* Boston MA: Little, Brown and Co., 1950.

—, *The Rising Sun in the Pacific 1931–April 1942 [History of the United States Naval Operations in World War II, vol. 3].* Boston MA: Little, Brown and Co., 1948.

Morton, Louis. *Fall of the Philippines [United States Army in World War II: The War in the Pacific].* Washington DC: Office of the Chief of Military History, Department of the Army, 1953.

—. *Strategy and Command: The First Two Years United States Army in World War II: The War in the Pacific]* Washington DC: Office of the Chief of Military History, Department of the Army, 1962

Mukherjee, Janam. *Hungry Bengal: War, Famine and the End of Empire.* Oxford: Oxford University Press, 2015.

Muscolino, Micah S. "Violence Against People and the Land: The Environment and Refugee Migration From China's Henan Province, 1938–1945." *Environment and History*, vol. 17, no. 2 (May 2011).

Najita Tetsuo. "Nakano Seigō and the Spirit of the Meiji Restoration in Twentieth-Century Japan." In *Dilemmas of Growth in Prewar Japan,* edited by James W. Morley. Princeton NJ: Princeton University Press, 1971.

Newell, Clayton R. *Burma, 1942.* Washington DC: United States Army Center of Military History, 1995.

Nicholson, Arthur. *Hostages of Fortune: Winston Churchill and the Loss of the Prince of Wales and Repulse.* Stroud: Sutton Publishing, 2005.

van Nooten, Barend A. "The Mouse-Deer and the Tiger." In *The Defining Years of the Dutch East Indies, 1942–1949: Survivors' Accounts of Japanese Invasion and Enslavement of Europeans and the Revolution That Created Free Indonesia,* edited by Jan A. Krancher. Jefferson NC and London: MacFarland & Co., 1996.

Ó Gráda, Cormac. "'Sufficiency and Sufficiency and Sufficiency': Revisiting the Bengal Famine of 1943–44." UCD Centre for Economic Research, *Working Paper Series* (2010).

Office of Naval Intelligence. *Combat Report Coral Sea.* Washington DC: Navy Department, 1943.

Ohmae Toshikazu. "Japanese Operations in the Indian Ocean." In *The Japanese Navy in World War Two: In the Words of Former Japanese Naval Officers,* edited by David C. Evans. Annapolis MD: Naval Institute Press, 1986.

—. "The Battle of Savo Island." In *The Japanese Navy in World War Two: In the Words of Former Japanese Naval Officers,* edited by David C. Evans. Annapolis MD: Naval Institute Press, 1986.

Okumiya Masatake and Horikoshi Jiro with Martin Caidin. *Zero! The Story of Japan's Air War in the Pacific 1941–45.* New York NY: Ballantine Books, 1957.

Ostlund, Mike. *Find 'Em, Chase 'Em, Sink 'Em: The Mysterious Loss of the WWII Submarine USS Gudgeon.* Guilford CT: Lyons Press, 2012.

Papuan Campaign: the Buna-Sanananda Operation. Washington DC: Historical Division, War Department, 1945.

Parillo, Mark P. *The Japanese Merchant Marine in World War II.* Annapolis MD: Naval Institute Press, 1993.

Parshall, Jonathan and Anthony Tully. *Shattered Sword: The Untold Story of the Battle of Midway.* Herndon VA: Potomac Books, 2005.

Paull, Raymond. *Retreat from Kokoda: The Australian Campaign in New Guinea 1942*. London: Secker & Warburg, 1983.

Peattie, Mark R. *Sunburst: The Rise of Japanese Naval Air Power, 1909–1941*. Annapolis MD: Naval Institute Press, 2001.

Percival, Arthur. "Operations of Malaya Command, From 8th December, 1941 to 15th February, 1942." *Second Supplement to the London Gazette*, January 27, 1948.

Perret, Geoffrey. *Old Soldiers Never Die*. Avon MA: Adams Media, 1996.

Petillo, Carol Morris. "Douglas MacArthur and Manuel Quezon: A Note on an Imperial Bond." *Pacific Historical Review*, vol. 48, no. 1 (February 1979): 107–117.

—. *Douglas MacArthur: The Philippine Years*. Bloomington IN: Indiana University Press, 1981.

Petty, Bruce M. *Voices from the Pacific War: Bluejackets Remember*. Annapolis MD: Naval Institute Press, 2004.

Plating, John D. *The Hump: America's Strategy for Keeping China in World War II*. College Station TX: Texas A&M Press, 2011.

Poeze, Harry A. "The Road to Hell: The Construction of a Railway Line in West Java during the Japanese Occupation." In *Asian Labor in the Wartime Japanese Empire: Unknown Histories*, edited by Paul H. Kratoska. Armonk NY: Sharpe, 2005.

Pogue, Forrest C. *George C. Marshall: Ordeal and Hope 1939–1942*. New York NY: Viking, 1966.

Ponder, Frans J. Nicholaas. "A Soldier in the Royal Netherlands-Indies Army." In *The Defining Years of the Dutch East Indies, 1942–1949: Survivors' Accounts of Japanese Invasion and Enslavement of Europeans and the Revolution That Created Free Indonesia*, edited by Jan A. Krancher. Jefferson NC and London: MacFarland & Co., 1996.

Potter, E. B. *Nimitz*. Annapolis MD: Naval Institute Press, 1976.

Prados, John. *Combined Fleet Decoded: The Secret History of American Intelligence and the Japanese Navy in World War II*. New York NY: Random House, 1995.

Pratt, Fletcher. *Sea Power and Today's War*. New York NY: Harrison-Hilton Book, 1939.

Pu Yi, Aisin-Gioro. *From Emperor to Citizen*. Beijing: Foreign Languages Press, 1979.

Raghavan, Srinath. *India's War: The Making of Modern South Asia 1939–1945*. London: Allen Lane, 2016.

Ramsey, Edwin Price and Stephen J. Rivele. *Lieutenant Ramsey's War: From Horse Soldier to Guerrilla Commander*. New York NY: Knightsbridge, 1990.

Reid, Richard. *Laden, Fevered, Starved: The POWs of Sandakan, North Borneo, 1945*. Canberra: Commonwealth Department of Veterans' Affairs, 1999.

Reporting World War II, Part One: American Journalism 1938–1944. New York NY: Library of America, 1995.

Reports of General MacArthur: Japanese Operations in the Southwest Pacific Area. Washington DC: United States Government Printing Office, 1966.

Rohfleisch, Kramer J. "Drawing the Battle Line in the Pacific." In *Plans and Early Operations, January 1939 to August 1942 [The Army Air Forces in World War II]*, edited by Wesley Frank Craven and James Lea Cate. Chicago IL: University of Chicago Press, 1948.

—. "The Central Solomons." In *The Pacific: Guadalcanal to Saipan, August 1942 to July 1944 [The Army Air Forces in World War II]*, edited by Wesley Frank Craven and James Lea Cate. Chicago IL: University of Chicago Press, 1948.

Roland, Charles G. "Massacre and Rape in Hong Kong: Two Case Studies Involving Medical Personnel and Patients." *Journal of Contemporary History*, vol. 32, no. 1 (January 1997).

Romanus, Charles F. and Riley Sunderland. *Stilwell's Mission to China [United States Army in World War II: China-Burma-India Theater]*. Washington DC: United States Army Center of Military History, 1953.

Roosevelt, Elliott. *As He Saw It*. New York NY: Duell, Sloan and Pearce, 1945.

Roscoe, Theodore. *United States Submarine Operations in World War II*. Annapolis MD: Naval Institute Press, 1949.

Roskill, S. W. *The War At Sea 1939–1945, Volume 1: The Defensive*. London: Her Majesty's Stationery Office, 1954.

Rottman, Gordon L. *World War II Pacific Island Guide: A Geo-Military Study*. Westport CT: Grenwood Press, 2002.

Roy, Kaushik. *Sepoys against the Rising Sun: The Indian Army in Far East and South-East Asia, 1941–45*. Leiden: Brill, 2016.

Sainsbury, Keith. *The Turning Point: Roosevelt, Stalin, Churchill and Chiang-Kai-Shek, 1943: The Moscow, Cairo, and Teheran Conferences*. Oxford: Oxford University Press, 1985.

Samarani, Guido. "An Historical Turning Point: Italy's Relations with China before and after 8 September 1943." *Journal of Modern Italian Studies*, vol. 15, no. 4 (2010).

—. "Shaping the Future of Asia: Chiang Kai-shek, Nehru and China-India Relations During the Second World War Period." *Working papers in contemporary Asian studies*, No. 11, Centre for East and South-East Asian Studies, Lund University, (2005).

Samuels, Richard J. *Special Duty: A History of the Japanese Intelligence Community*. Ithaca NY: Cornell University Press, 2019.

Sato Shigeru. "'Economic soldiers' in Java: Indonesian Laborers Mobilized for Agricultural Projects." In *Asian Labor in the Wartime Japanese Empire: Unknown Histories*, edited by Paul H. Kratoska. Armonk NY: Sharpe, 2005.

Sawyer, L. A. and W. H. Mitchell. *The Liberty Ships: The History of the 'Emergency' Cargo Ships Constructed in the United States during World War II*. Newton Abbot: David & Charles, 1970.

Sayre, Mary Geneva. *Missionary Triumphs in Occupied China*. Winona Lake IN: The Women's Missionary Society of the Free Methodist Church, 1945.

Scott, James M. *Target Tokyo: Jimmy Doolittle and the Raid that Avenged Pearl Harbor*. New York NY: W. W. Norton, 2015.

Seagrave, Gordon S. *Burma Surgeon*. London: Victor Gollancz, 1944.

Shaw Jr., Henry I., Bernard C. Nalty, and Edwin J. Turnbladh. *Central Pacific Drive [History of U.S. Marine Corps Operations in World War II, vol. 3]*. Washington DC: U.S. Government Printing Office, 1966.

Sherrod, Robert. *Tarawa: The Story of a Battle*. New York NY: Duell, Sloan and Pearce, 1944.

Sherwood, Robert E. *Roosevelt and Hopkins: An Intimate History*. New York NY: Harper, 1948.

Shi Linxian, "Personal Experience." In *Under the Same Army Flag*, edited by Deng Xian. Beijing: China Intercontinental Press, 2005.

Shillony, Ben-Ami. *Politics and Culture in Wartime Japan*. Oxford: Clarendon Press, 1981.

—. "Wartime Japan: A Military Dictatorship." In *Military and State in Modern Asia*, edited by Harold Z. Schiffrin. Jerusalem: Academic Press, 1976.

Shimada Kōichi. "The Opening Air Offensive Against the Philippines." In *The Japanese Navy in World War Two*, edited by David C. Evans. Annapolis MD: Naval Institute Press, 1986.

Shindo Hiroyuki, "The Japanese Army's Search for a New South Pacific Strategy, 1943," in *Australia 1943: The Liberation of New Guinea*, ed. Peter J. Dean (Port Melbourne: Cambridge University Press, 2014), 69–70.

—, "The Japanese Army's 'Unplanned' South Pacific Campaign." In *Australia 1942: In the Shadow of War*. Ed. Peter J. Dean. Port Melbourne: Cambridge University Press, 2013.

Shores, Christopher and Brian Cull with Yasuho Izawa. *Bloody Shambles*. London: Grub Street, 1992.

Shukla, S. P. "Chiang Kai Shek in India: An episode in the Sino-Indian relationship." *Proceedings of the Indian History Congress*, vol. 36 (1975).

Slim, William. *Defeat into Victory*. London: Cassell & Co., 1956.

Smith, Holland M. and Percy Finch. *Coral and Brass*. New York NY: Charles Scribner's Sons, 1949.

Smith, Michael S. *Bloody Ridge: The Battle That Saved Guadalcanal*. New York NY: Presidio Press, 2000.

Song Zhixin. *1942: Henan dajihuang [1942: The Great Henan Famine]*. Wuhan: Hubei renmin chubanshe, 2012.

Spector, Ronald H. *Eagle Against the Sun: The American War with Japan*. New York NY: Vintage Books, 1985.

Stacey, C. P. *Six Years of War: The Army in Canada, Britain and the Pacific [Official History of the Canadian Army in the Second World War, vol. 1]*. Ottawa: Queen's Printer, 1955.

Stewart, Adrian. *The Underrated Enemy: Britain's War with Japan, December 1941–May 1942*. London: William Kimber, 1987.

Stilwell, Joseph W. *The Stilwell Papers*. New York NY. William Sloane Associates, 1948.

Straus, Ulrich A. *The Anguish of Surrender: Japanese POWs of World War II*. Seattle: University of Washington Press, 2005.

Symonds, Craig L. *The Battle of Midway*. Oxford: Oxford University Press, 2011.

Tanaka Raizō. "The Struggle for Guadalcanal." In *The Japanese Navy in World War Two*, edited by David C. Evans. Annapolis MD: Naval Institute Press, 1986.

Tanaka Yukiko. *Hidden Horrors Japanese War Crimes In World War II*. Boulder CO: Westview Press, 1996.

Thorpe, Elliott R. *East Wind, Rain*. Boston MA: Gambit, 1969.

Tinker, Hugh. "A Forgotten Long March: The Indian Exodus from Burma, 1942." *Journal of Southeast Asian Studies*, vol. 6, no. 1 (March 1975).

Tipton, Elise. *The Japanese Police State: The Tokkō in Interwar Japan*. Honolulu HI: University of Hawaii Press, 1990.

Toland, John. *The Rising Sun: The Decline and Fall of the Japanese Empire 1936–1945*. New York NY: Random House, 1970.

Tolischus, Otto D. *Tokyo Record*. New York NY: Reynal and Hitchcock, 1943.

Tregaskis, Richard. *Guadalcanal Diary*. New York NY: Modern Library, 2000.

Tsuji Masanobu. *Singapore 1941–1942: The Japanese Version of the Malayan Campaign of World War II*. Singapore: Oxford University Press, 1988.

Tucker, David. "Labor Policy and the Construction Industry in Manchukuo: Systems of Recruitment, Management, and Control." In *Asian Labor in the Wartime Japanese Empire: Unknown Histories*, edited by Paul H. Kratoska. Armonk NY: Sharpe, 2005.

Tyng, Sewell T., Nelson L. Drummond and Robert J. Mitchell. *The Capture of Attu As Told by the Men Who Fought There*. Washington DC: War Department, 1944.

Ugaki Matome. *Fading Victory: The Diary of Admiral Matome Ugaki 1941–1945*, edited by Donald M. Goldstein and Katherine V. Dillon. Annapolis MD: Naval Institute Press, 1991.

United States Department of State. *Foreign relations of the United States diplomatic papers: The Conferences at Cairo and Tehran*. Washington DC: US Government Printing Office, 1943.

United States Strategic Bombing Survey (Pacific), Naval Analysis Division. *Interrogations of Japanese Officials*. Washington DC: United States Government Printing Office, 1946.

Uno Kazumaro. *Corregidor: Island of Delusion*. Shanghai: Mercury Press, 1942.

Urquhart, Alistair. *The Forgotten Highlander*. London: Abacus, 2010.

Urwin, Gregory J. W. *Victory in Defeat: The Wake Island Defenders in Captivity*. Annapolis MD: Naval Institute Press, 2011.

Utinsky, Margaret. *Miss U*. San Antonio TX: The Naylor Company, 1948.

Vandenbroek, Johannes. "A Teacher Turned Soldier and Imprisoned." In *The Defining Years of the Dutch East Indies, 1942–1949: Survivors' Accounts of Japanese Invasion and Enslavement of Europeans and the Revolution That Created Free Indonesia*, edited by Jan A. Krancher. Jefferson NC and London: MacFarland & Co., 1996.

van de Ven, Hans. *War and Nationalism in China 1925–1945*. London: RoutledgeCurzon, 2003.

Venkataramani, M. S. and B. K. Shrivastava. *Quit India: The American Response to the 1942 Struggle*. New Delhi: Vikas Publishing House, 1979.

Wainwright, Jonathan M. *General Wainwright's Story: The Account of Four Years of Humiliating Defeat, Surrender, and Captivity*. Garden City NY: Doubleday, 1946.

Walker, Allan S. *The Island Campaigns [Australia in the War of 1939–1945, Series 5 (Medical), vol. 3]*. Canberra: Australian War Memorial, 1957.

Walker, Charles H. *Combat Officer: A Memoir of War in the South Pacific*. New York NY: Ballantine Books, 2004.

Wampler, Ernest. *China Suffers: Or, My Six Years of Work During the Incident*. Elgin IL: Brethren Publishing, 1945.

War History Office of the National Defense College of Japan. *The Invasion of the Dutch East Indies*, edited and translated by Willem Remmelink. Leiden: Leiden University Press, 2015.

Watson, Richard L. "Battle of the Bismarck Sea." In *The Pacific: Guadalcanal to Saipan, August 1942 to July 1944 [The Army Air Forces in World War II]*, edited by Wesley Frank Craven and James Lea Cate. Chicago IL: University of Chicago Press, 1951.

White, Theodore H. and Annalee Jacoby. *Thunder out of China*. New York NY: William Sloane Associates, 1946.

Wickert, Ernst. *Mut und Übermut: Geschichten aus meinem Leben*. Stuttgart: Deutsche Verlags-Anstalt, 1992.

Wigmore, Lionel. *The Japanese Thrust [Australia in the War of 1939–1945, Series 1 (Army), vol. 4]*. Canberra: Australian War Memorial, 1957.

Williams, Mary H. *Chronology [United States Army in World War II: Special Studies]*. Washington DC: Office of the Chief of Military History, Department of the Army, 1960.

Williams, Peter. *The Kokoda Campaign 1942: Myth and Reality*. Cambridge: Cambridge University Press, 2012.

Willmott, H. P. *Empires in the Balance: Japanese and Allied Pacific Strategies to April 1942*. Annapolis MD: Naval Institute Press, 1989.

—, *The Barrier and the Javelin: Japanese and Allied Pacific Strategies, February to June 1942*. Annapolis MD: Naval Institute Press, 1983.

—, *The Second World War in the Far East*. London: Cassell, 1999.

Wooldridge, E. T., ed. *Carrier Warfare in the Pacific: An Oral History Collection*. Washington DC: Smithsonian Institution Press, 1993.

Wukovits, John. *One Square Mile of Hell: The Battle for Tarawa*. New York NY: NAL Caliber, 2007.

Xiao Ruping. "Kangzhan shiqi Jiang Jieshi fangwen Yindu de zai kaocha" ["A Reassessment of Chiang Kai-shek's visit to India during the War of Resistance"]. *Zhejiang Daxue Xuebao*, vol. 48, no. 5 (September 2018).

Yamashita, Samuel Hideo. *Daily Life in Wartime Japan*. Lawrence KS: University Press of Kansas, 2015.

Yang Zhenghua. "Changsha baoweizhan shimo" ["The Defense of Changsha from Beginning to End"]. In *Hunan Sida Huizhan: Yuan Guomindang jiangling Kangri Zhanzheng qinliji [The Four Big Battles of Hunan: Personal Recollections from the War of Resistance against Japan by Former Nationalist Commanders]*. Beijing: Zhongguo Wenshi Chubanshe, 1995.

Yenne, Bill. *When Tigers Ruled the Sky: The Flying Tigers American Outlaw Pilots over China in World War II*. New York NY: Berkley Caliber, 2016.

Zhou Wenxing. "Wenxing (Literary Star), Wuxing (Military Star), and a Patriotic Heart." In *Under the Same Army Flag*, edited by Deng Xian. Beijing: China Intercontinental Press, 2005.

Zimmermann, John L. *The Guadalcanal Campaign*. Washington DC: Historical Division United States Marine Corps, 1949.

Newspapers

Canberra Times
Daily Telegraph
New York Times
Nippon Times Evening
Völkischer Beobachter

Oral Histories

United States Marine Corps

Henry W. Buse
Justice M. Chambers
Lewis J. Fields
Norman T. Hatch
Carl W. Hoffman
Wood B. Kyle
John P. Leonard
Raymond L. Murray
Edwin Pollock
Julian C. Smith

US Naval Institute Oral History Program

Noel A. M. Gayler
Cecil S. King
Edwin T. Layton
Henri Smith-Hutton
Paul D. Stroop
John Muse Worthington

Australian War Memorial

Leslie Gordon Gaffney. Accession number S01738

Imperial War Museum

Neville Hogan (IWM SR 12342)
Pearl "Prue" Brewis, Imperial War Museum (IWM SR 22741)

Oral History Centre, National Archives of Singapore

Winston Arthur Reginald Mathews. Accession no. 002685
Elizabeth Yu. Accession no. 000597

Index